ALSO BY THE AUTHOR

Sting Like a Butterfly
The Eye of the Tigress

CHASING THE CHAMELEON

A CASH MCCAHILL NOVEL BY

PAUL COGGINS

SAVIO REPUBLIC

A SAVIO REPUBLIC BOOK
An Imprint of Post Hill Press
ISBN: 979-8-89565-396-8
ISBN (eBook): 979-8-89565-397-5

Chasing the Chameleon

Cover Design by Jim Villaflores

posthillpress.com
New York • Nashville
Published in the United States of America

1 2 3 4 5 6 7 8 9 10

As always, to Regina and Jessica,
whose love of books is second only
to their love of family

PROLOGUE

The lies of married men follow a predictable pattern, as Veronica Stoddard had come to learn. In her line of work, that lesson had kept her alive.

Tonight's "date" fit the pattern. Homer Donahue, surely not his real name, claimed to be single (one Pinocchio), a CEO (two Pinocchios), and looking for a long-term relationship (a whopping four Pinocchios).

The makeup mirror in the bedroom stared back at Veronica with two faces: the flawless one the world saw and a work in progress by a magician named Dr. Solomon Katzenbach. Instead of marveling at the miracle of her transformation from the effeminate Ronnie Stockton to the ultra-feminine Veronica Stoddard, she obsessed over a tiny bump on the bridge of her nose.

The Stockton schnoz had been the only thing her strict Baptist parents had passed down to her. To the outside world, the bump appeared as minor as a mole. To her, it loomed as large as a mountain.

First thing tomorrow, she would schedule her next surgery and haggle with Katzenbach over his standard fee of fifteen thousand for the simple procedure. Her bank account had less than half that amount, with rent on the apartment due Friday. As a frequent patient and an influencer among the trans community, she counted on the doctor to shave one or two thou from the price tag.

Regardless, a prospect dangled on the hook, an admirer with the wherewithal to bankroll this operation and the next several down the line. Homer emitted the sweet smell of Old Spice, instant infatuation, and repeat business.

Veronica retouched her ruby red lipstick. The color matched her nail polish, her toes on display in black, strappy sandals. Both the shade and sandals reflected the client's request.

She stood and smoothed the black dress, chosen for an evening of eclectic events. A flirty dinner with Homer at the East Wind Restaurant in Deep Ellum, followed by a solemn service at the Dallas Public Library for her slain sisters.

Five years since deciding to transition and three since coming out to the world, she still suffered bouts of anxiety before the first face-to-face meeting with a new client. Serial slayings in Dallas of trans women had her on edge.

Veronica took several deep breaths to slow her heartbeat. The panic attacks were coming more frequently.

Everything will be fine.

She had vetted Homer vocally and virtually, by chatting online and by phone for two weeks. During the daily sessions, for which he paid by the minute, she had leveled with him about who she was, where she had been, and where she was going.

In contrast, Homer had surely lied about everything. Well, almost everything. Homer might turn out to be his real first name. If so, Veronica chalked up the rare truth to caution on his part, not honesty. Experience had taught her that even the cleverest cons risked a delayed response to an alias, and Homer was far from clever.

Running late for the date, Veronica reached the apartment door when her iPhone rang. She recognized the number and took the call.

***

Marvin Upjohn, a rookie on patrol and riding solo, cruised lower Greenville Avenue. A dispatcher called with a report of a one eighty-seven in Deep Ellum that sent him speeding east, his heart pounding and siren screaming.

The first cop on the scene, he parked the cherry top at the corner of Commerce and Hall and sprinted toward a dark alley. He stumbled over something in the street and went down hard. His hands swept the pavement for what had tripped him.

He picked up a shoe. A woman's shoe. A black, strappy sandal.

CHAPTER ONE

Cash McCahill stood outside the Dallas Public Library, transfixed by the image in the glass entrance: his reflection. Then again, not his.

A forty-four-year-old lawyer stared into the glass. A seventy-four-year-old ex-cop stared back. His jowls sagged. Wrinkles creased his forehead and swallowed blue eyes turned brown by contact lenses. His hair was patchy, thinned out, and dyed gray. Fake liver spots dotted his temples.

Cash's transformation hadn't ended with the face. He had packed on twenty-five pounds, mostly at the gut, and gone from buff to beefy. A steady diet of milkshakes and Mars bars will do that.

Aging took a toll. Aging overnight, a brutal one.

Bang.

Cash wheeled around and traced the sound to a backfiring car in the parking lot. A year ago, he wouldn't have been so jumpy. Then again, a year ago, *Los Lobos,* a Mexican drug cartel, had yet to place a seven-figure contract on his head for refusing to betray *La Tigra*, a rival cartel leader and his client.

La Tigra was now dead, leaving Cash on his own to elude a swarm of *sicarios* combing the streets and back alleys in search of a big payday. He had two choices: run until his legs and his luck gave out or hide in plain sight in the city he knew.

He went with the latter and remained in Dallas. Not that he really had a choice. He had what passed for a family here, with his father figure and law partner Gary Goldberg, aka Goldy; his longtime assistant Eva Martinez; and Tina Campos, who straddled two roles: sometime client and full-time surrogate daughter.

Cash had sheltered Tina since her days as a trans teen living on the mean streets of Dallas. Given her background, it was a miracle she was still alive. Disowned by family at fifteen. In and out of lockup. Preyed upon by the worst of inhumanity.

Cash had played no small role in the miracle of Tina's survival. He had protected her from the law and the lawless. No way would he abandon her now, not when the greatest threat came from the latter. Not even with his life on the line.

Pissing away thirty years in his prime was a high price to pay, but Cash had paid it. Staying off a cartel's radar didn't come cheap or easy. Invisibility was the key to survival. In Dallas, the only thing more inconspicuous than a seventy-four-year-old man was a seventy-four-year-old woman.

After erasing thousands of years from the faces of the rich and vain, Dr. Katzenbach had finally found a place to park some of those lost years. Cash had been the surgeon's guinea pig, the first patient to go under the knife and emerge older, by design.

With a heavy sigh, Cash broke the spell cast by his reflection and went inside. Acting old was getting old.

Despite the danger of appearing in public, he needed to be here for Tina, who had been there for him. Not only had she hooked him up with Katzenbach, but she was also guarding his new identity. Other than the doctor, she alone knew that Cash McCahill and Carl Meadows were the one and the same.

Tonight's memorial service might be too wrenching for Tina. Even worse, the gathering of trans activists and their allies might prove too tempting for the serial killer targeting Tina's kind.

***

At the annual Transgender Day of Remembrance, Tina Campos pinched the wick and doused the flame. "The candle of life expires." She stood before a crowd of a hundred or so, seated on folding chairs in the Dallas Public Library. Women of color predominated, with a half-dozen males sprinkled among the audience.

Cash appeared to be the oldest person in the room and probably the only straight, white, cis male. Like most attendees, he had a new name: Carl Meadows.

Held every November 20th, the memorial service celebrated the lives of transgender men and women who had been killed that year, simply for being who they were. Martyred occasionally by strangers, more often by those closest to them.

Surrounded by scores of lit candles on a long table, the lone burnout would have gone unnoticed if Tina had not hovered over it. A sea of flickering flames were the only lights in the room and turned the speaker into a shadowy presence.

Like the candles before her, Tina had a slender frame topped by a fiery red mane. Also like the candles, she was a spark of light and energy—in constant motion but always on the brink of darkness.

With the click of a remote control, Tina brought the smiling face of Cassandra McCoy into focus on a large screen and relit the deceased's candle. "The candle of memory lives on."

The ceremony honored the victims chronologically, according to the dates of their deaths. Cassandra had been a spring killing, so her image appeared early in the program.

"Cassandra McCoy was killed in April in Boston, stabbed to death and dumped in the Charles River. The murder remains unsolved. Her friends called her Cassie and described her as the life of every party and a rabid Red Sox fan."

For a full thirty seconds, Cassie's face filled the screen before the next victim bumped her. With sixty-eight lives to spotlight, the parade of ghosts moved at a rapid clip. The next face of tragedy belonged to a black teen who had been gunned down in Scottsdale, Arizona, four days after Cassie's killing. The crime was also unsolved.

Cash slouched on the back row. He had slipped into the ceremony without speaking to anyone and planned to exit the same way. As spring killings gave way to a summer of carnage, a police detective entered the room and sat next to Cash. A case of gaydar in reverse. One straight dude drawn to another.

Cash quelled an instinct to bolt. In his past life as a crack criminal defense lawyer, he had racked up a slew of enemies in the police department. Based on a brutal cross-examination a decade ago, the cop at his side would fall squarely into the enemy camp.

The detective introduced himself to Cash as Robert Gamez and shook hands, betraying no hint of recognition. A pre-surgery Cash had last seen Gamez a year ago at the morgue, where Tina had identified Brandi Foxx as victim number four of the serial killer dubbed the Dice Cold Killer, or DCK for short. The men had stood on either side of Tina, ready to catch her if she collapsed.

She hadn't.

Cash was slow to give his name. Even after months of rehearsal, the new name still rang foreign to him. The voice sounded equally strange. After altering the face, Katzenbach had sent Cash to a specialist for pitch lowering surgery. Cash's voice had migrated from his head to his chest. He had gone from a baritone to a bass.

Cash still spoke as sparingly as possible, to Gamez and everyone else. Every word, every syllable, threatened to give him away, and for all he knew, Gamez could be bent. Cops had a long, lethal history of moonlighting as assassins, and a five-million-dollar hit fee would tempt even the cleanest cop.

Cash broke eye contact with Gamez and sat stone still, suffering through a thousand deaths. Actually, more like forty-two deaths, each with a separate screenshot, as Tina launched into the fall line of victims.

"What a waste," Gamez said. "Hard to sit through this."

Cash grunted in assent.

"Are you here for one of the victims?" the cop said.

"Here for all of them."

Gamez squirmed. "I meant, are you related to one of them?"

Cash pointed to Tina. "Related to her." He kept one eye on the screen, the other on the cop.

Gamez had an olive complexion and a square jaw. His barrel chest and biceps strained his blue blazer. He turned heads in a crowd, much as Cash had done in his youth, all of six months ago. Tonight, all eyes were on the detective, and Cash was invisible.

Gamez seemed oblivious to the attention. He sat ramrod straight. The bags under his eyes telegraphed the stress of being the lead officer in a high-profile investigation that was roiling the city. DCK had taken out six sisters in Dallas in the past two years.

Cash wondered whether the detective had turned up any fresh leads. Whether he was any closer to catching Brandi's killer. Whether he had come to the service out of a sense of duty, guilt, sympathy, all or none of the above.

Like most serial killers, DCK had a type. The victims had all been white, between the ages of twenty-five and thirty-five, and active in LGBTQ causes. The killer passed over the mild and meek—those who hid their candles under baskets. He went after fireballs—those who burned candles at both ends.

Like Brandi Foxx had done in the past. Or like Tina was doing now.

Speak of the angel, Brandi appeared on screen, sparking a sharp intake of breath by the detective. His jaw tensed, and his eyes narrowed.

Gamez must have known that Brandi was teed up as her death date neared, but he couldn't mask the triple shock of seeing her smiling face, hearing her name called, and watching her candle expire.

"Brandi Foxx was born in Ada, Oklahoma." Tina's voice broke. She pulled herself together and went on. "Brandi wasn't the name given her at birth, but she was a Brandi from day one." Her voice cracked again. "She was my best friend and my beacon."

Tina's tears flowed. "When I was coming out to family, friends, and coworkers, Brandi stood by me every inch of the way. On days I wanted to run away or hide under the covers, she forced me to face the world."

"Brandi was murdered by a serial killer who has taken from us six sisters in two years. We are working with the Dallas Police Department and the FBI to catch the monster terrorizing our community."

Scattered hissing greeted the shout out to law enforcement. Gamez sank lower in his seat.

"I want to thank especially Detective Robert Gamez of the Dallas Police Department for taking the lead in tracking down Brandi's killer and for being with us here tonight. Please stand, Detective Gamez."

Cash smiled. As if Gamez didn't already stand out in the rainbow-colored crowd with his Marine Corps crewcut, off-the-rack coat, and Dudley Do-Right demeanor.

Gamez blanched and remained seated.

"Don't be shy, detective." Tina motioned for him to stand.

A spotlight nailed him. He stood slowly and sat quickly. Stony silence greeted his curtain call, interrupted only by a stray hiss or two. Things were getting ugly between the community and the cops, what with six unsolved murders on the books.

A surge of sympathy for Gamez swept over Cash. Whatever the cop's motive for coming tonight, it sure as hell wasn't to see and be seen. He wasn't here for show.

With the detective on the defensive and distracted, Cash slipped from the room and the building. The moon had no-showed tonight. A cloak of darkness settled his nerves, but the calm proved short-lived.

Dozens of protesters congregated outside, chanting and carrying placards. They swarmed the parking lot and massed between Cash and his car. The kill-a-queer-for-Christ crowd added another flash point for a city on edge.

Cash recognized the mountain of a man with the megaphone. At six-six and two eighty, Reverend Gideon Bragg towered over his flock. With his gray beard and flowing mane, he looked like a throwback to the Civil War era.

A decade ago, he had split from the Southern Baptist Convention, finding the old guard too leftist, liberal, and libertine for his liking. Bragg had founded an offshoot brand of Bible thuggery, sometimes called The Sword of the Lord but more often dubbed The Sword of Gideon. It was an army forged for a religious war and committed to disrupting LGBTQ events, like tonight's memorial service.

Halfway to the lot, Cash made out the chant: *Pluck it out!* The message made no sense to him until he read both sides of a placard. "If Thine Eye Offend Thee" on one side. "Pluck It Out" on the other.

The sound of running footsteps prompted Cash to look back. Gamez was sprinting toward him. Cash picked up his pace, but the cop blew past him without a word and badged his way through the protesters.

The chant died down. Cash followed in the cop's wake and made it safely to his tan Chevy Malibu, the most forgettable car on the road. Gamez jumped into an unmarked Dodge Charger and peeled from the lot. Cash would have trailed him had Tina not emerged from the library.

The crowd smelled blood, while Cash smelled trouble. Gideon's disciples resumed the chant, louder than before, and hoisted their placards higher. Tina froze in the no-man's-land between the library and the lot. Cash motioned for her to go back inside. She ignored his warning and moved toward the mob.

Cash intercepted her before she passed the point of no return. "Go back to the library and wait this out," he shouted over the chanting.

Tina shook her head. She looked as if she had seen a ghost. That, or one was chasing her. "They found another body," she shouted back.

CHAPTER TWO

Their backs to the Dallas Public Library, Tina and Cash faced south toward Interstate 30. Beyond the highway loomed police headquarters, not that its denizens would lift a finger to protect Tina from the mob in the parking lot.

That job fell to Cash tonight. And every night.

No one from the memorial service joined Tina outside. Despite the death of another trans woman in Dallas tonight, the remembrance went on. This year's dead deserved their due, even as next year's honorees lined up for their star turns.

Cash shivered, and not just because the temperature had dived. November couldn't decide whether to cling to fall or slide into early winter. Seventy-two degrees yesterday, twenty-seven now.

Tina's rainbow-colored blouse fired up the protesters. The chanting intensified. Cash took the crowd's call to "pluck it out" as a threat to take her out.

"Go back inside," he told her. "Finish what you came here to do."

"Amber will wrap up." Trails of tears had eroded the mascara on Tina's face. "I'm going to Deep Ellum to identify the victim."

Her tone brooked no debate. It would be a waste of time trying to talk her out of the suicide mission of wading into the mob. She would head to the crime scene, with or without him.

It had to be with him. He hadn't protected her all these years to lose her tonight in a parking lot. "Who's the new victim?" he said.

Tina shook her head. "Gamez took off before I could get to him."

"Yeah, the cop shot out of here like his ass was on fire."

"I have to catch him," she said.

"How do you know the body is in Deep Ellum?"

"That's where DCK left the others." She held up her iPhone. "Plus, there's a media alert."

"First things first," he said. "Let's get you out of here before things turn ugly."

A glass bottle sailed toward them and crashed at their feet. Shards sprayed their shoes. *Too late.*

"I'm not afraid of them." Tina flipped a finger to the crowd.

"That's okay," Cash said. "I've got enough fear for both of us."

She rummaged through her bottomless purse. "Can't find my fucking keys."

He pulled her hand from the purse. "You're not going alone. Follow me and don't let go."

He cleared a lane for her, reverting to the form of his glory days as a fullback for the SMU Mustangs. Fortunately, most of Gideon's army were overweight and well past their prime. Still, roughly a dozen or so looked as if they could bench press their weight, and even the weakest in the flock had strong lungs to warn Tina where she would spend eternity.

Extended families, ranging in color from white to off-white and running in age from moppets to Medicare, clustered among the scores of protesters. A toxic mix of cousins marrying cousins. The family that mates together hates together.

It was easy to pick out the leader of the pack. Reverend Gideon Bragg held the power and the only megaphone.

Cash set out to prevent casualties tonight, on either side of the holy war. He plowed through the crowd, stiff-arming with his left hand, while his right hand clamped onto Tina's wrist. He took the brunt of the blows from placards. His legs kept churning, and he leaned into the hits.

The press of bodies slowed but never stopped him. He zigzagged through the lot, eyes ahead except for brief glances back at Tina. Though largely spared the gauntlet of placards, she suffered the sting of taunts ("Burn in hell, tranny!" and "Repent or die!" being the most common). Spat on and shoved, she soldiered on.

Their abuse backfired. With each step, Tina seemed stronger, becoming less of a drag on Cash and more of a spur forward.

Together they made it to the Chevy. Cash gassed and braked through the lot, inching through a crowd that parted like the Red Sea. When the Malibu finally broke free at the exit, it took an eternity for the car to reach sixty miles an hour.

***

Cop cars and crime tape kept Cash and Tina a half-block from the body. They joined a line of gawkers and reporters jockeying for a better view. A forensic team huddled around the deceased, shielding the victim from the press and public. When the forensic folks shifted positions, Cash caught glimpses of the corpse.

Tina accosted every cop who came within shouting distance with the bogus claim that she was there to assist Detective Gamez. None bought it, or if they did, none gave a shit.

She grabbed the arm of a uniformed officer as he passed by. He pulled free. "Touch me again, lady, and I'll arrest you for assaulting an officer."

"I have to talk to Detective Gamez," Tina said.

"He's busy," the uniformed officer said.

She pressed a card into his hand. "Please give it to him."

Five minutes later, Gamez trudged to the tape, moving like he had aged a decade in the past hour. Cash knew how that felt.

The detective stopped outside Tina's reach. "What are you doing here?"

"I came to identify the victim."

"If we need your help, we'll call." His tone told her not to wait by the phone. He walked a step or two away before turning back to her. "The formal identification will take place at the morgue. You should know the drill by now."

"Does she have any ID on her?" Cash asked as if he already knew the answer.

The detective turned toward Cash. "Who are you?"

"Meet Carl Meadows," Tina said. "My grandfather."

Gamez nodded. "You were at the memorial service." He looked around. No cop was within earshot. "There was no ID on her."

"I did you a solid by identifying Brandi Foxx," she said. "I need to know who the new victim is."

Tina had one thing going for her. The cops needed to know that too. The sooner, the better.

"I asked for your help with Brandi because she was your roommate." The detective's tone softened. Less hard-ass. More human. "Please tell me you haven't lost another roommate."

She patted Cash on the back. "Paw Paw is rooming with me until he gets settled."

The cop gave Cash a look that said, *Good luck with that, buddy.* "If I let you see the body, you don't touch anything."

Tina nodded.

"Don't talk to anyone but me."

She kept nodding.

Gamez lifted the tape. "And you leave as soon as I tell you to."

Tina and Cash ducked under the tape and squeezed into the scrum around the body. A sheet covered the corpse to the neck. It was still more than Cash wanted to see. A scene he couldn't unsee.

Gamez and Cash bookended Tina for support. When her knees buckled, the cop caught her. Her tears left no doubt she could make a positive ID.

* * *

Cash and Tina sat in the parked Malibu. Minutes passed in silence. With the body gone, the crowd had drifted away. Cops cleared out. Tonight's mission accomplished: Tina had managed to make the identification of her trans friend Veronica Stoddard, despite the mutilation.

"The eyes," she said.

Cash closed his. "I know." The less said about them, the better. "Do you want to go back to the library?"

Tina shook her head. "The service will be over."

"How about home?"

She nodded. “I think I made a mistake.”

“On the identification?” he said.

“On bringing you into my private hell.”

Not your call, mijita.

No way would he leave her side, not with a killer on the loose.

CHAPTER THREE

Freddy the Forger hadn't changed. Same shaggy hair and pitted complexion. Same skin-and-bones body. Same bloodshot eyes that never settled on anyone or anything longer than a nanosecond.

If not in need of Freddy's services, Cash would never have risked an encounter with a client from his past life at the defense bar. Then again, if Freddy saw through the surgeries, Cash was as good as dead anyway.

Freddy, a two-time loser, sank deeper into the darkness of a back booth at a Maple Avenue dive called Rosita's. The forger hunched over the house special: a frozen blue margarita and *chalupas poblanas*, no charge for the extra grease.

Cops, the ultimate connoisseurs of cheap grub, gave the joint a four-roach rating and avoided it like the plague. The absence of police made Rosita's a perfect sanctuary for Freddy and his customers.

"Who the hell are you?" A string of cheese dangled from Freddy's mouth as he spoke.

Cash breathed easier. Dr. Katzenbach's handiwork had passed the Freddy test. Granted, a low bar.

"I may be in need of your services," Cash said.

"Buzz off." Freddy's spindly arms circled his plate. Cash had seen the defensive posture before, while doing time in Club Fed on a bum rap for jury tampering. An attempt by weaker prisoners to block the stronger from filching their food. It hadn't worked for Cash at FCI Seagoville. He doubted it had worked any better for Freddy, at any of his joints.

A frumpy waitress shuffled to the booth for Cash's order. "I'll have what he's not having," he said. "Surprise me."

She waddled away.

"What did you say your name was?" Freddy sounded suspicious.

"I didn't." Cash placed a large envelope on the table and leaned back to show he had no designs on the *chalupas*. "But for the record, it's Carl Meadows."

"You smell like pork," Freddy said. "The cop hangout is down the street."

"Ex," Cash said, "and no longer a fan of the boys in blue, which gives us something in common. I checked your background. You picked up a pair of felonies a couple of decades back. Forging passports."

Freddy shrugged, as if the convictions were no biggie.

Cash went on. "Since then, though, you've beaten two raps. Hats off to you. Fucking over the feds two times is no small feat."

Freddy's eyes narrowed. "It was no small *fee*, that's for damn sure. Cost me a fortune to beat those bullshit charges."

Not exactly how Cash remembered it. Neither the part about Freddy forking over a fortune for his defense, nor the bit about the government's cases being bogus. Cash had worked miracles for those acquittals.

The waitress returned with a Dos Equis and three cheese enchiladas atop refried beans and Spanish rice. "Anything else?" she said.

"Just a smile and a kind word, my lovely."

She left without a smile or a word, kind or otherwise.

"Who gave you my name?" Freddy said.

"A friend of yours. Cash McCahill."

Freddy shook his head. "I don't know any Cash McCahill."

"That's odd, because he represented you at your last two trials. He's the reason you're not doing life as a three-time loser."

"Oh, that Cash McCahill."

As if there were so many.

Cash had to hand it to Freddy. Caught in an obvious lie, he didn't blush or miss a beat. Instead, he rushed to the next whopper. "A name from the distant past. Must've slipped my mind, having left that life behind long ago."

Make that his next *two* lies.

Freddy lied often but not well, which explained why Cash had avoided the mistake made by the forger's first lawyer: Tony Dial, aka Terrible Negotiator Tony. TNT for short.

Regina Delgado, then an assistant US attorney in Dallas and now the deputy attorney general, had run circles around the hapless defense. Regina had stuck Freddy and a flunky in separate interrogation rooms and left it to defense counsel to do the rest. Tony had obliged by spooking Freddy into believing his partner had turned on him. Simultaneously, a public defender sold the same crock of shit to the flunky. As a result, the co-conspirators ratted out each other and, in the process, screwed themselves.

Freddy and Tony had fallen for the oldest trick in the prosecutors' playbook: the prisoners' dilemma game. The ploy was old but effective, netting not one but two convictions and cementing Regina's reputation as the GOAT of the gotcha game.

Cash had his own history with Regina, but he didn't dwell on it. It was too painful. He returned to the task before him. "McCahill claimed you were the best in the business."

Freddy belched. "What business would that be?"

"He called you an artist. The da Vinci of fake documents." A pause for Freddy to take a bow. When he didn't, Cash continued. "If someone needs an ID that'll pass the tightest security on the planet, you're the man to see."

"I'm out of the business," Freddy said, "that I was never into."

Cash smiled. A prosecutor would have a field day with Freddy. "I understand your caution. You don't know me, and you can't call Cash to check me out. With him being gone and probably dead, you sure don't want to take on the feds a fourth time."

Cash emptied the contents of the envelope onto the table. "Maybe this will ease your mind." He spread out four items: a Texas driver's license, a social security card, a voter ID, and a passport. All in the name of Carl Meadows and part of a go bag he had put together upon getting in bed with a cartel. He had left the cash from the go bag in a safe place.

"What do you expect me to do with these?" Freddy said.

"Tell me how good they are. Nothing dicey or dangerous about that. I'm simply asking for your expert opinion on the quality of my documents."

Freddy picked up the driver's license, looked at both sides, and put it down. "Experts get paid for their opinions."

Cash had come prepared. "Will you take a check?"

"Sure. As soon as it clears, I'll send you my written opinion by snail mail."

Cash pulled out his wallet and placed a hundred-dollar bill on the table. Freddy tapped the table. Cash laid out another hundred. Freddy tapped again.

Cash balked at paying more than his hourly rate back in his heyday as a defense lawyer. "Two hundred bucks for ten minutes of your precious time is more than fair."

Freddy pocketed the bills. "Okay, Mister Big Spender, I'm feeling generous today." He picked up the driver's license again. "Where'd you get this?"

"I know a man who knows a man," Cash said.

"It should get you past security at the airport." Freddy looked up from the license. "I'll go you double or nothing that the man you know, the one who knows the other man, met you outside the *Fiesta Mercado* on Ross Avenue."

Cash didn't take the bet. "Can you do better?"

"In my sleep."

Freddy rated the fakes by who they would fool. The driver's license scored highest as TSA-proof. The passport, lowest as likely to bump a sleepy bank teller.

"I'm considering a job at a law firm," Cash said. "Will these documents get my foot in the door?"

"As a lawyer?"

Cash shook his head. "Investigator."

"Fifty-fifty."

"What's your fee for a set of documents that moves the odds in my favor?"

"Like I said before, I'm no longer in the business that I was never into."

Cash swept the items into the envelope and started to rise. Freddy grabbed his arm. "But speaking strictly hypothetically, someone in that line of work could whip out a set for a K, payment in cash and up front."

"How good would the docs be?"

"Good enough to get you into the White House."

"Last place on the planet I want to go." Cash pretended to weigh the offer before counting out five more bills and placing them on the table. "Half now. The rest on delivery."

***

"Business at the firm has gone from bad to worse." Tina broke the news to Cash while clearing the breakfast dishes in her apartment. The smell of chicory coffee and cinnamon buns lingered in a kitchen decorated in powder blues and hot pinks. The toaster, coffee maker, place mats, cups, and dishes bore the Hello Kitty logo. "If work doesn't pick up soon, I don't know what I'll do."

Cash stayed at the kitchen table. She filled his coffee cup. "No sweat," he said. "Carl Meadows to the rescue." He pushed an envelope to her. She picked up the envelope but didn't count the bills.

"Carl Meadows is nothing but the name of an old man who needs to keep a low profile and spend as little as possible. Make that, no profile and spend nothing. That means you don't leave the apartment without clearing it with me first, Paw Paw, and you don't need to pay rent."

Cash winced. "I'll pay double if we can agree on another nickname?"

"No way. You chose Carl Meadows to keep the same initials. Makes sense. Possible that something from your past will turn up with your initials on it. Same reason you're stuck with what I called *mi abuelo*, God rest his soul. Someone from my past might remember my nickname for him."

She pushed the envelope toward him. "You took me off the streets and never charged me a dime. Not for the legal fees. Not for room and board. Not for risking a beating or worse from Rocky."

Cash frowned at the name of her former pimp. He made no move to pick up the envelope.

"Our situations are totally different," he said. "You were a kid with no means of support." At least, no means that didn't make his skin crawl. "Once I got involved with a cartel, I put together a go bag stuffed with bills. I can afford rent and board."

What he didn't tell her was that the bag had gotten considerably lighter. When Cash McCahill dropped out of sight, the bag bulged with $379,571 in small bills. The transformation from Cash to Carl had cost one hundred grand, and it would cost a like amount to undo the process.

"Six or seven K a month is no sweat," he lied. "Just don't deposit ten K or more at one time and trigger an IRS reporting requirement."

She nodded.

"What I can't do is stay cooped up here. I'm going stir crazy."

"As long as there's a contract out on you, it's too dangerous for you to be on the streets. Besides, Carl Meadows doesn't exist, except in your head."

"In three days, I'll have a set of documents that proves otherwise."

"Those documents and three dollars will get you a cup of coffee at Starbucks."

"Those documents," Cash said, "will get me a job. While we're on the subject, maybe it's time for you to look for a new one."

Tina stopped loading the dishwasher and turned toward him. "I can't abandon Goldy and Eva in their hour of need."

"It's not really abandonment if they can't afford to keep you on, and it sounds like their need will last a damn sight longer than an hour. If we both have paying gigs, we can help them more." He shifted in his seat. "How's Goldy's health?"

"Lousy," she said. "He drinks too much. Sleeps too little. Smokes on the sly. Worries all the time. You know how he gets when he doesn't have a case to chew on."

Cash certainly did. Exactly how he suffered when he didn't have a trial in the works.

"He hides cigars behind the law books in his office," Cash said. "You need to sneak into his office and confiscate them. What about Eva? How's she doing?"

"She worries all the time too, mostly about you." Tina sat at the table across from him. "I'm not okay with keeping Eva and Goldy in the dark. We should tell them you're alive."

He shook his head. "You need to brush up on your Sherlock Holmes canon."

"You lost me."

"Holmes faked his death and disappeared for years without telling his sidekick Dr. Watson where he was or even that he was alive. He had to do it that way. Watson's grief sold the notion that Holmes was dead."

"Then I guess I should feel honored that you let *me* know."

"You hooked me up with Dr. Katzenbach. Without him, I couldn't have disappeared in plain sight. If there had been any way to keep you in the dark, I would have."

She wrapped both hands around her coffee cup and stared into the drink. "Truth is, I've been thinking about making a change."

"Great minds," he said.

"I'm considering applying to the Dallas Police Department."

Cash choked on the coffee. Veronica Stoddard's murder must have pushed Tina over the edge. "Not the worst idea you've ever had, but it definitely ranks in the bottom five."

Her nostrils flared, but before she could fire back, there was a knock on the door. She rose and headed to the foyer.

"Look through the peephole first." He had a premonition and raced toward the door.

The knob turned in Tina's hand. "It's the police," she said.

He picked up speed. It wouldn't be the first time a cop turned hitman. Nor the first time a hitman impersonated a cop.

CHAPTER FOUR

On Saturday, Tina screwed herself six ways to Sunday.

First mistake, she invited the uninvited visitors into the apartment. Detective Robert Gamez and FBI Special Agent Stanley Bowers made an odd couple. Gamez was fit and twenty years younger than the pasty, pear-shaped Bowers.

Cash distrusted both, but for different reasons and with different intensities. Though he barely knew Gamez, how could he trust anyone with the bad judgment to team up with Bowers the backstabber?

While the cop set off a single alarm, Bowers triggered all five. The toxic agent had been behind the banishment to Bismarck of Maggie Burns, Cash's ex-lover. Gamez could rot in the hallway, but Bowers should rot in hell.

Moreover, Cash operated under a strict quota of law enforcement types allowed inside the home without a warrant, and that number was zero.

Both men wore blue blazers, starched white shirts, and gray slacks. They were color coordinated and on the clock. Nothing about the visit spelled check-the-box. Not the day, time, or place.

In his prior life, Cash had cross-examined Bowers twice, in the process picking up two important tidbits. One, Bowers lied like the politician he was, oath or no oath. Most agents strayed reluctantly from the truth, but Bowers reveled in falsehoods.

Two, when both cases went south on the feds, Bowers lined up a fall guy for one and a fall gal for the other. When it came to passing the buck, he didn't discriminate based on race, creed, religion, sex, or color.

Gamez had better watch his back.

Cash stopped Bowers in the foyer. "Is your visit personal or professional?"

Bowers made no effort to hide his disappointment at finding a man in the apartment. Agents always wanted to confront a witness or target alone and outnumbered.

"Are you asking in a personal or professional capacity?" Bowers said.

"Strictly personal. I'm Tina's grandfather. Carl Meadows." Cash extended his hand.

Bowers didn't shake. "Then it's strictly professional on our part."

Gamez spoke to Bowers, "I met Mr. Meadows a couple of days ago." He didn't say where or under what circumstances.

Barefoot and showing too much skin in hot pink pajamas, Tina invited everyone into the kitchen. Her nails matched the pjs and the Hello Kitty motif. She offered breakfast to the visitors.

Mistake number two. Bad enough to bring Johnny Law inside the walls. Worse to prolong the stay.

Gamez ceded the last cinnamon bun to Bowers. Both men nodded to the offer of coffee. Before they could settle down at the breakfast table, Cash herded everyone into the living room.

In contrast to the cozy kitchen, the living room was stark and chilly. Black leather, shiny chrome, and polished glass gave it an office vibe. A collection of souvenir shot glasses on the fireplace mantle tracked Tina's travels, pre-transition to the present.

Cash guided the men to the couch and Tina to the chair farthest from them. He sat between her and the law and said, "How can we help you?" The offer to help rang hollow. He had shepherded Tina through scrapes with cops for a decade and had no intention of aiding anyone but her.

"There's no *we* to it," Bowers said. "Detective Gamez and I are here to see Miss Campos, and we'll talk to her alone. We can do it here or at headquarters."

Tina started to speak, but Cash cut her off. "We'll do it here, and I stay."

Bowers gave stony silence a chance to turn Cash around. It didn't. The agent blinked. "Are you an attorney?" The way he said "attorney" made it sound like a bad thing.

"Hell no," Cash said. "What gave you that idea?"

"You act like one." Bowers turned his attention to Tina. "I won't take much of your time, Miss Campos, but I have a few questions about Veronica Stoddard."

Tina tensed, as did Cash. An image of trans victim number seven haunted both. The killer had dumped her body in a Deep Ellum alley, taking her eyes as souvenirs.

Like the shot glasses on the mantle.

Cash didn't buy the bullshit about the interview not taking much time. Agents always said that before subjecting a sap to the third degree.

Relegated to the note-taking role, Gamez held a pen in one hand and a pad in the other. Dollars to donuts, Bowers had told the cop to let the big, bad agent do all the talking.

The Bureau rarely recorded interviews, opting instead to churn out self-serving memoranda from handwritten notes. Less chance that way of exculpatory nuggets cropping up in their works of creative fiction.

Bowers lobbed a softball. "I understand that you knew Veronica."

Tina nodded. "She went by Ronnie."

"How long did you know her?"

"Four…five years…as long as she'd been in Dallas. She moved here from Jackson, Mississippi. We ran in the same circles."

"When was the last time you saw her?"

Cash cut in, hoping to break the rhythm of the interview. "You mean while Veronica was alive?"

The agent made a show of exasperation. "Yes."

"About a week ago," she said.

"When and where was that?"

"A mutual friend threw a fundraiser for a candidate from the Valley. Ronnie and I were there to show our support."

Bowers stayed silent. This time the pause paid off.

"Carole Donovan," Tina said. "It was her fundraiser."

Mistake number three: volunteering information.

"Did you talk to Miss Stoddard at the fundraiser?"

Tina nodded. She pulled her knees to her chest, her heels resting on the edge of the chair. She was getting too comfortable in the presence of the enemy.

Mistake number four.

"What did you two talk about?" Bowers said.

"I don't recall anything specific," she said. "Just the usual chitchat about work, movies, TV, that sort of thing."

"Maybe I can jog your memory." Bowers's tone suggested there was no maybe to it. "Did you two discuss the remembrance ceremony that took place at the library last week?"

Tina nodded.

"Tell me about that," Bowers said.

Cash's discomfort level spiked. This didn't have the feel of a drive-by debriefing. The agent was breaking ground and about to dig deep and hard.

Cash considered shutting down the interview. If he could afford to out himself as a lawyer, he would have pulled the plug long before now. However, he was walking a fine line with a fake identity. He needed to protect Tina like an asshole attorney without coming off as one.

"Tina, our guests are running low on coffee," Cash said.

She slid off the chair and took a step toward the couch.

Bowers held up a palm, signaling her to stop. "*No más.*" Gamez followed the agent's lead.

She retreated to the chair and resumed the position. Arms wrapped around her legs. Chin tucked into the valley between her knees.

"Did you and Veronica argue about the ceremony?" Bowers said.

Tina hugged her knees tighter to her chest, curling into a smaller target. Her mouth opened, but no words came out.

Bowers leaned forward. "Did you strike Stoddard at the fundraiser?"

Tina blanched. Cash couldn't contain himself any longer. "Are you treating Tina as a suspect in Stoddard's murder?"

Bowers went silent again, which told Cash all he needed to know. The interview was over. Cash sensed that Gamez had something to say but didn't dare.

"She's a person of interest," Bowers said.

Tina looked from the agent to Cash. "What does that mean?"

"It means," Cash said, "that you're talking to an attorney before answering any more questions."

"But I have nothing to hide," she said.

In Cash's world, everyone had something to hide, and those who claimed otherwise hid the deepest, darkest secrets. Besides, talking to the law was always a crapshoot, with the odds favoring the house. Not Tina's home but the big house.

A target was a thousand times more likely to talk her way into trouble than weasel out of it. Despite Bowers's ploy of calling her a person of interest rather than a suspect, he had painted a bull's-eye on her back.

"I have only one or two more questions," Bowers said.

Cash didn't buy that either. He had pulled the same stunt on scores of judges. Whenever Her Honor threatened to shut down a cross-examination, Cash promised only a few more questions. Anything to keep it going. And going. And going.

"We can clear this up now," Bowers said, "or do it at headquarters. Your choice, Miss Campos."

Tina looked lost. "I really don't have anything to—"

"I need to talk to my granddaughter alone." Cash dragged Tina into her bedroom and closed the door behind them. She sat on a canopy bed. He stood by the door. "Have you forgotten everything Goldy and I taught you about talking to the cops? Lesson number one: don't do it."

She went pale. Cash chalked it up to nerves.

"I can clear this up in two minutes," she said.

"Then you *have* forgotten everything. I'm booting them out, and we're calling Goldy."

"This is totally insane. They can't really believe I had anything to do with Ronnie's death!"

"Keep your voice down," he said. "We don't know what they believe or what they know. Until we do, you say nothing."

"You saw me at the memorial service. A hundred people were there, including Gamez. What do those guys think? That I killed her and then raced back to the library?" Her voice rose with every word.

He warned her again to lower her voice. "Here's a quick lesson in Criminal Law 101. Whenever an agent describes you as a target, suspect, or person of interest, shut the fuck up and call a lawyer."

"Speaking of lawyers," she said, "you'd better stop acting like one. You're about to blow your cover."

Cash moved away from the door. "Which is why we're calling in Goldy."

"We'll call him right after I remind the big, dumb cop out there that he's my alibi. He can place me in the library when Ronnie's body was found in Deep Ellum."

"Two problems with that plan," Cash said. "First, Gamez doesn't strike me as dumb. Bit of a plodder maybe, but not dumb. Second, there's nothing you can tell them that Goldy can't relay with less risk to you. Your statements are admissible in court against you. Goldy's aren't."

Her shoulders slumped in surrender. "Okay, when we go back to the living room, I'll let you do the talking."

Cash knew her better than that. "You stay here. I'll handle our guests and report back when they're gone."

Cash found Bowers at the fireplace mantle, holding a shot glass. "Your granddaughter gets around. Hong Kong, Portugal, Ireland, Amsterdam, New Zealand, South Africa, and I'm just halfway down the row." He replaced one glass and picked up another. "Here we go. Thailand. I knew she'd have this one."

"Tina is done talking to you," Cash said, "until we hire a lawyer."

Bowers returned the glass to the mantle. "Her decision or yours?"

"Mine. You must be desperate for leads if you're running down this dead end."

"Every once in a while," the agent said, "a dead end leads to a dead body."

"Get real. Your silent partner there saw Tina at the library the night Stoddard was murdered. He's a witness *for* her."

"I'm not a witness for or against anyone." Gamez did his best impersonation of Switzerland. It wasn't very good.

While it was never wise for a witness to talk to cops, a lawyer could learn a lot if he got the boys in blue talking. Time to pump the pair for info.

"What led you to question my granddaughter in the first place?" Cash said.

Bowers didn't respond right away. When he did, it sounded cold, clinical, and confident. "For starters, Tina is connected to every one of the victims. They all knew her, and we believe the killer is someone the vics knew and trusted. Two of them lived for a time with Tina, including Stoddard. Did you know that Stoddard and your granddaughter shacked up for six months? I hear they fought like wildcats and had a nasty breakup."

Cash hadn't known that but didn't let on. "Is that it?" he asked.

"Not by a long shot," Bowers said. "Did you know that Stoddard and your granddaughter turned tricks together?"

In a fever dream that came and went in a flash, Cash lunged for Bowers and choked the life from him. Instead, Cash settled for setting the record straight. "Tina works at a law firm now."

"So same thing," Bowers said. "Once a whore, always a whore."

"I heard it differently," Cash said. "Once an asshole, always an asshole."

Bowers's face turned red. "Finally, serial killers often try to get involved in the investigation of their crimes. Allows them to monitor the goings-on. Tina has been pushing to assist our task force for months, even to the point of crashing crime scenes."

Cash scoffed. "You don't have a shred of evidence tying Tina to Stoddard's murder, and she has an air-tight alibi."

"Who says she acted alone?" Bowers said.

Tina reappeared in the living room without waiting for the green light from Cash.

Mistake number five.

"This may be an awkward time to ask for a favor, Detective Gamez," she said, "but I'd like to go on a ride-along with you."

Gamez looked flustered. Cash silently screamed at Tina to shut the fuck up.

Bowers smiled and said, "I see you're still eager to *assist* our investigation, Miss Campos."

"I can be your liaison to the transgender community," she said.

Mistake number six.

CHAPTER FIVE

"You're late." Bunkered behind his boomerang-shaped desk, Goldy glared at Cash but spoke to Tina. "And it ain't bring-your-grandpappy-to-work day."

Not since Cash had disappeared six months ago and resurfaced as Carl Meadows had he seen Goldy at close range. In that time, the old man seemed to have shrunk, making his head too large for the withering body. A walking cane lay across the desk. That was new.

Cash invited himself to sit and said, "It doesn't look like you can afford to run off any prospects."

Though Eva had banned smoking in the office years ago, decades of cigar smoke had seeped into the walls. A sepia haze fogged the room. The framed photos and newspaper articles of Goldy's courtroom triumphs looked like relics in a musty museum.

Tina sat. "Goldy, meet Carl Meadows, *mi abuelo*. He'll be staying with me for a while."

Goldy's eyebrows arched. "You never mentioned a grandfather," he said.

Tina blushed. "We were kind of estranged."

Faced with the ultimate test of his new identity, Cash made no move to shake hands or speak more than necessary. He had accompanied Tina, thereby risking recognition, only because he didn't trust her to convey the gravity of her plight.

If he could fool Goldy and Eva, both of whom had worked at his side for years, he owed Dr. Katzenbach a five-star rating on Yelp. If not, he was on the next plane to New Zealand.

Goldy grunted in what passed for hello. "Bringing gramps to the office won't spare you from an ass-chewing for being late."

Cash breathed easier. He was halfway home.

"I'm late because—"

Goldy cut her off. "And no bullshit excuses. Nothing short of death, and by that, I mean *your* death, gets you off the hook."

"The reason I'm late," she said, "is that I had a visit this morning from the Dallas Police Department and—"

Goldy cut her off again. "If you're back on the streets, your timing sucks. This is election season, when vice pumps up the stats to drive the church crowd to the polls. Even meth whores zonked out of their skulls know to lie low during the run-up to a vote."

"It's a little more serious than a vice bust, but thanks for the vote of confidence." Tina sounded more hurt than pissed. "A homicide detective and an FBI agent dropped by the apartment, which got my day off to a great start."

Goldy rocked forward in his chair. "Now you've got my attention."

Evidently, Eva's too. The paralegal appeared in the doorway. It was the first time Cash had seen her up close in six months. Previous sightings had been covert and at a distance, for her safety and his. He counted on daily updates from Tina to keep him in the loop.

Eva hugged Tina and introduced herself to Cash. No hint of recognition in her voice or eyes. Final and toughest test, passed.

Or was it?

He caught Eva eyeing him and tried hard not to stare back. It wasn't easy. He had watched her transform from a street kid to a skilled paralegal. The old Cash would have mocked her outfit, but Carl Meadows had to hold his tongue. That also wasn't easy, given her puffy blouse and parachute pants. In their fifteen years together, she had gone through about a hundred phases. Hippie chick, goth girl, boho, biker babe, deb, cowgirl, on and on.

She changed looks more often than Goldy switched socks. Her current choice registered as one of the more comical.

Hammer called and wants his pants back.

"Don't forget your ten-thirty appointment," Eva said to her boss.

Cash placed the odds of Goldy having such an appointment at less than fifty-fifty. More likely, she had given the old man an opening to put Tina to work and send Cash home.

"To the surprise of absolutely no one," Goldy said to Eva, "our part-time receptionist and full-time problem child has gotten her brand new tits in a wringer." He winked at Tina. "Don't think for a minute I haven't noticed."

Cash rolled his eyes. An old dog up to his old tricks.

Cash stood and walked to the window facing Griffin Street. The packed parking lot behind the federal courthouse meant multiple trials in the works, putting parking spaces at a premium.

God, how he missed the courtroom. The worst day in trial was better than the best day behind a desk. Jonesing for a fix of courtroom action, he promised himself a blitz through the courthouse after the meeting with Goldy. No tarrying. No talking. Simply a chance to feel the heat of whatever trial generated the most sparks.

For old crime's sake.

Tina relayed the early morning visit almost word for word. Cash picked up the narrative at the point of Tina's banishment to the bedroom.

Goldy sat through the story stoically, while Eva's face registered greater outrage by the word. "I'm going to cut off Bowers's balls," she said, "and feed them to Gamez."

A pre-op Tina stiffened in her seat. "Hold off on the talk of surgery below the belt until Gamez does me a solid. I asked him to take me on a ride-along."

Goldy rose to his feet. "Worst. Idea. Ever."

"Thank you," Cash said.

"The plan is," Goldy told Tina, "that you stay as far away from the police as possible. That means no riding around with cops, no sleeping with them, zero contact of any kind with the boys in blue. Don't even watch cop shows on TV."

Tina stood eye to eye with Goldy, three feet of mahogany between them. "Okay. I'll put you down as undecided." She left the office in a huff.

On the way out, Cash passed by his empty office. It looked untouched since the day he had jettisoned his old life. He thought about asking Eva about the missing occupant but decided not to push his luck.

On the steps outside Founders' Square, Cash ran into Freddy the Forger, who was about to enter the building. The two men stopped and stared at each other. After an awkward silence, Cash said, "Are you going to see Goldy?"

Freddy sighed. "Once again I find myself unjustly accused by an overzealous government."

By Cash's calculation, that happened roughly every five to ten years. "Do me a solid and don't mention our little transaction to Goldy."

"Funny," Freddy said, "I was about to tell you the same thing."

***

The federal courthouse featured a distinctive odor for each floor. By smell alone, Cash bailed from the elevator at the sixteenth floor. The fiefdom of federal judges with lifetime tenure reeked of raw power. A protected preserve for a rare breed who would never sweat the loss of a paycheck.

Cash had tried cases in every courtroom in the building and ventured into the chambers of every judge in the courthouse. Often invited there for conferences among counsel. Occasionally summoned for a tongue-lashing. The chambers all featured a photo of the kingmaker behind the appointment of every jurist in the building. Whenever Stewart Powell whispered a name to the president, a new judge got a black robe.

The sixteenth floor also offered lockup cells for prisoners in transport to and from court, some of whom would score lifetime gigs. A not-so-rare breed who would never sweat room or board.

Twice, Cash had landed in a cell called "Suite Sixteen," which was set aside for attorneys sanctioned for contempt. Strike one had drawn a lunch hour behind bars. Strike two had led to lockup for a full day. So far, no strike three.

Today, the halls also carried a whiff of justice—at least the rough brand handed down by juries. That morning, three criminal trials had reached the deliberation stage. The rare trifecta meant heavy foot traffic on the floor. Thirty-six jurors took frequent breaks from deciding defendants' fates to roam the halls, check their messages, kick vending machines, and clog the restrooms.

The jurors wore badges identifying them as such. No need for a badge to pick out the accused. At one end of the hall, a pair of suit-and-tie defendants huddled with friends, families, and attorneys armed with leather attaches. The combined stroke of the counsel and their clients scored an audience with Jenna Powell, the US attorney.

Jenna worked the hallway like a politician, shaking hands with the connected and hugging the well-connected. The politicking made sense, given her open campaign to replace Karen Belton as attorney general. Regina Delgado, number two in the Justice Department, loomed as Jenna's biggest rival.

Belton had crossed the president in a way that would not go unpunished. Cash had a history with both leading candidates for the top job. He also had dirt on both but no plan to use his ammo against either.

At the other end of the hall sat a defendant, eyes down and slumped on a bench. Alone. Looking like he had lost his last friend in the world. He wore black boots, black pants, and a white Mexican wedding shirt. A day laborer in his Sunday best.

Cash gravitated to the loner. "Mind if I share a bench with you?"

The Latino scooted over. At close range, he looked younger, maybe mid-thirties. He was short and stocky. Not a gym-hardened body but a compact build, courtesy of physical labor. Calloused hands pegged him as a construction worker or landscaper.

The defendant waited to speak until a gaggle of jurors had passed out of earshot. "Are you a lawyer?"

"No, but I've watched more trials than most lawyers will in a lifetime. I come to the courthouse for entertainment. Sort of like watching Judge Judy in the flesh." Cash suspected the TV reference flew over the head of one who toiled dawn to dusk, seven days a week. "Who's your attorney?"

"Lawyer Helms."

"He's one of the good guys." Cash looked around. No Helms in sight. "Where is he now?"

"He's talking to the prosecutor."

The defendant's silver wedding ring tempted Cash to ask why the wife wasn't here to show support. Jurors noticed the absence. Going through a criminal trial is hell. Doing so alone is hell squared.

Cash nixed the question. Too personal. Might hit a nerve and make things worse.

The defendant must have read Cash's mind. "*Mi esposa* is with our kids. Me being out of work during the trial...." He didn't finish the sentence.

"What are you charged with?" Cash said.

"Harboring illegals."

"*Familia*?"

The defendant nodded. "*Mis primos*."

"What time did the jury start deliberating?"

"Nine."

Cash checked his watch. "They've been out almost three hours. Good sign. Helms gave them something to think about."

The Latino mustered a faint smile.

Cash stood. "The meeting between your lawyer and the prosecutor, whose idea was it?"

"The prosecutor's. Miss Martin came here about ten minutes ago and asked Lawyer Helms to meet in her office."

"That is a *very* good sign."

The defendant's smile widened.

Jenna Powell walked past Cash. He took two steps toward her, aiming to bust her chops over the shameless jockeying for the AG job but stopped short. That would have been a Cash move, not one by a stranger like Carl Meadows.

Rumors of Jenna's recent engagement to Lou Watson, the CEO of Longhorn Investments, had reached Cash. Watson was twenty years her senior and twenty times wealthier than her father. Here again, Cash would have had something to say about that, but Carl couldn't.

The emergence of FBI Agent Stanley Bowers from Judge Tapia's chambers ended Cash's stay at the courthouse. He hauled ass to the elevator bank.

* * *

That night, Cash swung by his house on Lakewood Avenue. Despite his absence for six months, the place still looked lived in. The yard, maintained. But only because Eva had a key and looked after the house and grounds.

Cash didn't stop or slow down on the street. A dark van with dark windows made sure of that. He had seen the same van before, parked in the same place, a half-block from his house.

Dollars to donuts, a hitman was staking out his house in the hope that Cash would return for clothes or whatever. Getting sloppy like that would cost Cash his life and net the *sicario* a cool five mil from the cartel.

CHAPTER SIX

Skyler Patterson's article in the Dallas Morning News on the Dice Cold Killer put Cash off his breakfast burrito. Across the table, Tina sucked the dregs of a strawberry smoothie through a straw and said, "It's been more than two weeks since Gamez came by."

"So?" He knew where she was going with this. The same place she had gone yesterday and the day before.

"I'm going to ask again for a ride-along."

"Over my dead body."

"Don't tempt me. Not with a bounty on your head and rent due tomorrow."

Cash pushed aside his plate. The steel in her green-gray eyes told him the debate had already been lost. When he had rescued her from the streets, she had been a stubborn, feral creature. The feral had worn off. The stubbornness stuck. "You're not going to drop this damn fool idea, are you?"

She raised her right hand. "I solemnly swear not to say an incriminating word to the detective all night."

"Oh, I know you won't," he said, "because I'll be at your side the whole time."

***

Gamez knocked on the door to Tina's apartment at precisely 8:00 p.m. Cash answered the door, ready to roll. Tina wasn't.

The two men sat in the living room. Cash broke the awkward silence with the news that he would accompany his granddaughter on the ride-along.

Gamez frowned. "I brought only one waiver form."

"No problem," Cash said. "We can sign the same CYA document. That'll give the department cover if one or both of us stubs a toe."

The detective's frown deepened. "You should've been a lawyer," he said. It didn't come off as a compliment.

"He's not a lawyer," Tina said from the hallway, heels clicking on the wooden floor. "Just a run of the mill asshole. Rule of thumb: While all lawyers are assholes, not all assholes are lawyers."

Gamez laughed. "I'll try to remember that."

She made an entrance into the living room, dolled up and dressed more for a date than a descent onto the mean streets of Dallas. Makeup meticulously applied. Red hair brushing her shoulders. A clingy, crimson dress that fell inches north of her knees, its color matching her lipstick and nails. Heeled sandals that would be a serious handicap in chasing down criminals.

"You look…." Whatever Gamez started to say, second thoughts silenced him.

"Ridiculous," Cash said. "Is that the word you were going for?"

The cop rose from the couch. "I was going to say overdressed."

She looked crushed. "What's wrong with what I'm wearing? I thought we might stop at some nice places."

"You thought wrong," Gamez said.

"See what I've got on." Cash stood to model sneakers, jeans, and a Texas Rangers T-shirt.

"Your grandfather is a tad underdressed," said the detective, who had on the same by-the-book blue blazer, white shirt, and gray slacks he'd been wearing during his visit with Bowers.

"Since it took her forever and a day to get ready," Cash said, "let's roll as-is. If we run into trouble, Beat Cop Barbie can stay in the car."

Gamez had commandeered a Caddie from the department's fleet of forfeited vehicles. Tina rode shotgun, while Cash stretched out in the back. They cruised Uptown, a hive of temptation for the hot and horny. Bars and restaurants lit up the area. The patrons were on their way to being lit up as well.

"We don't get many requests for a ride-along these days," the detective said, "and civilians generally want to hang with patrol. Why did you ask for me?"

He braked for a gaggle of college-age kids jaywalking across McKinney Avenue and snarling traffic both ways. He picked up the phone to call in the violation but let it slide.

Tina held her response until the party made it safely to the other side. "You're still in charge of the DCK investigation, right?"

Gamez nodded.

"Then we're on the same team," she said, "whether you realize it or not."

The detective snickered. He caught a red light at the intersection of Cedar Springs and Oak Lawn, which gave Cash a chance to torpedo any talk of a team. "What part of 'person of interest' do you not understand?" he asked Tina. "And by the way, Gamez, shouldn't you give her the *Miranda* warning?"

That should get our evening off to a great start.

"I don't have to Mirandize her. She's not in custody."

"Could've fooled me," Cash said.

The light turned green, and Gamez gunned the Caddie. He took a left at Throckmorton and stopped outside an upscale club called *Cherchez La Femme*. Pink and purple neon letters spelled out the name of the nightclub.

"Why are we stopping here?" Tina said.

"I've had trouble gaining the trust of the trans community," the cop confessed. "The least you can do in return for the ride-along is help me break the ice. Operation Icebreaker starts here and now."

Cash didn't need to see Tina's face to know her eyes were rolling. What Cash didn't know about the trans network in Dallas could fill a book. What Gamez didn't know could fill a library.

"Okay, *La Femme* is definitely a trans-friendly club." Tina sounded like a teacher lecturing a slow child. "But it's a lesbian bar, and the trans women who hang out—"

"Hold that thought." Gamez reached for his vibrating phone.

Cash looked over the cop's shoulder and read the text message: 10-62, 9700 block of Harry Hines. "What does that mean?"

"B and E in progress." Gamez revved the engine. "You guys want to see patrol in action?"

Before Cash could veto the idea, Tina shouted, "Yes!"

"Okay," the cop said, "but we watch from the cheap seats."

"What does that mean?" Cash said.

"We stay in the car and observe from a safe distance."

The Caddie peeled from the lot and rocketed north. Gamez didn't say a word on the wild ride.

***

Gamez beat patrol to the scene of the crime in progress. The targeted site was a massive one-story warehouse with a sign that read: THE PILL BOX. The nondescript structure squeezed into a shotgun lot between a used tire store and a fleabag motel. The latter flashed a flickering sign: $29 a day and free H_O.

Cash doubted the hos were free.

It was dark inside the building. No sign of anything wrong, except for a silent alarm that had alerted the police.

"What is this place?" Tina asked.

"An online pharmacy." The cop called in his location. "With stockpiles of every drug you can imagine and some you can't." He opened his door.

Cash grabbed his arm. "Shouldn't you wait for backup?"

"You know what they say about cops," Gamez said. "Never around when you need one. Well, that doesn't apply to this cop."

A shaft of light from inside the warehouse bounced around. Someone was on the move in the building.

Gamez pulled free of Cash's grip and grabbed his Glock. "You two stay in the car. I mean it. Do not leave the car."

"You know what they say about bold cops," Cash said.

The detective ignored Cash's warning and sprinted toward the warehouse. He checked the front door. Locked. He circled to the side and out of sight.

"What do they say about bold cops?" Tina said.

"There are old cops, and there are bold cops, but there aren't a lot of old, bold cops."

Tina opened her door and swiveled in her seat, facing the warehouse. She planted her feet on the curb and rocked back and forth, as if torn between sitting and standing. Each forward thrust brought her closer to the latter.

"You heard what Gamez said." Cash's voice had an edge. "Stay in the car."

She stood. "I'm just stretching my legs." When the light inside died, she took three steps toward the dark warehouse.

"You have ten seconds to get your ass back in the car," Cash said.

As it turned out, she didn't have ten seconds. A slender male dressed in black appeared on the roof, fifteen feet above the ground and maybe thirty feet from Tina. He aimed a gun at her.

She froze. A still target. The crimson dress stood out. The color of blood.

Cash calculated his odds at less than zero of reaching her before the gunman fired. A sudden movement might spook him into shooting. Best Cash could hope for was a miracle miss. Failing that, call for an ambulance and try to stop the bleeding. Failing all that, see that she didn't die alone.

Cash hit on a diversion play that doubled as a suicide mission. He bailed from the car and waved his arms wildly, shouting, "Over here, sucker." He jumped up and down, side to side, his movements erratic. A bigger but harder target.

The gun swept toward Cash and held on him for an eternity. The thief dropped the pistol to his side and took off toward the back of the roof.

Gamez sprinted to the front, Glock in hand, and shouted, "Where is he?"

"He's on the roof," Cash said, "and running toward the back."

Gamez disappeared around the building. He returned minutes later, empty-handed. “Sonovabitch got away.”

Tina was shaking. “We sent him toward you.”

“Bullshit.” Anger laced the detective’s voice. “You scared him away from me. If he had jumped off the roof from the front of the building, he would’ve been out in the open on Harry Hines, and I would’ve run him down. I told you idiots to stay in the car.”

Tina was on the verge of tears. “I was—”

“I don’t want to hear it,” Gamez said. “The ride-along is officially over.”

Two patrol cars pulled up, one from the north, the other from the south. Cash couldn’t resist. “Like you said, never around when you need one.”

Gamez glared at him. “You two get back in the car, and let me do the talking.”

For a change, Tina and Cash followed orders.

***

The next morning, Cash vacillated over which version of the “I told you so” speech to deliver: the grandfather knows best bromide or the fire and brimstone butt-kicking. At the breakfast table with Tina, he made his decision. Time for a good, old-fashioned butt-kicking.

“I hope you learned your lesson about playing detective last night,” he said.

Tina looked rested and ready to rumble. “I’ve never felt more alive.”

Uh oh.

CHAPTER SEVEN

May-December couples packed Ocean Prime Restaurant on Thursday night. The women were young enough to be their dates' granddaughters, which meant Tina and Cash fit right in. The lights were mercifully low, and fireplaces cast a romantic glow. With the outside temperature in the fifties, the faux logs generated more mood than heat.

In a black dress, Tina would have looked striking under any lighting. Her red hair brushed bare shoulders, and her green-gray eyes sparkled. Black lipstick matched the nail polish.

Cash lifted a flute of Cristal for a toast. "Here's to our half-year anniversary. Six months under the same roof, and we haven't killed each other."

Tina clinked flutes. "Yet." She sipped.

He raised the flute again. "And here's to my speedy return to the job market."

She scoffed. "Who's going to hire a seventy-four-year-old ex-cop?"

"Rhoden's law firm."

"Great plan," she said with sarcasm to spare, "except for two tiny details. Rhoden hated you, and he's dead. A cartel gunned him down a year ago, in case that slipped your mind."

"It might've been a cartel. Could've been a disgruntled client. Or maybe a jealous husband. The suspect list is a mile long, and the cops never bothered to find the killer or killers."

"Whatever, Rhoden's gone."

"But his firm has survived, sort of. Darrell Pendergass is trying to keep the ship afloat, and he could use a crack investigator to drum up business."

Her eyebrows arched. "You?"

He nodded.

Bettina Biddle passed by their table on the arm of Stewart Powell. The couple matched the demographic of the room, with Bettina in her late twenties and Powell, mid-sixties. She kept her head down and seemed eager to reach their table or booth. He shook hands and slapped backs along the way, displaying the widow like a prized possession.

Cash wished a hole would open on the floor and swallow him. The sight of Bettina took away his appetite. It had been more than six months since he had seen her at close range. She was paler and slimmer than the siren of his dreams. The fragrance of her perfume lingered.

"Roll your tongue back into your mouth," Tina said, "before someone trips over it."

"Sorry. I got distracted."

"By seeing her," she said, "or seeing her with him?"

"Both." Cash fell into a blue funk. Large as the age gap was between the widow of his cellmate and the silver-haired pillar of the bar, it loomed even larger between her and Carl Meadows.

Tina put her hand over his. "You're not responsible for her husband's suicide."

"*If* it was a suicide."

"Either way," she said, "Biddle's death isn't on you."

Cash needed something stronger than champagne and ordered a Jameson Irish Whiskey. "You share a cell with a man for a year, and you get close real fast. I promised to get Marty out alive, and I failed."

"You didn't let Marty down, and you don't owe his widow anything."

"I've got a bad feeling about Stewart Powell, and not just because he's trying to buy a cabinet post for his daughter."

"What you're feeling," she said, "is called jealousy."

Cash scoffed. "What could she see in him?"

"You mean other than wealth, good looks, and immense power. Face it, Paw Paw, they may be having an old-fashioned affair."

"In plain sight?" Cash said. "I don't think so."

"And if they started the affair before her husband's trial...." Tina didn't complete the sentence. She didn't have to.

Cash finished it for her, silently. If an affair had begun before the trial, Bettina might have been complicit in sacrificing her husband to save Longhorn Investments, Marty's employer and Powell's cash-cow client. Marty's trial had been a farce. Longhorn had hired Rocket Rhoden to defend him.

Or as it turned out, to not defend him.

Suspicion festered in the darkest recesses of Cash's mind, and there was plenty of it to spread around to multiple parties: Powell, Lou Watson, the CEO of Longhorn, and even Bettina.

"We need to plant someone inside Powell's law firm," Cash said.

Tina stiffened in her seat. “Don’t look at me.”

Cash stared straight at her. “A stint at Powell’s white-shoe firm would look good on your resume, and you admitted that Goldy and Eva are hurting for work.”

“I’ve got more important things to do than play cupid for you—like catching a serial killer.”

“I’ll make you a deal,” Cash said. “You spy on Powell’s firm for me, and I’ll work the Dice Cold Killer angle with you.”

Her eyes narrowed. “On one condition: DCK stays on the front burner.”

“Deal,” he said.

They clinked flutes.

***

Two weeks later, Tina and Cash returned to Ocean Prime to celebrate her new job. “I’m not surprised Powell’s firm hired you,” Cash said, “but I’m a little surprised it happened so fast.”

“I had three things going for me. First, the firm landed new bond work for DFW Airport, and they were desperate for bodies.”

“And the second thing?” Cash said.

“Turned out I had a champion in firm management. A kickass corporate partner named Paula Marshall.”

Caught mid-sip, Cash choked on a name from the past. Not one of his favorite people, and the feeling was mutual.

“Paula interviewed you?” he asked.

“More like she hijacked the whole interview process. As the partner in charge of hiring, she screens every resume sent to the firm. She saw that I worked for Goldy and ambushed me at the reception desk. Took me to Starbucks and grilled me for an hour."

"On what? Your qualifications? Favorite color? Likes and dislikes?"

Tina laughed. "There were maybe three questions about me and three hundred about Eva."

"Ah," Cash said, "so Paula's still hung up on our little girl."

"Big time." She sipped champagne. "Paula sees me as a way to keep tabs on the one who got away."

"You said you had three things going for you."

"Ah, here's the kicker. I did my homework on Powell's shop. Every year it ranks at or near the top on most measures of a law firm's success. Gross and net revenue. Revenue and profits per partner. Overall compensation. Top five in the nation across the board on the metrics that matter to money-grubbing lawyers."

"Is there any other kind?" Cash said.

She ignored his question and went on. "Every year the American Bar Association conducts a diversity study and ranks firms on their inclusiveness, taking into account race, religion, sexual and gender orientation, etcetera. Powell's old-boy bastion sucks on this score. No big whoop now, but soon it will be a deal breaker for the more woke clients."

"In other words, diversity gets taken seriously as soon as it impacts the bottom line," Cash said. "Like I asked before, any other kind?"

"You've gotten cynical in your old age, Mr. Meadows."

"I was cynical at a young age," he said. "But whatever the motives behind your hair-trigger hire, you offer the firm a boost in the ratings."

"With the hire of a Mexican-American trans woman, they check three boxes."

"Don't sell yourself short," Cash said. "You had a fourth factor in your favor."

"What's that?"

"You're a damn good paralegal."

"Wow, a rare compliment from you." She lifted her empty flute. "That calls for another round."

Cash summoned the waiter, who took their orders and left. "Feel free to return the compliment," he said, "after I land my new job tomorrow."

"What new job?" Tina said.

"As an investigator for Rhoden's old law firm. It's a miracle the firm has survived a year past the pariah's death. It'll be a greater miracle if it lasts another year."

Her brow furrowed. "Do you think that's safe?"

"Safer than sitting around and doing nothing. I'm going stir crazy." He picked up a loaf of sourdough bread and tore a heel for her. "We attack the snake from both ends." He took the other heel. "You from the head. Me from the tail."

***

Cash arrived fifteen minutes early for a 9:00 a.m. appointment with Darrell Pendergass, the sad sack who had spent nine years handling hot messes for Rhoden. A year ago, Darrell had inherited his mentor's practice but not his courtroom wizardry.

Rhoden had treated Darrell as cannon fodder, consigning him to sure losers—hearings and trials where the defense didn't stand a snowball's chance in Houston. While Darrell had proven he could take a punch, the big palooka couldn't counterpunch to save his life.

Or the life of a client.

Nor, apparently, could Pendergass keep the firm afloat much longer. There was no one in the waiting room save Cash. No calls in or out for Sami the secretary to field. Nothing but dead air and a bad vibe.

Rumors of the firm's imminent demise ran rampant. Long-time clients had defected. Retainers had dried up. Fresh clients were rarer than innocent ones. Cash couldn't decide which firm would fold first, Darrell's or Goldy's.

He brought to the interview a resume riddled with lies and a set of phony documents prepared by Freddy the Forger. His head throbbed from last night's rounds of champagne with Tina, and a breakfast burrito roiled his gut.

While waiting for Darrell to arrive, Cash made small talk with Sami. He had seen her at Rhoden's funeral, and the memory had stuck. Count on Rhoden to hire a former Dallas Cowboy cheerleader as his girl Friday. She had been a standout in the blonde, blue-eyed contingent of the cheer corps. At five-eight, she was tall for a gymnast but short for a model. In past lives, she had been both.

Two, four, six, eight. Give us dough to litigate.

Sami handed Cash a cup of coffee and returned to the receptionist's desk. He wondered how long she would hang around the dying shop. Why was she still here, when she could be the face of any firm in the city?

At 9:10, she said, "I'm sure Mr. Pendergass is caught in traffic."

Which would be a neat trick, given that Darrell's apartment was a five-minute walk from the office on McKinney Avenue. Three minutes if he hopped the free trolley.

Her bullshit excuse tipped off Cash to her tell. When Sami lied, her pitch rose toward the end of a sentence, turning a statement into a question. Like most liars, she struggled to commit fully to a falsehood, which was unlike her late boss Rhoden.

"I've got time," Cash said, "and your coffee is better than the swill I get at home."

"Hang out here as long as you like, but you're wasting your time. We won't be hiring additional staff until spring at the earliest."

There it went again. Her voice scaled higher as the lie took flight. Meaning, Darrell couldn't make payroll now, and the firm would never see spring. The mystery deepened as to why she hadn't bailed.

Darrell lumbered into the office. Up close, he was larger than Cash remembered. The former Longhorn linebacker stood six-four and tipped the scales at two-thirty plus. Beefy and square-jawed, he looked like a contender. Despite the advantages of size and youth, however, he played small in court. Prosecutors a foot shorter and a hundred pounds lighter routinely manhandled him.

"Let's talk in my office," Darrell said.

The "my office" part was a stretch. The room had Rhoden's prints all over it, literally and figuratively. Framed photos and articles of the deceased's courtroom exploits still covered every inch of wall space. No doubt because Darrell had nothing to put in their place.

Whatever the firm's budget for furniture had been, Rhoden must have sunk the bulk of it on his office. A rosewood desk took center stage. No surprise that Rocket's red lair included a crimson couch that converted into a king-size bed.

Darrell sat behind the desk and scanned Cash's resume. Make that Carl Meadows's resume. He looked up. "How can I help you, Mr. Meadows?"

Cash sat. "I'm new to Dallas. Moved here to be with my granddaughter. I've got a ton of experience as an investigator and an itch to get back to work. A few years ago, I helped your former boss, God rest his soul, with a sticky problem in Albany. He tried to talk me into moving to Dallas and working for him. Sorry he's no longer around."

"Me too." Darrell sounded like he almost meant it.

"Did they ever catch the ones who gunned him down?"

Darrell shook his head. "Not that the cops tried all that hard." He rustled the resume. "You've got an impressive background, Mr. Meadows, but the firm isn't in the market to hire now. If you're still interested in six months, come back to see me."

Same line as Sami. Delivered with a tad more conviction.

"I once had a boss," Cash said, "who imparted to me these words of wisdom: To make money, you have to spend money."

"What happened to him?"

"Oh, he went broke."

Darrell laughed. "My kind of lawyer."

"I'll level with you, Darrell. I have a nest egg from forty-five years on the beat and a place to hang my hat at night, so I don't have to work. But I'm going batty cooped up in my granddaughter's apartment all day, and we're already on each other's last nerve. Hire me on straight commission and pay me a percentage of the work I bring in. You've got nothing to lose."

"You're new to Dallas," Darrell said. "How will you land clients here?"

"I already have a live one on the line. Just need a place to reel him in and a lawyer to skin him."

"How did a newbie like you manage to snare a client so fast?" Darrell said.

"Like it says in the gospel according to Garth: I've got friends in low places."

CHAPTER EIGHT

A sunny Saturday morning saw a full parking lot at the prison. Visiting day at FCI Seagoville drew a crowd that skewed young, female, and dark-skinned. Among the steady stream of visitors of color, a white geezer like Cash stuck out like a sugar cube among coffee beans.

The flow of foot traffic swept Cash through the front gate and into the waiting room, where he committed his first felony of the day by entering an alias in the visitors' log. Headshots of the president, attorney general, director of the Bureau of Prisons, and warden stared disapprovingly as Cash signed in.

All were new to their jobs, except for the warden. For a decade, Marvin Stockman had ruled the prison with all the warmth and flexibility of a granite mountain. The hard-ass had bedeviled Cash for two years. Carl Meadows had no reason to expect better treatment at his hands.

Sitting face to face with Marcus Allen DuPree, aka Big Black, further stoked Cash's fears of a return trip to Seagoville. The inmate loomed large in Cash's memory and larger in life. He had to be six-five and close to three hundred pounds of muscle and mean. A lifetime of blows by everything from bats to bottles had dented and dinged a bald skull and scrambled the brain.

A second stretch in Seagoville would be a death sentence for Cash. An inch of reinforced glass between the men didn't seem like enough protection.

The prisoner picked up the receiver. "Make it fast. My old lady's on the way."

Cash didn't call bullshit on the claim. The inmate's dance card was as empty as a West Texas rain gauge in August. During Cash's two years as his cellmate, Big Black hadn't scored a single visit.

"Still fuzzy as to who you are and why you're here." The prisoner had a heavy East Texas drawl. "Have we crossed paths before?" Which was Big Black's way of asking if they had done time together, in this prison or another.

Cash shook his head and introduced himself as Martin Biddle's uncle from back east. He kept the background info vague. Less chance of tripping up on details.

Cash caught Big Black's fleeting reaction. The brute had witnessed bloody beatings without batting an eye and had inflicted more than a few himself, but he flinched at the mention of Biddle's name.

"If you came to ask about his death—"

Cash cut him off. "I'm here to ask about his life inside."

Big Black shook his head. Cash could almost hear the marbles rattle. "Me and him, we was friends. 'Bout all I can say."

All he could safely say anyway. Carl Meadows's status as a non-lawyer meant their conversation was fair game for taping by the feds.

"I heard you were more than friends," Cash said.

Big Black's grip on the receiver swelled the pinkish letters carved in scar tissue on four fingers: B-E-A-R. "You best not be saying what I think you're saying."

Nope, an inch of reinforced glass damn sure wasn't buffer enough. Cash rushed to defuse the situation. "If Marty had confided in anyone here, it would've been you."

The prisoner started to hang up but didn't. Cash went on. "The feds wrote off Marty's death as a suicide. That right?"

"What's done is done."

"Marty's wife and twin girls deserve to know the truth."

But not the whole truth. Not what Marty did to survive inside.

"The boy didn't off himself." The inmate sounded certain. "He wouldn't. Not with an appeal in the works."

Now came the tricky part. If Marty had been killed, Big would be the prime suspect. How do you ask in a subtle, non-threatening way if a stone-cold killer murdered his cellmate?

Big made it easy on Cash by adding, "If I find the fool who did him in." He stopped mid-threat. Good thing too. More than likely, tape was rolling.

Cash sensed the anger welling inside the brute. If it was an act, Big deserved an Oscar. He hadn't recovered from the loss of Marty any more than Cash had.

Big had kept Cash safe inside. Marty had kept him sane.

"Do you have a lawyer?" Cash said.

"My mouthpiece is dead."

"Do you need a lawyer?"

Big shrugged.

Cash rose. "I'll see what I can do."

* * *

On Monday morning, Cash brought two gifts to the office. He placed a six-pack of craft beer on Darrell's desk and planted Freddy the Forger in the hot seat. Cash remained standing.

"Thanks for the Dallas Blondes," Darrell said, "but it's a little early for a drink."

"Never too early to celebrate our first client together." Cash placed a hand on Freddy's shoulder. "Meet Fred Foster, aka Freddy the Forger, unjustly accused of forgery again and in need of a vigorous defense."

Freddy and Darrell shook hands. "What happened to the earlier charges?" the lawyer said.

"I kicked the government's ass the last two trials." Freddy failed to mention Cash McCahill's *minor* role in the acquittals.

"And took felonies on the others," Cash said.

"Tell me about your first conviction," Darrell said.

"My sorry excuse for a lawyer fucked up on that one." Freddy's voice swelled with outrage. "He convinced me that my partner was snitching me out and pushed me to tell my side to the feds. Huge fucking mistake."

Cash laid out the history, not trusting the forger to deliver the straight skinny. "At Freddy's first rodeo, a barracuda named Regina Delgado ran the prisoners' dilemma game on him and a cohort. Tony Dial, Freddy's low-rent lawyer at the time, bought Delgado's line that the flunky was spilling his guts in the other room, laying it all on Freddy. Likewise, the flunky's lawyer convinced him that Freddy was snitching him out. The suspects ratted on each other and in the process buried themselves."

Darrell shook his head. "Unfortunately, the felony record means we can't put you on the stand."

The least of our problems, Cash thought. No sane lawyer would put Freddy on the stand and under oath. "I'll leave you two alone," Cash said, "to work out the terms of engagement."

Darrell sat. "Where are you running off to?"

"He's my first catch of the day," Cash said, "but not the last."

On Cash's way out, Sami said, "My hero." Even if meant as a joke, it put a bounce in his step.

She rose from behind the reception desk and told him to follow her. She led him to the last door on the left and opened it to reveal a storage space for metal file cabinets. A musty odor whooshed from the windowless room. A metal desk and chair fit snugly in the center.

"An office for our new rainmaker," Sami said.

"I like what you've done to the place," he said. "It has that never-lived-in look."

CHAPTER NINE

Happy hour found Sami, Darrell, and Cash seated around a small table in a conference room. Darrell and Cash were working on their second Dallas Blondes, while Sami nursed her first.

"If you'd prefer tequila," Darrell said to Sami, "I've got a nice bottle of *Roca Patron*."

"I'll stick with beer." Her tone was frostier than the bottle. Cash suspected Darrell wasn't the first to try to loosen her up with liquor. Nor the first to fail.

He turned to Cash. "Do you trust Freddy?"

Cash laughed. "Freddy's like a stray dog. Throw him a bone, and you'll never be rid of him. On the good side, he's repeat business. The grift that keeps on giving."

Darrell lifted his bottle to toast. "To recidivists and their retainers." The trio clinked glass.

"While we're on the subject of repeat business," Cash said, "the best way to find new clients is by mining the golden oldies."

"Who told you that?" Sami's tone straddled amusement and skepticism.

"Let me guess," Darrell said. "The same financial genius who told you that to make money, you had to spend money. The one who went broke."

"Hey, nobody bats a thousand." Cash drained the defensiveness from his tone. "The idea is still solid. I suggest Sami and I go through the old files, looking for leads, loose change, whatever falls out."

She took a sip. "Not sure my ticker can take the excitement of the dead file detail."

"Beats sitting at the reception desk all day," Cash said, "like a potted plant."

Emboldened by beer, Darrell rushed to defend her from the slightest of slights. "Don't you dare diss our yellow rose of Texas."

Cash suppressed a smile. Chivalry might be dead, but lechery wasn't. The big lug was trying too hard to rescue a damsel in no distress.

Sami put down her bottle, a sign she had hit her limit—of booze and the games boys play.

The exchange confirmed Cash's read of the relationship between his new colleagues. Darrell would crawl over broken glass for a smile from her. Out of love or animal attraction or something in between.

The feelings ran one way. She tolerated his groveling just enough to keep hope alive. Not from love or animal attraction or anything in between.

What Cash couldn't fathom was why.

***

The next day, Sami arrived for work in sneakers, cutoffs, and an oversize T-shirt that read:

DON'T FLATTER
YOURSELF COWBOY

I WAS LOOKING AT YOUR HORSE.

Darrell had a convenient court appearance in the morning and a mystery meeting out of the office in the afternoon, leaving Sami and Cash alone in a windowless conference room crowded with files. Every folder represented a life upended by Johnny Law. More than a few, lives ended by the law.

Cash had eyes for only one file—Marty Biddle's—but he couldn't be too obvious about his target. He planned to paw around in the papers for a couple of hours before pouncing on Biddle's records.

A couple of hours stretched into three to four. Three to four, into five or six. Every hour or so, as they whittled down a stack of folders, Sami would disappear for a few minutes and return with a fresh batch of old cases.

Ten hours of drudgery and still no sign of Biddle's files. Tempted as Cash was to short-circuit the search and ask outright for the records, he fought the urge. Given Carl Meadows's newness to Dallas, how would he know to flag a specific case?

At 7:47 p.m., Cash called it a day. "We're not going to make it through all the files today. What say we grab a bite to eat and hit it hard again mañana?"

Sami rubbed her bloodshot eyes. "What do you have in mind?"

"Your choice," he said, "but my treat."

She chose fast and cheap. An act of mercy, given the hard day behind and ahead of them. Moreover, his comp hadn't kicked in, as she knew.

In Dallas, fast and cheap generally meant Tex-Mex, and Sami took him to Mattito's on Oak Lawn. A young crowd packed the place and kept the decibel level at rock concert reverb. An endless parade of waiters bore pitchers of rainbow-colored margaritas.

Cash steered Sami to a table near the bar, counting on liquor to loosen her tongue. Throughout the day, he had teed up plenty of openings for her to bitch about the job, bad mouth Darrell or the not-so-dearly-departed Rhoden, and commiserate about life in general.

She hadn't gone there. Vague as his responses to her questions had been, her answers to his were even more evasive. They were like boxers circling the ring, feeling each other out, feinting now and then, but going all day without landing a single, solid blow.

He ordered two swirl margaritas and an appetizer of bean and cheese nachos before lobbing a softball. "Do you miss being a Dallas Cowboy cheerleader? I understand Texans rank the cheerleaders several rungs above the governor."

"The parking lot attendants at the stadium poll higher than our Austin politicians."

Cash waited for a straight answer and finally got one.

"Not in the least," she said.

His smile said he wasn't buying it.

She went on. "That was a lot of work for very little pay."

"You don't strike me as being averse to work."

"The little pay part turned me off."

The nachos and drinks arrived, giving Cash a break to calibrate how hard and deep to push into personal territory. "From the outside looking in, I can't see that you've improved your lot all that much. Seems like Darrell bounces between slow pay and no pay."

"You're on the inside now too," she said.

"Well, I've got one foot in and one out, but you appear to have jumped in with both feet."

She licked salt from the rim of her glass. "In for a penny...."

"Literally," he said.

Her frown signaled that he had gone too far. While she would never take Darrell's hand, she had his back. Cash eased off. "I couldn't help noticing something today. We've gone through a mountain of files and face another shitload tomorrow. Rhoden attracted a ton of business and pulled in a steady stream of big retainers."

"And you're wondering if Darrell can do the same," she said.

"Aren't you?"

"The jury's out." She nibbled around the edge of a nacho, steering clear of the cheesy center. "He's young. Still has time to come into his own."

Cash gauged her to be a couple of years younger than Darrell but light years ahead of him. "Rhoden will be a tough act to follow." He made it through the compliment without gagging. Among the defense bar, the deceased had earned his status as a pariah.

"Yes and no," she said.

"You lost me."

"Darrell will never be the courtroom wizard Rocket was, but then who is?"

Cash could think of one attorney. Make that two.

“On the other hand,” she said, “Darrell’s a better man.”

“In what way?”

She shrugged. “They say not to speak ill of the dead.”

“I say why the hell not. They can’t hear you.” He lifted his glass for a toast. They tapped. “Here’s to hoping my critics hold their fire until I’m six feet under.”

“For starters, Darrell is loyal to a fault. Rocket didn’t share that virtue. Or handicap.”

Cash banked on silence wheedling more from her. When it didn’t, he prodded. “What other handicaps did Rhoden have?”

“He had an incurable zipper problem. Couldn’t keep it up to save his life.”

“With anyone in particular?”

“With everyone in general.” Her bitterness finally surfaced.

Cash waited for her to name names, to throw shade on her late boss’s sexual partners. He expected a long list and prayed for one name not to be on it: Bettina Biddle.

Not that Cash could judge either Bettina or Rhoden. Given his past, he was in no position to do so. Given his present, he had no call to.

Throughout drinks, dinner, and more drinks, she spilled nothing. Not a drop of margarita, nor a single name. The after-hours Sami proved to be as tight-lipped as the workday model.

***

Cash returned to the apartment around 10:00 p.m. and waited up for Tina, anxious to hear if she had learned anything at the new job at Powell’s firm. When midnight arrived with no word from her, he went to bed.

At 2:17 a.m., he gave up on sleep and rose to check on Tina. She still wasn't in. He texted her: *where r u?*

She texted back: *in good hands.*

He: *Whose?*

There was no reply, which translated into no sleep for Cash.

CHAPTER TEN

With Tina AWOL and not answering her phone, Cash couldn't sleep. Visits from ghosts of deaths past compounded his fears for her. Images of Brandi Foxx on a slab in the morgue and Veronica Stoddard in a Deep Ellum alley haunted him.

Brandi and Veronica had been roughly Tina's age and had run in her circles. Like Tina, they had been outspoken leaders for LGBTQ causes. With the murderer still on the loose, Tina couldn't have picked a worse time to be out, in both senses of the word.

Cash worried that she had reverted to the line of work that had brought them together in the first place. If so, her survival hinged on whether the cops or the killer pinched her first, putting Cash in the awkward position of rooting for the police.

If DCK got to her first, she was dead. Then again, lockup could be a death sentence as well. Tina's last night in the trans tank had almost proved fatal.

At 5:00 a.m., Cash fixed a pot of industrial strength coffee. The aroma worked its magic, luring Tina back to the apartment at 5:13. Shoes in hand, she eased open the door and tiptoed inside.

He busted her in the foyer. "Where the hell have you been?" The anger in his tone swamped the undercurrent of relief.

She looked a mess. Not like she'd taken a beating. More like her dance card had been full tonight. Her auburn hair hung in limp strands. Sweat or tears had eroded her makeup. Purple lipstick smudged her chin.

Cash's defense lawyer instincts jumped to the conclusion that she had gone back to the life. His instincts as a friend told him to keep his suspicions to himself.

She jettisoned the shoes and headed for the kitchen. "I need a cup of coffee before you begin the third degree."

"I'll get you a cup." He pulled out a chair for her at the kitchen table. "You need to get off your feet. It's been a while since you walked the streets in heels."

She sat. "What's that crack supposed to mean?"

He handed her a cup of coffee. "You picked a helluva time to put yourself back on the meat market. Bad enough that you broke a promise to me. Worse that you're supposed to be at the law firm in about…." He checked his watch. "Four hours."

"I'll be at my desk when the bell rings." She took a long drink. "We're going to need a bigger cup."

"You think this is funny?" His anger spiked. "Have you forgotten there's a monster out there targeting your type?"

"Not for one second." She raised the decibel level. "And fuck you for the vote of no confidence."

A tinge of regret stilled his tongue. Maybe he had jumped to the wrong conclusion. "I just thought that—"

She cut him off. "I know what you thought, and I thought you were my friend. I guess we were both wrong."

If her goal had been to make him feel like shit, she had succeeded. He walked to the counter, putting enough distance between them that if she threw a cup, he stood a chance of dodging it.

"We've been through so many trials together, in and out of the courtroom," he said, "that we're more than friends."

"You really shouldn't talk about trials. Takes you out of character."

"It's just the two of us here talking." He tried to toss off the next question casually. "By the way, where were you last night?"

"None of your fucking business. We need to get something straight. You're playing my grandfather, but you're not my blood."

"Now look who's stepping out of character." He doubled down on the show of concern. "Sorry I ambushed you at the door, but I was worried sick. Didn't sleep last night."

She massaged her temples. His headache must be contagious.

"Don't worry about me," she said. "Last night I was one hundred percent safe."

He topped off her cup and said, "No one is ever one hundred percent safe."

***

The morning of day two in dead file gulch hit more dry holes on the Biddle front but turned up a surprise shortly before lunch. Cash came across a thin file for Dr. Solomon Katzenbach. The only items in the file were an engagement letter dated two years earlier with a vague description of the matter as a "potential criminal issue" and a copy of a retainer check for $750,000.

The Katzenbach matter could be anything or nothing. Taxes. A sexual harassment allegation by a patient. No lawsuit or indictment had been filed against the doctor, but that hadn't stopped Rhoden from burning through the whole retainer. Cash expected nothing less.

He went back to work on the files with two new mysteries unsolved. Why had Katzenbach retained Rhoden? And the bigger mystery: Why would the doctor have hired Rhoden over Cash or Goldy?

By 3:30 p.m., he and Sami had gone through all the records on the premises, finding few leads to follow up on and no sign of Biddle's files. Cash still hadn't come up with a way to ask specifically for Biddle's records without raising Sami's suspicions.

Someone must have removed or destroyed them, and Cash had three main suspects: Rhoden, Darrell, and Sami. In that order. When he factored in the risk of cutting the skirt too much slack, the order shifted to Rhoden, Sami, and Darrell.

Darrell barged into the conference room. Good timing, with the dead file review now done. He told Cash to go to Goldberg's office and pick up Freddy the Forger's records.

The assignment set off alarms. Sure, Carl Meadows had already visited Goldy's office, but Darrell and Sami had taken the lead then. This time he would be flying solo. A word, a gesture, might blow his cover.

Cash came up with a dodge. "There are messenger services for that."

Darrell handed him an envelope. "You've got two legs for that."

"What's this?"

"A letter signed by Freddy, authorizing us to take custody of his files."

"Got any advice for me if Goldberg pulls out his trusty musket and starts blasting away?"

"Duck," Darrell said.

* * *

It was almost closing time when Cash reached Goldberg's office at Founders' Square. He found no clients in the waiting room and Eva at the reception desk. No surprise on either count. She was the office hyphenate: receptionist-assistant-paralegal-shadow lawyer-bookkeeper-babysitter.

Also not surprising that she had a new look. Well, an old new look. She had done cowgirl before but had decided to give it another go. Not her first rodeo. Boots, jeans, a plain white shirt, and a black Stetson completed her western apparel.

Her eyes were bloodshot. Her stare, unblinking. His sweat glands gushed. He let her have the first word. The less said by him, the better.

"Tina's not here, Mr. Meadows." She sounded tired.

"I'm not here for Tina." He handed Eva the envelope. "Mr. Pendergass sent me to pick up Fred Foster's files. This letter authorizes me to take them."

If the news of Freddy's defection surprised or upset Eva, she didn't let on. Well, other than by staring at the letter longer than it would take her to read it twice.

Cash suffered over what he was doing to her and Goldy. They were struggling to keep the firm afloat without him as a draw. He had spent two years behind bars, followed by a year back in the saddle before disappearing again six months ago. Clients couldn't count on him.

Nor could Eva.

Goldy's firm was faltering, along with his health. A stream of clients had bailed, with Freddy being the latest. Much as Cash hated to bear more bad news, poaching Freddy gained him access to Rhoden's firm and files. Those files might be the key to solving the mystery of Marty Biddle's death—if he could find them.

Eva glanced at the closed door to Goldy's office before turning back to Cash. Given a choice, he would have preferred a beating at her hands to the pained look in her eyes. She didn't give him a choice. Cash broke eye contact.

"It will take me an hour or so to gather the files and download the emails." Her tone of resignation was more torture for Cash. "I'll do it after Mr. Goldberg leaves for the day. Come back tomorrow morning at eight, and the files will be ready for you."

Good for her to compile the documents while Goldy was out tonight and turn them over before he rolled into work tomorrow. Bad for Cash, because it meant another sleepless night and a second run through the ringer tomorrow.

CHAPTER ELEVEN

The following morning, Cash braced for a battering from Hurricane Eva, fearful that the Category 1 storm had gathered strength during the night. The fear proved unfounded, and the pickup of Freddy the Forger's files went smoothly, with no destruction of life or property in the wake. Well, other than the psychic damage inflicted by Eva's glare. A smoldering rage had replaced the pain clouding her eyes yesterday.

Cash couldn't flee Goldy's office fast enough. After putting the files in the trunk of his car, he walked a block to the Bank of America Tower on Main Street.

He took an elevator to the top floor with three goals in mind: Make amends to Tina for busting her chops yesterday; settle his nerves after the encounter with Eva; get an update on Tina's progress in finding the files on Marty Biddle and Longhorn Investments, the company that had thrown Biddle under the bus.

A redhead at the reception desk greeted Cash. An engraved nameplate identified her as Carrie Scarborough. No wedding ring, but that would come soon. She had the look of the presentable second or third wife she was destined to become. In a hotbed of type-A personalities (where the A stood for adultery), the partners at Powell, Ingram & Gardner retained clients longer than spouses.

"May I help you?" Carrie had mastered the art of sounding sincere.

"I'm here to see Tina Campos."

"We don't have an attorney by that name."

"She's a paralegal," Cash said, "who started with the firm two weeks ago."

Carrie swiveled to her computer screen and scrolled the firm directory. "Miss Campos no longer works here."

Cash did a double take. "Please check again. It might be under Cristina Campos. Or maybe she's so new that she hasn't made the directory."

"She worked at the firm for a short time but isn't with us now."

"Since when? Did she quit? Was she fired?" His voice swelled by the question.

"Even if I knew the answers to your questions, I wouldn't be at liberty to say."

Cash backed away from the desk and whipped out his phone. His first instinct was to call Tina. His second, pocket the phone and cool off before confronting her.

***

Cash made small talk at dinner, postponing his cross-examination until he had polished off a second slice of apple pie a la mode and a third glass of Malbec. "How's the new job going?" The opening question set the trap.

Tina cleared the dishes from the table. The question lingered. She spoke from the sink, her back to him. "Fine."

"The big firm lawyers, are they treating you well?"

She turned off the faucet and faced him. "You know, don't you?"

"Yep."

"How did you find out?" she said.

"Does it matter?"

She shrugged. "Guess not."

He let the silence wear on her. That usually fared better than words, and tonight it did.

"On my second day at Powell's firm," she said, "I understood why Eva hadn't stayed there more than a month or so. By day three, I knew I wouldn't last a month. Sure enough, the next day HR gave me a choice: Resign or be fired. Same choice they gave Eva, and I made the same call."

"What grounds did they have to fire you?"

"They called it insubordination."

Cash perked up. "Now I have to hear the whole story."

"Not much to tell. It happened so fast."

"I'm waiting."

"Besides, what's done is done."

"I need to know who you pissed off," he said, "in order to figure out how to get your job back."

Her eyes narrowed. "I'll go into the gory details, but there's no fucking way I'm going back there." She poured herself a glass of wine and returned to the kitchen table. "Do you know a lawyer named Gerry Freeman?"

"By reputation," Cash said. "A scorched-earth litigator at Powell's shop."

"Which is another way of saying he's a royal asshole." She took a sip. "Unfortunately, I got assigned to work on a matter for his big bank client. A Greek couple owned a family restaurant in North Dallas. They'd been doing well and making their payments until last spring's tornado shut them down for six months."

"Please tell me you didn't side with the borrowers against the bank."

"Of course not." She didn't sound convincing. "I simply took issue with Freeman's legal strategy."

"And being brand new and the most junior member of the team, you managed to keep that issue to yourself, right?"

"Wrong."

He knew where this was heading but pumped for more details anyway.

"Freeman gathers the troops in a huge conference room. The dude's barely five-five, but he's strutting around and barking out orders like the little general. He stops at my chair and tries to tower over me, but he's more of a toadstool than a tower. He tells the room that I used to work for you and Goldy. For some reason, that gets a big laugh."

Now Cash definitely knew where it was going.

"The prick tells me to put my criminal background to use by combing through every document the Greeks had sent the bank to cherry pick two or three mistakes. The firm would seize on the errors to threaten the couple with a bank fraud indictment, acting like Jenna Powell and her prosecutors were working for the firm."

Cash didn't react. Tina went on. "Freeman would hit them with an ultimatum: Cough up every penny of collateral or spend their last dollar on a criminal lawyer. Either way, the feds would take their freedom, and the bank would take their restaurant. I had qualms about that tactic."

"And you couldn't keep those qualms to yourself?"

"Would you?"

He didn't answer.

"All I did was make a simple observation." A smile curled her lips. "I might've said something about using a bazooka to blast two ants."

Cash refilled their wine glasses and waited for the story to get worse. Or better.

"And I might've said it in front of a couple of bankers."

"You called out your boss in the presence of his client?"

She shrugged. "The little prick chased me from the conference room and out of the firm."

Cash had half a mind to unload on her. After all, she had blown their access to the files at Powell's firm, putting them back at square zero. Instead, he swallowed his anger, compensating for being too hard on her yesterday. Besides, in the same position, he might have popped off as well. Perhaps not now, but certainly twenty years ago, when he was her age.

"Since leaving the firm, where have you been spending your days?" His tone turned more paternal, less pissed off.

"I've been helping out at Goldy's shop, not that there's a lot to do there. Just mostly hanging with Eva."

"And at night," he said, "where have you been going?"

"Out."

"Where are you going tonight?"

"Same."

Her evasions stirred the anger festering inside him, but he held it in check. If Powell's firm had the juice to sic the feds on two small borrowers bedeviled by bad luck, what could it have done to Tina if she had been caught spying?

Serial killer be damned, maybe she was safer on the streets than at the firm.

CHAPTER TWELVE

Cash spent another restless night worrying over where Tina was, what she was doing, and who was with her. The water stains on the ceiling morphed into dragons in a makeshift Rorschach test. Not that he needed more dragons to slay, what with a serial killer on the loose, Biddle's death still a mystery, and a cartel out for his scalp.

Around 3:00 a.m., he hit on a way to ask about Biddle's files without arousing Sami's suspicion. Six hours later, Operation Widow Whisperer went into effect. Cash followed Sami into the breakroom. Freed from the drudgery of dead file duty, she had dressed for the receptionist role in a dark blue outfit.

"That's two days of our lives we'll never get back," he told her. "We didn't harvest many leads."

"We found one or two worth running down." She offered him an espresso.

"No thanks. I got up early today." A stretch since he hadn't slept at all. "More caffeine and you'll have to peel me from the ceiling. While I was up, though, I googled Rhoden. Still searching for leads on future work."

"Don't believe everything you read about Rocket," she said. "There was no middle ground on him. People either loved or loathed him."

"I came across several articles on a recent trial of his, one that went south. A white-collar case for a bean counter named Biddle. Martin Biddle. Ring any bells?"

The color flushed from her face. The name must have rung more than bells. It had set off alarms. Her voice came back before her color did. "Biddle died in prison. He won't need our services again."

"But his widow might," Cash said. "I checked the docket on Biddle's federal case, and the bastards with gold badges are trying to squeeze blood money from her. She's in a nasty forfeiture fight and needs help."

"She's off limits." Sami's tone had a ring of finality.

Cash feigned surprise. "Why?"

She stood at the counter, her back to him. "Ancient history. Best left in the past."

He sat at the table. She joined him, armed with a double espresso.

"History was my best subject in school," he said. "Not that I got high marks in it, but I managed to stay awake in that class."

"When I said folks either loved or loathed Rocket, I should've added that a lot of people who started out loving him came to loath him. He was an acquired distaste."

"Are we talking about you now?"

Her fingers wrapped around the cup and squeezed. "Rocket pissed me off more times than I can count. Cheated on me whenever the opportunity arose, which was often. But I never worked up a healthy hatred for him." She broke her death grip on the cup. "For a time, I thought I loved him. Guess I was wrong because it never evolved to hate."

"What about Mrs. Biddle? Did she cheat on her husband with Rhoden? Is that why we can't pitch her?"

"That relationship was doomed from the start," she said.

"Which relationship? The one between Rhoden and Mrs. Biddle? Or between her and the late husband?"

"Both." She took a sip. "You don't know Bettina Biddle. Pray that you never will. She's a manipulative bitch."

Cash chalked up the vitriol to jealousy. It pained him to think that Bettina might have fallen for Rhoden, even for a brief fling. Cash McCahill would have pushed back on the suggestion, but Carl Meadows couldn't. "Sounds like she and Rhoden were a perfect match."

Sami scoffed. "In his dreams. Everything started out great between them. Rocket was the white knight, riding in to save her husband."

"What went wrong?"

"Rocket didn't rescue Biddle, but that didn't stop him from hitting on Bettina before, during, and after the trial." Her voice dripped venom. "What kind of lawyer does that?"

Cash squirmed. That hit close to home. Mariposa Benanti had been a client's wife and Cash's lover before and during her hubby's trial for tax evasion. Not after the trial, though. He leaned on that thin reed to distinguish his bad behavior from Rhoden's worse behavior.

Then again, after Larry Benanti's mistrial, Cash had gone to prison for jury tampering. Thus, he never really got a chance to bed Mariposa post-trial.

The reed snapped.

With Cash's history of hopping in and out of bed with all the wrong women, he could hardly slam Rhoden for sinking into the same toxic cycle. As a young assistant US attorney, Cash had slept with two fellow prosecutors: Jenna Powell, now the US attorney in Dallas, and Regina Delgado, currently the deputy attorney general in DC.

One of the two women would soon replace Karen Belton as the attorney general. Cash stood to lose either way.

Cash McCahill had no call to criticize Rhoden's lapses. Fortunately, the older and wiser Carl Meadows could. "Sounds like one fucked up lawyer," he said.

***

Nordstrom's was busy for a Tuesday afternoon. The shoppers skewed white, well-to-do, and with time on their manicured hands.

Cash beelined to the perfume wing on the second floor. Despite Sami's warning, he had to see Bettina Biddle and make sure she was doing well or at least getting by.

He wound through a maze of glass counters, each stocked with a name brand and guarded by a seller armed with a spritzer. No sign of Bettina. He widened the search to all three floors before returning to the starting point. He approached a perky brunette pushing Estée Lauder products. Her nametag read: Nikki.

Nikki closed a deal on the *Spellbound* special before turning to Cash. "May I help you, sir?" She reached for a spritzer.

Given Nikki's shoot-first-ask-questions-later vibe, Cash backed away from the counter. "I'm looking for an employee named Bettina Biddle. Last time I was here, she was working your turf."

"Oh, I know Bettina. Very cool lady and super popular with the customers."

He looked around. "Is she here today?"

"She quit about a month ago."

Cash reeled from a sense of *déjà vu*. First Tina took a powder from Powell's firm. Now Bettina bails from Nordstrom's. What was it with the women in his life? Today's news drove home a hard lesson from his childhood: Women leave. Even mothers.

"Do you know where she went?" he asked. "Why she quit?"

Nikki shook her head. "She just up and left. I didn't hear about it until she was gone."

"What did you hear after she left? There's bound to be gossip."

Nikki leaned over the counter, drawing Cash closer. "Cheryl at the Chanel station heard that Bettina had a sugar daddy. I say good for her." A shopper showed up, and Nikki went back to spritzing and selling.

Cash went to Cheryl's counter and waited for her to close a sale. She had a ready smile that made him warm to her instantly. She hadn't talked to Bettina since her abrupt departure. She had tried to call her, but the old number no longer worked. She didn't have Bettina's current number or address.

Cheryl added little to Nikki's account, except for one detail. She recalled a scene between Bettina and an older man. Heated words had ended with Bettina in tears and the stranger storming from the store. The entire exchange had lasted five minutes, tops.

"Do you know what they were arguing about?" Cash said.

Cheryl shook her head. "I couldn't hear them."

"Can you describe him?"

"Gray-haired, tall, handsome, distinguished-looking."

"How old was he?"

She stroked her chin. "Younger than you, but closer to your age than hers."

"Anything else you remember about him?"

"Yeah," she said, "the suit."

"What about it?"

"It was silk, Italian-cut, and cost way more than anything we carry."

"Think he could be her sugar daddy?"

She handed him a business card. "If you find him and he's not with Bettina, tell him to give me a call."

***

Phase two of Operation Widow Whisperer started with a stake-out at Michael Hinojosa Elementary School. Following her husband's death in prison, Bettina had pulled the twins from Hockaday, a private and pricey school for young ladies, and placed them in public school. Saved her $50K a year, easy.

As grade school let out for the day, Cash slouched in his parked car and watched the kids pour onto the playground. He had no chance of spotting Bettina's SUV among the caravan of like models lining the pickup lane, better than even odds of picking out the twins, and absolute certainty of identifying Bettina. He stayed on stakeout until the last child boarded the last SUV.

***

As dusk fell, Cash pulled to the curb and parked. The ranch style house in Richardson looked deserted. Bettina and the kids had moved in after the feds seized the Southlake showplace. He left the car and circled the house, peering through dust-coated windows without drapes. It was dark inside. The lawn needed work.

Cash took a photo of the For Sale sign, capturing the realtor's name and number. Maybe something had gone terribly wrong for Bettina, and the squeeze by the feds had forced her to downsize again. Alternatively, things could have gone terribly right for her, and the sugar daddy rumor had legs.

* * *

Cash reached the apartment as Tina was leaving. He had promised himself not to ask where she was going. To give her space. Trust her judgment. He immediately broke that promise and asked where she was going.

"To see a friend." She didn't try to sell it.

"Who?"

She stopped at the door. "You missed your true calling."

"As a grandfather?"

"As a prison guard. Don't wait up for me." She closed the door behind her.

CHAPTER THIRTEEN

After giving Tina a thirty-second head start, Cash rocketed from the apartment and down the staircase. His sprint downstairs beat her elevator ride. From the lobby, he watched her turn left outside the building.

He trailed her from a safe distance of a half-block. Traffic on Cedar Springs was light. Foot traffic on the sidewalks, lighter. A gold Mercedes convertible pulled alongside Tina. The driver opened the passenger door. His vanity plate read: AM BENZ. Cash took an instant dislike to Sam.

Tina walked on. The Mercedes coasted at her speed to the end of the block. The driver stuck his hand out the window and flipped her a farewell finger.

She crossed the street at Wycliff Avenue and hurried to a silver Lexus 350 parked at the curb. She got in without hesitation. Cash pulled out his phone and took several shots of the license plate as the Lexus headed south.

The smooth pickup meant that Tina knew Mr. Lexus. She wouldn't hop into a car with a stranger. Not with a serial killer out there.

Whether by luck or design, Tina had shaken Cash tonight. No chance for him to backtrack to the apartment building, jump in his car, and catch the Lexus.

On the slow walk home, a pack of questions dogged Cash. Why had Tina arranged to meet Mr. Lexus two blocks from their building? Was it to keep Cash in the dark? Who was she with tonight, and where were they going? Had she left a clue in the apartment that could shed light on any of this?

One question sank its teeth into Cash and wouldn't let go: Would Tina make it home safely? He reminded himself that he was merely playing the role of her grandfather. She wasn't blood, but that didn't ease his mind. Like it or not, she was family. She had been since he rescued the teenage Tina from the streets, and she would be so for the rest of his days.

Surveillance on foot had been a bust, but he wouldn't make the same mistake twice. Tomorrow night when she left the apartment, his car would be gassed and on the starting block. Game face and track shoes on.

He scrolled through the photos of the Lexus and froze on the one with the best view of the license plate. No vanity here. Just the standard letters and numbers above the legend: THE LONE STAR STATE.

He sent the image to the cloud. Had to save that one.

Back in the apartment, he searched the internet for the name of the owner of the Lexus. He was Maurice "Mo" Howard. Another database disclosed Mo's many aliases and lengthy criminal record, including a conviction last year on a drug conspiracy charge.

Given Mo's current residence at FCI Beaumont, he wasn't tonight's driver, but one of his fellow gangbangers could be. Cash tried to identify Mo's associates but hit one dry hole after another. He couldn't think of a cop who owed him a solid, but there was a federal agent in the wings—one with access to that kind of information.

Duane "Leroy" Lee of the DEA specialized in staging buy-busts, bending the rules, and guzzling beer. Back when Cash had been a federal prosecutor, they had worked dope cases together, racking up a string of mid-level convictions. Today, the only cases Leroy cleared contained Coronas.

While Cash McCahill and Leroy had been drinking buddies, Carl Meadows and the agent had shared only a brief exchange months ago at the Ritz bar. No way would a liquored-up Leroy remember a random conversation or be able to pick Carl from a lineup.

Cash shelved the idea of contacting the agent tonight. However, the photos would come in handy in an investigation if Tina came home hurt.

Or didn't come home at all.

***

Cash spent the next morning working on Bettina Biddle's whereabouts. He accessed the docket sheet for the federal forfeiture case and scrolled through every entry. Because Marty Biddle had gone to trial, the docket entries ran into the hundreds.

He found no listing of Bettina's current address because all the pleadings went through her attorneys. Her original lawyer had been Tony Dial, aka Terrible Negotiator Tony, or TNT for short. The bloated bottom feeder brought zero leverage to the bargaining table, due to his deathly fear of going to trial. It was a fear the feds routinely exploited to screw his hapless clients.

Court records indicated that Gerry Freeman of Powell, Ingram & Gardner had bumped TNT as Bettina's counsel about a month ago. That was like trading a pet hamster for a python.

The change in counsel presented the classic good news/bad news tradeoff. Good news for Bettina on the settlement front. Her newfound bargaining strength, backed by a scorched-earth litigator and the heavyweight firm behind him, boded well for her.

It was bad news for Cash in his search for Bettina. He could wring the truth from Tony—or at least come as close as the fat man could get to the straight skinny. Freeman and his partners, however, would be tough nuts to crack. The powerhouse firm of Powell, Ingram & Gardner had already bounced Eva and Tina, and Cash saw no way in for himself.

He set out to sweat Tony on the theory that stale news beat no news at all and tracked him to the sixth floor of the Frank Crowley Courthouse. TNT was schlepping files from courtroom to courtroom and searching for the next shit-out-of-luck client on the assembly line of justice. The defense counsel had a one in ten chance of landing in the right courtroom and worse odds of identifying his client among the scrum of defendants.

Cash approached Tony in the lobby. Poor wretches packed benches along both walls. The stench of sweat and cheap cologne made Cash long for the relative peace and prosperity of the federal courthouse.

"Can I help with those files, buddy?" Cash said.

"Sure thing." Tony unloaded the whole stack on Cash. "Follow me to Snipes's courtroom. I'll set up shop there."

Tony waddled. Cash trailed. They reached Judge Snipes's turf, but instead of entering the courtroom, they took a hard left into a windowless conference room. The room served as a hotbox for counsel to browbeat defendants into taking whatever shitty deal the state had put on the table.

The rotund Tony didn't breathe so much as wheeze. "Say, do I know you?"

Cash dumped the files onto a metal table. "Doubt it. I'm new in town. Name's Carl Meadows." Cash and Tony shook. "I'm a private investigator, making the rounds to introduce myself to the defense bar."

Tony panted from the exertion of a fifty-foot walk. Sweat stains darkened the armpits of his shiny blue blazer.

Cash handed him a business card. "Call if I can help you with a case."

Tony pocketed the card. "I don't have much need for an investigator."

Which explained why TNT was not so much a defense counsel as a defenseless one.

"Then maybe you can help me on a matter," Cash said. "You had a client named Bettina Biddle. I'm looking for her."

Tony plopped onto a chair. The chair groaned. "Who are you working for?"

"Now that Bettina is single again, an old flame wants to reconnect with her." Not far from the truth. "Beyond that, I can't say."

"Tell your client to steer clear of that cold-hearted bitch."

"My client is smart in business matters. Not so smart in affairs of the heart. You know the type. Learns hard lessons the hard way."

"I was this close." Tony held up his right hand, the thumb and forefinger an inch apart. "This close to working out a great deal for her with the feds."

The docket said otherwise. Cash said nothing.

"But she shitcanned me for some big firm attorney, who wouldn't know an indictment from an anchovy."

"If I wanted to get hold of her," Cash said, "how would I go about doing that?"

"And she and her new asshole lawyer." Tony's face turned two shades of red. "They cut me off cold. Not a penny for all my time and effort."

"Do you know her new address or not?"

TNT was too far gone in the tirade. "Miss high and mighty has enough dough to put the princesses back in Hockaday but not enough to take care of good old Tony."

Cash didn't bother sitting. With the news that the twins were Hockadaisies again, he had the lead he needed, and back-to-back stakeouts filled his dance card.

CHAPTER FOURTEEN

The next night, Tina left the apartment at 7:45 again without divulging where she was going, with whom, or when she would return. Cash waved goodbye, feigning interest in the shouting heads on ESPN.

He spotted her a minute's head start before dashing from the apartment, sprinting down the staircase to the underground garage, and speeding to the intersection of Cedar Springs and Wycliff. Reaching the presumptive hookup spot before she did, he cooled his jets.

He didn't have a long wait. Two minutes and ten seconds, to be exact. The silver Lexus arrived at straight up 8:00, as did Tina on foot. The Lexus and the lady had choreographed the dance. She entered the car without hesitation.

Mr. Lexus made it easy on Cash by obeying speed limits, using turn signals, and avoiding counter-surveillance measures. No cutting across lanes of traffic, sudden U-turns, or backtracking to reverse the roles of hunter and hunted. Either the driver didn't notice the tail or didn't care. Cash's stealth vehicle gave him an edge, never drawing a second look and seldom much of a first.

The deeper south the cars wound, the farther back in time they traveled. The roads became rougher. The houses, older. More abandoned buildings appeared per block. South Dallas had always gotten the short end of the stick from the city.

Fourteen minutes after picking up Tina, Mr. Lexus parked outside a one-story building on Martin Luther King Boulevard, close enough to Fair Park to see the crown of the Ferris wheel. If not for a few lights inside, the building would have looked deserted. Just another faded dream on a boulevard of broken ones.

Cash drove past the Lexus and parked in the next block. He waited five minutes before leaving the car. Most of the streetlights had burned out, and clouds shrouded tonight's sliver of a moon. The hood had a way of turning a dark street darker.

Cash counted eight cars parked outside the building that Tina and the driver had entered, for what smelled like a buy-bust. Or maybe not. The Lexus had more resale value than the other seven vehicles combined. Drug gangs generally sported slicker rides.

He circled the structure twice. Quickly the first time. More slowly the second. He picked up voices inside. They were female and occasionally raised. He made out random words and phrases but couldn't piece together a conversation or even a context.

A crying jag started and stopped abruptly. Window shades hid the goings-on inside. Whatever, a woman was hurting and needed help. And it could be Tina.

Cash had a problem. He was unarmed in a state that worshipped firearms. Carrying a weapon risked a felony conviction and a return trip to prison. Meaning he never…well, almost never, went to a gunfight with a gun.

Texas being Texas, the odds were less than zero of there being no weapons inside. That left Cash with two options: bail and live to fight another day or try to talk his way in and out of trouble. With Tina possibly in danger, he went with the latter, trusting his tongue to keep them both alive.

The porch creaked underfoot, the closest thing to an alarm on the property. Cash froze and held his breath. No one came or called out. He tested the door. Locked. He circled to the back door. Also locked.

He found an open window on the west side of the building and pulled himself up and over the sill. He landed in a dark room and slowly stood. Smell told him where he was before his eyes adjusted. The room reeked of air freshener.

The door banged open, and a shadowy figure stood at the threshold. The steady breathing of the shadow contrasted with the pounding of Cash's heart. His vocal cords locked down, sparing him the indignity of a scream.

The light flipped on, and Cash stared into the barrel of a Glock pointed at his forehead. He blinked. The gun didn't.

A sicario has come to collect the bounty on my head.

Sweat glands gushing, Cash instinctively raised both arms above his head and slowly peeled his eyes from the gun to the gunman. The hand that held the pistol belonged to Detective Robert Gamez. Cash breathed easier. The cop could be here to rescue Tina, in which case Cash would gladly stand down.

Gamez did a double take. "Hey, aren't you—"

"Yeah, Tina's grandfather." Cash started to shake hands but thought better of it and kept both arms in the air. "Carl Meadows."

Gamez lowered the gun. Cash took that as a green light to drop his arms to his side.

"Don't you think you're being a tad overprotective?" the cop said.

"That depends on what my little darling is up to out here."

Tina entered the bathroom and stood behind Gamez, her hand on his shoulder and her lips inches from his ear. Whatever was going down tonight, the two were in it together and joined at the hip.

Gamez was the mysterious Mr. Lexus. The detective must have boosted the car from DPD's forfeiture fleet. An upgrade to impress Tina.

"If you're not going to shoot him," she told Gamez, "give me the gun, and I will."

"This seems like a good time for a family meeting," the detective said. "I'll leave you two alone to sort this out."

"Take the gun with you," Cash said.

Gamez laughed on his way out. Tina stood her ground, arms folded at her chest. He had seen warmer expressions on Warden Stockman.

"Follow me." Her tone brooked no debate.

In the hallway, they passed by a room on the right, where three black women were on calls. The room was bare but for six small tables, each with a folding chair and a phone. To the left was a closed door with a posted sign that read: SESSION IN PROGRESS.

Tina led him to a breakroom, shut the door behind them, and told Cash to sit. The room smelled of burnt coffee. Empty pizza boxes covered the table.

"How about a cup of coffee?" Cash said.

"Coffee is for closers." She snapped her fingers. "Quick old man, what film is that from?"

"Too easy. *Glengarry Glen Ross*."

The right answer evidently didn't score points with her. "What the fuck are you doing here?" she said.

He took a shot at changing the dynamics of who was grilling whom. "I was about to ask you the same question, only in a nicer way."

She sat at the table across from him. "What do you think is happening here?"

He said the first thing that came to mind. "The women on the calls…is this some kind of phone sex operation?" The second thing on his mind didn't come off any better. "Or a boiler room?"

She rolled her eyes. "With a mind mired in the gutter, how do you manage to get up in the morning? Those women, who started their shifts at six and will be here past midnight, volunteer on a hotline for at-risk kids. They're saving lives."

"And the session behind the closed door," he said, "what's that all about?"

"A counselor is holding a free group meeting for kids who are wrestling with gender identity issues. Most are homeless, and almost all have been tempted to give up and…."

Cash knew why Tina didn't finish the sentence. She had been there. Her most recent brush with suicide followed a lockup at the Dallas County Jail. Guards had paraded her in bra and panties up and down the men's cellblocks before tossing her in a cold cell, naked and alone. A crushing sense of helplessness had pushed her to the brink.

"We're trying to help them cope," she said, "convince them that their lives matter."

She had Cash on the ropes, but he still swung wildly. "And the cop, why are you hanging out with him?"

"Not that it's any of your business, but unlike you, Robbie knows he has a lot to learn about the trans community and not much time to do it. I'm his guide to the other side. Introducing him to my sisters. Taking him to our hangouts. Showing him the shit we deal with. Even from so-called friends and allies."

"Tonight is what? A stop on the trans around town tour?"

"He's trying to catch the killer who's terrorizing our community, and I'm all in to help any way I can."

"Tina, not every battle is yours to fight. Leave the police work to the police."

"I couldn't agree with you more," she said.

"Wait, what?" Something was wrong. She never surrendered this quickly. Hell, she never surrendered at all.

That's when she dropped the bombshell on him.

CHAPTER FIFTEEN

Tina's bombshell extended Cash's streak of sleepless nights. She planned to apply to the Dallas Police Department. He held his tongue at breakfast until he no longer could. "Don't get your hopes up."

Her bloodshot eyes blinked. The oversize T-shirt bore an image of bare buttocks and a message clearly aimed at him: BUTT OUT. She took a bite of wheat toast and chewed angrily. "You spoke your piece last night. Give it a rest this morning."

Someone had to talk sense to her, and it fell to him. "Those felony charges a while back must've slipped your mind. You assaulted a federal officer." He paused for effect. "Three times."

"And you seem to have forgotten that I was acquitted." She dropped the toast to the plate. "Three times. Of course, back then you had a law license and a pair of balls."

Low blow. The balls were still intact. Granted, the bar had pulled his ticket for three years. Two while he was behind bars and a third on supervised release. However, he now possessed a valid Texas law license. The only glitch: Carl Meadows couldn't practice law under a license issued to Cash McCahill.

"If you're going through with this," he said, "at least let me review your application forms. Putting anything false or misleading on them is a new crime, and Cash McCahill isn't around to save your ass now."

"Why don't you want me to be a cop?"

"I don't want you to get hurt. If you shoot straight on the application, you won't reach the interview stage."

The fire in Tina's eyes told Cash to back the fuck off. "Robbie says I have a shot."

"Then he's as delusional as you." Cash put down the coffee cup. The brew tasted bitter. "And it's Robbie now?"

She shrugged. "We're working together as a team. We've bonded."

"Look," Cash said, "I know cops, and—"

She cut him off. "Like I don't?"

A good point that segued into his next one. "Which brings up another problem from your past. You spent many nights on the street and more than a few of them behind bars. Odds are that a cop or two who busted you then will be judging your fitness to serve now."

"Robbie doesn't think my past will sink my chances. I was a minor for most of those arrests, and I've cleaned up my act and gone straight." She smiled. "Well, maybe straight's not the right word here. At any rate, I have you to thank for my career as a paralegal, which looks damn good on the resume."

"Regardless of what I do or say, you're going to apply, aren't you?"

She nodded.

"Just don't get your hopes up."

They finished breakfast the way it had started. In silence.

***

The second stakeout in two days didn't end with a gun pointed at Cash like the night before had, but it still ended badly. He parked two hundred feet from the morning drop-off point for Hockadaisies. After a semester in public school, Bettina Biddle's twins had returned to the most expensive private school for girls in Dallas.

Cash waited and watched. Not that it would be easy to spot Bettina or the twins. Like a pea under a pod in a shell game, she drove one in a long line of SUVs, most of them black, stretching halfway down the block.

The twins hopped from a black Escalade and merged into a sea of students, most of them white and all in identical uniforms. Oxford shirt. Green and white plaid skirt. Saddle shoes. White blazer with green trim.

After the twins disappeared into the science center, Cash followed the Caddie for about ten minutes until it entered a gated community called Preston Hollow Estates. He failed to talk his way past the posted guard and turned back onto the street. He pulled into a cul-de-sac and parked.

Cash ran the math in his head. Hockaday tuition for two set back Bettina $50K or more a year. A new Escalade ran close to a hundred grand. The gated community offered showplaces in the mid seven figures. All of which added up to flush times for Bettina and a bad vibe for Cash.

He had two options for the rest of the morning. Wait near the gate and ambush Bettina when she left the compound or set Johnny Law straight.

Business before pleasure.

* * *

The sixth time was the charm. Gamez finally took the call. "I was afraid you were screening my calls," Cash said.

"I was."

Give the cop credit for honesty. "What made you change your mind?"

"We need to clear the air," Gamez said.

Cash and the cop met at Lucky's Café on Oak Lawn. Gamez didn't look happy to see him. After last night's scene at the community center, that came as no surprise.

Cash opened with a little levity. "What are your intentions toward my granddaughter?" The detective blanched. Cash backtracked. "I need your help to convince Tina that applying to the DPD is a terrible idea."

"Does Tina know you're talking to me about this?"

"Of course not."

Gamez shifted in the chair. "I gave her the idea to apply."

Cash recoiled. "Why would you do that? Why set her up to fail?"

"I don't see it playing out that way."

"How many trans officers are on the force?" Cash asked as if he knew the answer.

"Zero, and that's the point. The department is taking heat from activists, which is bad enough, as well as from the media, which is worse. The killings have the mayor and city council shitting bricks."

"And shit rolls downhill," Cash said.

"Chief Thomas is up to her neck in it. I told her last year that we should hire a trans officer, and she's been scouring the state for one since then."

"I get it," Cash said. "The brass wants to hire someone to play a cop on TV. Snow some gullible tool into wearing a uniform and serving as window dressing, all to fool the press and placate a handful of protestors. Yeah, that ought to work. For about five minutes."

Gamez smiled. "You've known Tina all her life. You tell me, Paw Paw, would you describe her as a gullible tool?"

Damn. It was not supposed to be this hard to roll the detective.

"Why does Tina have to be the first?" Cash said.

"She stepped up when others didn't. I've been chasing this killer for almost two years. In that time, the tension between the department and the trans community has worsened by the day. Tina has been a game changer. She's taking me on the rounds. Introducing me to her friends. Showing me where they hang out."

"And in return," Cash said, "you're going to get her killed."

Gamez leaned forward and lowered his voice. "I don't want her going anywhere close to real danger."

"That makes two of us."

"But she would make a great ambassador for the department. A liaison to the LGBTQ community. Our little media star."

Cash played his final card. He didn't want to go there, but Gamez had left him with no choice. "Have you run Tina on NCIC?" A few clicks on the law enforcement database would flood the screen with her history of arrests, charges, and dispositions."

"You're getting desperate, old man."

You have no idea.

Not only would a thorough background check sink Tina's shot at the force, but it might also reveal the inconvenient truth that both of her grandfathers were dead. That would terminate Cash's alter ego and put a nail in his coffin.

"If she applies," Cash said, "they'll have to do a background check on her."

"Correction. It's been done."

"And she passed?" Incredulity pitched Cash's voice higher and louder.

"The brass graded her on a curve. Like I said, the chief has been looking for a trans recruit for a year."

Cash was out of coffee and ammo. "Are you two playing Benson and Stabler again tonight?"

"That's the plan." Gamez dropped a five-dollar bill on the table and rose. "And for your sake, I won't mention our conversation."

After the cop left, Cash put another fiver on the table, doubling the tip and hoping karma snapped his losing streak.

***

Gas tank and confidence low, Cash followed Bettina to Central Market on Royal Lane in the afternoon. The gift of gab had failed him today. He had already lost rounds to Tina and Gamez and had failed to talk his way past a rent-a-cop at Preston Hollow Estates.

He sidled toward Bettina in the produce section and caught a whiff of her favorite perfume. She looked antsy. Her high forehead was furrowed. Traces of worry lines bracketed her lips.

"Mrs. Biddle, my name is Carl Meadows, and I work with Rocket Rhoden's law firm." He flashed a smile. "Well, I suppose it's Darrell Pendergass's firm now."

She took a step back. The tomato fell from her hand to the floor and bled out.

Cash never got any closer. Two goons converged and blocked his path to her. With their dark suits, short hair, and ear buds, they could pass for a Secret Service detail.

He tried to hand a business card to Bettina, but the taller goon snatched it. “She won’t need this,” he said. “She’s well represented.”

“Well guarded too,” Cash said, as the bodyguards hustled her to the exit.

CHAPTER SIXTEEN

Upon opening the door to his makeshift office, the smell hit Cash. More accurately, the absence of a familiar odor did. Every morning, the storage space that doubled as Cash's office exhaled a musty mix of mites and mildew. Today, only a faint whiff wafted from the room.

His office had aired out overnight, which spelled trouble. Someone had violated his space, no doubt to search the records there. His surefire way of checking involved three steps: going to file cabinet number four of the six that stood side by side along the western wall, thumbing through the Ks, and lifting the Kendall file.

Cash had a daily ritual. Before locking the office in the evening, he selected one file for the ass-backward treatment. A new file for each day. Yesterday had been Marvin Kendall's turn. He had placed the thin file backward, making it the only one in all six cabinets whose tab ran against the grain.

This morning the tab faced forward like all the others. Someone had removed the file last night. There was no reason to believe it had been the lone one pulled for inspection and put back.

Cash called an all-hands meeting in the conference room but later switched the venue to the Starbuck's in the building. A precaution in case the intruder had bugged their offices.

"Did either of you circle back to the office last night?" Cash said.

Darrell was too busy texting to look away from his iPhone. "Not me."

"Me neither," said Sami.

"Are you sure neither of you went into my office last night?"

"Technically, they are all my offices." When Darrell didn't snivel like an abused associate, he swaggered like an abusive partner. This morning, he played the partner role.

Sami's brow furrowed. "What gives?"

"Someone broke into my office last night and went through the files," Cash said. "Odds are, your offices were searched too."

Darrell looked up from the phone. "I didn't see any sign of a break-in."

"You aren't meant to." While a federal prosecutor, Cash had let slide an off-the-books search by the Bureau of a child predator's lair. He had kept that secret fifteen years and planned to take it to the grave. "Smells like a black-bag job," he said.

Sami looked puzzled. "What's that?"

"When agents stage a search on the sly. They blitz in and out of your place before you know it. If they do it right, you never know it."

"Why do you believe we had a break-in?" Darrell doubled down on skepticism.

Cash laid out his wrong-way file practice. Darrell's left eyebrow arched, signaling he wasn't sold. "Have you found anything missing?"

"That might not be the point," Cash said. "Maybe they copied what they came for. Maybe their goal was to plant something, like a bug or two. Or maybe they were here to confirm we don't have something."

"That's a lot of maybes," Sami said.

"We're in the dark until we know why they hit us." Cash let that sink in before confronting them. "What were they looking for?"

Sami and Darrell exchanged a look, but not the same look. Darrell stared blankly, as if struck dumb by the question. Sami's steely glint kept him quiet and in tow. Whatever secret they shared would stay between them for now.

Cash remained the odd man out and the voice of experience. "When was the last time you had the office swept for bugs?"

"It was back when Rocket was alive," Sami said. "Last October, I think."

"Have it done today." Cash chugged coffee. "In the meantime, assume everything you say in the office is being recorded."

"Aren't you being a little paranoid?" Darrell said.

Cash stood. "Have your cars and residences swept as well."

***

If Cash could be in two places at the same time, he would lock Sami and Darrell in side-by-side rooms and grill them about Biddle. Run the prisoners' dilemma game on the pair. Better yet, let Regina Delgado break them. No one played the game better than she did. In a bet on who would break first, the smart money would be on Darrell.

For that reason, Cash peeled off Darrell, convincing him to meet for drinks after work. Compromise led them to Sixty

Vines in The Crescent Complex near downtown. Darrell had proposed the Ritz. Cash had balked at returning to the site of his arrest for jury tampering and countered with Sammy's BBQ.

Sixty Vines split the difference. Sufficiently chic to attract eye candy for Darrell's entertainment. Casual enough to allow Cash to kick back in boots and jeans. A wide selection of wines to loosen Darrell's tongue. Craft beer catered to Cash's taste.

With a female-to-male ratio of three to one in the restaurant, capturing and keeping Darrell's attention was like trying to grasp liquid mercury. His eyes flowed from one temptation to the next. Scores of women returned Darrell's eye contact, all looking past or through Cash.

It sucked to be old. Even to play old.

"How's Freddy's defense coming along?" Cash said.

"He's talking about testifying, but I don't think that's a good idea."

"He's posturing." Cash could say the same about most defendants. "Come nut-cutting time, he'll be happy to let you do the talking."

A waiter took their orders. A 2018 Syrah for Darrell and a Local Buzz for Cash.

"How big a retainer did you get?" Cash said.

"Asked for a hundred K."

"And got?"

"He's working on it."

Translation: Dumbass Darrell had banked zero. Cash took a deep breath and exhaled slowly. Where to begin? Answer: Criminal Law 101. "With no money up front," he said, "you wind up with nothing but experience, and you know what they say about experience."

Darrell shook his head.

"It's what you get when you were looking for something else." Cash's mind defaulted to the worst-case scenario. "Tell me you haven't filed a notice of appearance in the case."

"Filed it yesterday," Darrell said.

"Then we're on the hook, even if Freddy stiffs us. Make that *when* Freddy stiffs us. The judge can keep us on the case as unpaid counsel. Didn't Rhoden teach you the golden rule? No gold, no go."

"He's good for it," Darrell said, his voice and temper rising.

Cash could swear to the opposite, but Carl Meadows couldn't, not to the same degree of certainty. He switched subjects. "Just for the sake of argument, let's say Freddy turns out to be slow pay or no pay. What other hooks have you got in the water?"

Darrell's eyes lingered on a nearby table of newcomers. "I'm working on a habeas petition for a state prisoner."

If that was meant to impress Cash, it didn't. "That can't pay much."

"I have a trial for a bank robber in two months." Darrell sounded defensive.

"Retained or court appointed?" Cash said.

"Latter."

"That will pay less." Cash snapped his fingers to capture Darrell's attention. Not his full attention. That would never happen, not with the talent on display. Just the minimum needed to ensure Cash's words registered. "Surely Rhoden had a few rich clients we can tap."

"Dopers were our biggest paydays."

Cash knew the drill. Rhoden had made a fortune on cartel work, paid to keep low-level scum from flipping. Over the years, Cash had encountered scores of Rhoden's expendable clients, serving out their sentences in federal joints. If one of the expendables broke the code of silence or even hinted at doing so, Rhoden alerted higher-ups, and the inmate got his wish to leave prison early.

In a body bag.

The image of Marty Biddle hanging in the prison chapel returned to haunt Cash, and he needed something stronger than beer. Much stronger than wine. Not that anything he swallowed, snorted, or shot up would banish Biddle's ghost. Cash had failed on his promise to get Marty out alive. He wouldn't fail to find his killer.

"How about white-collar work?" Cash said. "Did Rhoden have any clients we wouldn't be ashamed to be seen with in a place like this?"

Darrell shrugged. "One or two."

"Let's hear about them," Cash said.

"Not much to tell. We had a brother-sister team of inside traders, but we settled with the SEC last year. They paid a fine and took a lifetime ban on serving as officers or directors of a public company."

"What others?" Cash said.

"Can't think of any."

Cash could. The question was whether to drop Biddle's name. Doing so might tip off Darrell that Carl Meadows knew too much to be who or what he purported to be. On the other hand, if he didn't bring up Biddle now, when would he? Better to float the trial balloon before the dull and distracted Darrell, rather than the sharp and suspicious Sami.

"I ran into a looker at Central Market," Cash said. "We got to talking, and she asked where I worked. When I told her, she said to say hello to you."

Darrell's eyes fixed on Cash. "You had me at *looker*. Who was she?"

"Funny name. Bettina something." For the first time tonight, Cash had Darrell's full attention.

***

Dropping the Bettina bombshell had two immediate effects: one intended, the other not. The upside—Darrell stopped scanning the room and began thinking with his other head. The downside—he called in reinforcements.

Sami arrived in time for the third round of drinks and stood out in a restaurant teeming with beautiful women. She moved the party from the see-and-be-seen table of Darrell's choice to the most private booth in the back. Darrell never made it to the booth. Sent away by Sami, he slinked into the night.

"I told you to stay away from Bettina Biddle," Sami said. "Why did you disobey me?"

A waiter took Sami's order, giving Cash time to come up with a cover story. "I researched Rhoden on the internet, keying on his big trials. I hoped to impress you and Darrell by finding a former client in need of our services."

"And what makes you think Mrs. Biddle is a good candidate?"

"She's fighting the feds over forfeiture, with millions at stake. Thought we could take the matter on contingency and score a nice cut of whatever we saved her."

"And you would score a nice cut of what the firm took in," she said. Her look softened from skeptical to dubious. Cash hoped she would see him as more dim than devious.

"Don't approach our exes," she said, "without clearing it with me first."

Cash nodded, eyes down. Playing the penitent.

"And do not contact Mrs. Biddle. Ever. Understood?"

"May I ask why?"

"No."

CHAPTER SEVENTEEN

Cash needed time and space to float theories and found the perfect place: the spare bedroom Tina had converted into a study. There was little to no chance of an interruption over the weekend. Tina had called Friday with a crock about caring for a sick friend.

For the past month, she had spent less and less time in the apartment and more and more time with Gamez. They had sidelined Cash from their investigation of the Dice Cold Killer, leaving him free to chase Marty Biddle's ghost on his own.

He loaded his playlist with the perfect soundtrack for a gray Sunday morning. The complete Johnny Cash collection kicked off with a classic about ringing church bells, frying chicken, kicking cans, and getting stoned.

His self-imposed isolation dredged up memories of a week in solitary at Seagoville. Seven days and six nights of staring at blank walls and playing mind games to keep from freaking out. His prison punishment had left unseen wounds that would never heal.

What Warden Stockman had dished out was a love tap compared to the blow *Los Lobos* had delivered to Cash. The cartel had given him an ultimatum: Betray his client *La Tigra* or die. He had crossed the cartel and now faced the consequences. The warden had isolated him for a week. The cartel had erased his past, perhaps forever.

He wrote two names atop a large white sheet on an easel. Rocket Rhoden in blue marker on the left and Stewart Powell in red on the right. A sea of blank space surrounded the names. A black line bisected the board from top to bottom, running like a dark river of death between the men. Rhoden had wound up on the wrong side of the divide.

The empty expanse on the sheet illustrated the failure of Cash's two-step strategy for investigating Marty Biddle's hanging. Step one had been to plant Tina in Stewart Powell's law firm. She had lasted only days there, with nothing to show for her short stint.

Step two had been his infiltration of Rhoden's law firm, run by Darrell in name and Sami in fact. Cash had failed to hit pay dirt, and his outreach to Bettina Biddle made his footing shaky at the firm.

Two steps forward, four steps back.

He shelved his frustration over past failures and focused on solving the mystery of Biddle's death. Changing the coroner's ruling from suicide to homicide would bring a windfall to Bettina, courtesy of an insurance company. More important, the twins would not write off their father as having committed suicide. Or what would be worse for them, to never really know how or why he had died. The not knowing part would haunt them forever.

Cash could testify to the toll of not knowing. Orphaned at eight, he remained in the dark as to his mother's fate.

As morning wore on, the twelve-by-fifteen-foot room morphed into a confessional, where Cash copped to the deeper goal of playing the white knight. He would ride to Bettina's rescue and pick up where they had left off six months ago.

Currently, a series of hurdles separated them. When Bettina ventured outside her gated community, goons guarded her. In addition, Sami had ordered Cash to stay away from her. Finally, Cash could hardly resume a relationship when he no longer existed.

The longer he stared at the board, the more convinced he became of one thing. The key to the mystery lay in the unlikely intersection between two lawyers. He wrote in a frenzy, filling the sheet with lists under both names. Putting down clients, friends and foes, strengths and weaknesses, assets and liabilities. He went at it until his hand cramped.

He stepped back and stared at the outpouring of words and phrases. There had been no eureka moment. It still made no sense. No natural or rational connection between the lawyers had emerged. Rhoden and Powell lived in different worlds. A Who's Who of Fortune 500 companies filled Powell's expanding client list, while Rhoden had catered to whichever kingpin paid top dollar.

Only rarely had Rhoden managed to land a white-collar client. Marty Biddle had been one. Dr. Katzenbach, another. The surgeon had hired Rhoden for some unknown reason. On paper, both Biddle and Katzenbach would seem to belong on Powell's side of the ledger.

In one respect, however, the two lawyers were similar. Both had amassed fortunes.

Rhoden had a net worth in the high seven figures according to probate records found at the firm. Cash suspected the deceased had parked more money in tax havens. Being a pariah of the bar had paid well.

Powell had done even better. A net worth of eight figures allowed his sole heir, Jenna, to occupy the US attorney post without sacrificing the lifestyle of a trust fund baby. Hefty political contributions fueled her bid to fill the top spot at Justice.

Cash returned to the easel, unleashing his mind and hand to free associate about the two men, their money, and their motives. By morning's end, swirls of red and blue had left only small patches of white on the sheet. Arrows flew up and down and from side to side. Semicircles ran clockwise and counterclockwise.

He ended the session certain of one thing. There had been only one reason for Powell to have chosen Rhoden to represent Biddle. Rhoden had a history of keeping defendants from cooperating, even at the cost of their lives.

Cash left the red, white, and blue of the sheet in search of another color: black, as in The Man in Black. The morning soundtrack reached a song recorded live at Folsom Prison, reminding Cash of an inmate closer at hand: Big Black.

***

Weather and warden permitting, Seagoville allowed visits in the yard on weekends. While Texas weather was unpredictable, Marvin Stockman was not. He approved regular visits for prisoners who toed the line and yard visits for those who enforced the peace.

With North Texas baking in a late summer heat wave, Cash staked claim to a shaded table outside. The prisoners in the yard cleared a path as Big Black hobbled to the table, constricted by chains running wrist to wrist, ankle to ankle, and wrist to ankle.

Despite patchy cloud cover, Big wore shades. Though it had been only a month since Cash's prior visit as Carl, the prisoner looked different. Whoever had shaved his bald, battered skull had been more of a butcher than a barber. Fresh scabs criss-crossed the flesh.

Big landed hard on the chair. The chains jangled.

"What's with the Hannibal Lecter treatment?" Cash said.

"That's to protect you."

"Do I need it?"

Big snorted. "If you came back to accuse me of murder again, you damn sure do." He stared hard at Cash. "You remind me of someone. Ever pull a stretch?"

Cash shook his head. "I've got that kind of face." *Thanks to Dr. Katzenbach.* "Like I said before, I'm Marty's uncle. Could be a family resemblance."

"Nope, that ain't it." Big's smile bared a gold front tooth. "Didn't expect to see you again. Thought we was one and done."

"We didn't finish our conversation last time," Cash said.

"You got more questions about Marty?"

"There are a lot of unanswered questions."

"I didn't kill him." Big sounded resigned to disbelief by everyone on everything. The story of his life, inside and out.

Cash bucked the trend. "I believe you." Big hadn't fallen completely off the suspect list, but he no longer topped it.

"Marty wouldn't…." Big clammed up.

Cash looked over his shoulder. A one-eyed guard swaggered toward their table and crashed the party. The asshole's name was Parker, but everyone called him *The Pirate*. The eye patch explained the nickname.

"Warden wants to see you," Parker said.

"Why?" Big asked.

"Not you," the guard said. "He wants to talk to your visitor."

The Pirate had never brought good news in the past, and Cash doubted that today would prove any different. If Big almost saw through the facial surgeries, the warden might nail him in no time.

CHAPTER EIGHTEEN

"Who are you?"

Those were the first words spoken by Warden Marvin Stockman to Cash since his last day in Seagoville, more than three years ago. Overcrowding across the federal system had triggered Cash's early release, a gift from a rare judge who gave a shit about prison conditions. The judge's order applied only to inmates in their last year of a sentence, freeing Cash but not Marty Biddle.

Cash froze at the doorway, fearful that his mask as Carl Meadows had slipped. Or that Stockman had seen through it.

"Who are you?" The question was louder the second time.

On the couch, Bettina Biddle shivered in a sleeveless dress. Stockman kept the room at meat-locker cold. A spark of recognition widened her eyes. She nodded to Cash.

Cash took the nod as a good sign. Sweating bullets, he nodded back but stayed silent. Stockman made no introductions, probably waiting for one or both to commit to knowing the other.

Cash had never put much stock in prayer, but he sent a silent one to the Guardian Angel of Perpetual Fuckups. He prayed for Bettina to remember Carl Meadows from their brief encounter at Central Market and to consign Cash McCahill to the purgatory of lost souls.

"I'm waiting for an answer." Stockman's tone hardened.

Moment of untruth time. A lesser liar might have cracked and confessed. A greater liar like Cash knew better. When in doubt, admit only to what the other side knows. Cash stalled. "What do you mean?"

"On your application to visit Big Black, I mean Marcus DuPree, you claimed to be a relative of Martin Biddle." Stockman pushed a single page across the desk. "Is that your signature?"

Cash didn't move. Stockman had opened with an ace, but Cash wanted to see the opponent's full hand before bluffing.

"You can't see from there," Stockman said. "Come closer."

Cash stepped forward and nodded. With little chance of surviving the high stakes showdown, he played the odds. That meant favoring nonverbal answers over verbal, verbal over written, and written over sworn.

The scribbled signature of Carl Meadows didn't unnerve Cash, but a chilling thought did. His fingerprints were all over the form. Dr. Katzenbach hadn't altered the prints, and the feds had a database that could end Cash's run as Carl Meadows.

Along with his life.

Cash waited for the warden to say more, and he did. "Was Martin Biddle your nephew?"

Cash doubled down on the strategy of silence.

"It's a federal crime to lie on this form." Stockman patted the single sheet that would be exhibit number one at Cash's second criminal trial in the dock. "Clamming up won't make this go away. I called Mrs. Biddle to ask if you really are her late husband's uncle."

Cash turned to Bettina, who stared at the floor. It was a bad sign when a juror wouldn't look him in the eye. Especially the lone juror.

"She didn't think so," Stockman said, "but wasn't sure. When I found out you were returning to Seagoville, I invited her to come and see for herself." He turned to Bettina. "What's the verdict, Mrs. Biddle? Is he your deceased husband's uncle?" he asked, as if he knew the answer.

She walked over to Cash and stood so close that her perfume clouded his judgment. For the first time, he noticed a small, white scar at her widow's peak. There had to be a story behind the scar, but he couldn't ask. Not now. Not here.

"Marty did mention a Dutch uncle back East," she said.

Stockman bolted to his feet. "Dutch uncle!"

The last time Cash had seen such outrage from the warden was over the court order that forced him to rubber stamp Cash's early release. Now it looked as if lightning was about to strike twice. Or, more accurately, miss Cash by a whisker twice.

Stockman hadn't held onto power for two decades by giving up easily. "Wait a second. A Dutch uncle isn't a real uncle."

Bettina returned to the couch and retrieved her purse. "To Marty he was."

The warden wheeled toward Cash. "Dutch uncle or not, what's your purpose here?"

"I want to find out who killed Marty Biddle," Cash said. "Do you?"

Stockman blanched, which told Cash all he needed to know. Marty's death also haunted the warden. After all, it had happened on his watch.

* * *

Bettina ambushed Cash in the prison reception area, which was empty except for them. "We need to talk," she said.

He pointed to monitors stationed at the four corners of the ceiling. "The warden's eyes and ears. Let's go to the parking lot. Your car or mine?"

"There are two bodyguards waiting in my SUV," she said. "Not the parking lot."

"The goons from Central Market?"

She nodded.

"Are they supposed to keep others away from you," Cash said, "or you away from others?"

"It works both ways." She managed a weak smile. "Mostly it's to keep people like you from getting to me."

"Why?"

"Apparently my late husband made powerful enemies, and I inherited his debts. If the feds have their way on forfeiture, that's all I'll inherit from him." She bit her lower lip, a sign she was holding back.

Cash led her to the outside steps, where they sat. The sun cast her complexion in a coppery glow. "As long as we stay low and keep our voices down," he said, "your guards can't see us, and Stockman can't hear us."

"You never answered the warden's question," she said, "but you gave him a hell of a fright. He turned white as a sheet when you brought up Marty. What's that about?"

"Guilt," Cash said. "The warden should have tried to release your husband early or at least transfer him to another prison. He didn't, and Marty wound up dead. Based on his reaction today, Stockman isn't over it."

Her eyes misted. "Back to the warden's original question. Who are you? Then we'll go to my questions, starting with why you're interested in what happened to Marty."

He came up with a new cover story. "It's Rhoden I'm looking into."

"He's dead," she said.

"He's in a grave, but that won't stop me from digging. I represent a client who made the mistake of hiring Rhoden to defend him in a criminal case. True to form, Rhoden sold him out. As a result, he's doing life. In my research into Rhoden's background, I came across your late husband's case. There are a lot of parallels between what happened to your spouse and my client."

"Who is your client?" she asked.

"I can't divulge that."

"I guess that also explains why you're working for Rhoden's firm."

Cash nodded. "My turn to ask a question. Why did you cover for me in the warden's office? I doubt your husband had a Dutch uncle, and if he did, it wasn't me."

There was a long pause. Cash gave her the benefit of the doubt by not assuming she was concocting a bullshit answer. More than likely, she really didn't know.

"You have a kind face," she said.

First time Cash had heard that. Then again, it was a new face. Still under warranty.

"And I find myself in need of the kindness of strangers," she said. "I too want someone to look into Marty's death."

"Why not hire a PI?"

She bit her lower lip again. "I can't. A friend was helping me investigate Marty's death, but he's...gone." Her voice dropped toward the end.

Maybe not forever.

"When he disappeared, I panicked. If Marty's enemies would kill a lawyer—maybe two lawyers—they wouldn't think twice about killing me and leaving my girls orphaned."

The word "orphaned" triggered Cash's memory of the day his mother vanished. At a loss for words, he simply nodded.

Bettina went on. "I signed a nondisclosure agreement with Marty's company to drop the investigation into his death, which had hit a dead end anyway. Without Cash…." She fell silent and looked away. "The NDA is keeping the girls and me afloat."

"Who drafted the agreement?" he asked.

"A woman in Stewart Powell's firm. I can't remember her name."

Cash took a stab. "Paula Marshall?"

She nodded. "That's the one."

"And who recommended you sign it?"

"Mr. Powell, Ms. Marshall, and Mr. Watson, Marty's boss."

"Did you have your own lawyer look over the NDA?"

She shook her head.

It was all Cash could do to keep from rolling his eyes. He resumed the cross-examination. "Who picked Rhoden to represent Marty at his criminal case?"

"They did."

"Who hired the muscle waiting in your SUV?"

"They work for Mr. Watson or his company."

Speak of the devils, the goons showed up and cast long shadows over the couple. They pulled Bettina to her feet. Cash tried to rise, but the taller goon shoved him down and said, "That's two strikes, gramps. A third and you're out."

They marched the widow to the lot and out of Cash's sight.

CHAPTER NINETEEN

The next morning, a cop with a gold badge in one hand and a Glock in the other greeted Cash at the door to Darrell's firm. Cash raised both arms in the air and said, "I'm not armed."

He was the only one in sight who wasn't. A wrecking crew in FBI, DEA, IRS, and DPD windbreakers stripped the room like a plague of locusts, seizing everything not nailed down. Computers. Cell phones. File cabinets. Day-timers. Papers. Post-it notes. Down to scraps from the shredder.

All safe and secure one minute. Tagged, boxed, and whisked away the next.

The cop holding the gun on Cash said, "Who are you, and what are you doing here?"

"Carl Meadows, and I work here."

"Get in our way, and I'll bust you for obstruction."

Cash had witnessed raids before, on both sides of the badge. He knew what was going down and how it would play out. "Can I see the warrant and your badge again?"

"Are you in charge of this firm?" the cop asked.

"No."

"Then no and no."

Unarmed and outnumbered, Cash didn't debate the point. The Glock pointed him toward the conference room. He moved in that direction, keeping his hands high.

On the way, he recognized the alpha agent in charge: Marty Shafer of the IRS. Shafer was the oldest person on site, other than Carl Meadows. The tax agent had briefly been Cash's ally, but that was long ago and in a different lifetime. It had been an enemy-of-my-enemy thing. Cash didn't count on any residue of goodwill, certainly not for Carl Meadows.

Mr. Glock prodded Cash into the conference room and closed the door, leaving him to face a seething Sami and a dumbfounded Darrell. No sympathetic smile or comforting word from either. It was going to be that kind of day.

"What's going on?" Cash said.

Darrell slid a document across the table. Cash flipped through all ten pages. He had seen hundreds of s

earch warrants and drafted dozens as a federal prosecutor. This one gave the search team the green light to seize all evidence of bribery, fraud, tax evasion, structuring, and money laundering. Those charges barely scratched the surface of Rhoden's criminal history. It would be quicker to list the crimes *not* committed by the late cartel mouthpiece.

The warrant didn't mention Rhoden by name, nor did it divulge the names of any live targets of the investigation.

Cash looked at his colleagues. They weren't prisoners, but they weren't free to go either, not until the raid wrapped. Walking out the door invited an obstruction charge.

Cash couldn't sit still. Technically, he remained in the conference room but pushed the boundary. He opened the door and recorded the action on his iPhone. A cop hustled over. The badge identified him as D. Benavides. He had a catcher's build. Short, squat, and solid enough to block the plate. "What do you think you're doing, asshole?" Benavides said.

"Recording the raid."

"Turn it off."

Cash ran a bluff. "The Supreme Court in *Campisi versus State* affirmed my absolute right to video this search." The fictitious citation drew a smile from Sami and Darrell, but not from Benavides.

"The case of my foot versus your ass overruled the Supreme Court," the cop said. He shoved Cash back into the conference room and slammed the door in his face. Cash returned to the table and sat.

An arrest would be bad news for Darrell and Sami, but it would be fatal for Cash. Running Carl Meadows's fingerprints through the database would blow Cash's cover and put him back in the crosshairs of the cartel.

The body language of Sami and Darrell told Cash that the two were together in one respect, worlds apart in another. They shared a distrust of him but differed in their reactions to the raid. Sami scrolled through the messages on her phone, while Darrell sweat and squirmed. A case of the blonde leading the bland.

Cash kicked off the blame game. "Who did you two manage to piss off?"

"Funny." Darrell didn't sound amused. "I was about to ask you the same thing."

"Me!" Cash feigned outrage. "You've got some nerve trying to turn this on me. You're the one who tied his reputation to the pariah of the bar." He shut up, having already said too much. "Pariah of the bar" sounded like something Cash would say about Rhoden. Indeed, it *was* something Cash had said about the not-so-dearly departed.

"We were doing just fine," Sami said. "You show up, and all hell breaks loose."

"Just fine is a stretch," Cash said. "Your firm is dying."

Sami stopped scrolling through her messages. "Where were you yesterday?"

"I had errands to run." Cash didn't trust them with the truth. Based on the vibe in the room, the feeling was mutual.

Questions were piling up in Cash's mind. The raid made no sense. Sure, everyone with a badge had a hundred reasons to hate Rhoden, but he had been dead for a year. Why go after his faltering firm now? Why take down a lightweight like Darrell?

"Did the agents try to interview either of you?" Cash said.

Sami nodded. "The old guy from the IRS did."

Shafer would have been Cash's guess. The old dog never missed a trick, and cornering an assistant in the heat of a search was a classic.

"Did you talk to him?" Cash said.

She scoffed. "What do you think?"

He thought not. *Good girl.*

The time for untruth had passed. They were holding back, as was he. Someone had to fess up first and begin the long, painful process of unraveling the ball of lies. "I talked to Bettina Biddle yesterday," Cash said.

Darrell slapped the table, the sound as sharp as gunfire. Sami glared at Cash and said, "Why the fuck did you do that?"

Cash had given them a dose of the truth. Any more would be an overdose. "To see if she would consider hiring our firm to handle her forfeiture case."

"It's *our* firm now?" Darrell said. "At least we know why we got raided."

"And now we know who gets fired for insubordination," she said.

Cash couldn't push back, not with the search coming hot on the heels of his brush with Bettina and not after Sami had ordered him to steer clear of the widow.

"Why is Mrs. Biddle off limits?" Cash said.

Sami and Darrell exchanged a look that spelled pure panic. Whatever secrets they were keeping from him wouldn't surface today, certainly not after Shafer entered the conference room and handed three pages to Cash. "Here you go, pops. Maybe you can convince Ken and Barbie that they're not cut out for a life of crime."

Cash flipped through the pages, the last one signed by Shafer, the first two initialed and dated by him. Line after line of seized items, described generically. He wondered what the team had looked for and not found, as well as what they had taken that didn't make the list.

"Does this mean we're free to go?" Sami asked.

Shafer grunted. Cash took that as a yes. All three rose from the table. The agent put a hand on Cash's shoulder and said, "Not you."

***

Cash McCahill knew better than to talk to an agent, especially a bulldog like Shafer. The only question was whether Carl Meadows would have to learn his lesson the hard way.

Sami and Darrell fled the conference room. Shafer and his sidekick took their seats at the table. Officer Danny Benavides, a generation younger than Shafer, looked like the silent type, leading Cash to expect the IRS agent to do the talking.

"Who are you?" Shafer said. "And what are you doing here?"

Against all odds, Cash gambled that he could wheedle more info than he gave up. "Since my participation in this interview is entirely voluntary, I'll answer a question for every one of mine you answer."

"You first," Shafer said.

"Carl Meadows. My turn. Can I see the affidavit supporting the search warrant?"

"No. The court sealed it. Back to me. What are you doing here?"

"I'm an investigator and new in town. Just trying to drum up business with the local bar." Cash went straight to the key question. "Since Main Justice has to sign off on the search of a lawyer's office, who had the stroke to get a green light for this fishing expedition?"

That question aborted the interview. Shafer left the room first. On his way out, Danny dropped a business card in Cash's lap—Carl Meadows's business card.

"You left this behind the other day," the cop said. "Mrs. Biddle won't need it."

Left alone in the room, Cash walked to the window and looked at the street below. Police vans loaded with plunder pulled away from the curb. TV vans jockeyed for empty parking spaces. First plague gone. Second plague on the way.

CHAPTER TWENTY

It looked like a tornado had torn through the law firm, leaving behind only the battered furniture. A cacophony of phones buzzed, beeped, and chirped. Carl Meadows alone silenced his iPhone. Unlike Cash, Carl hadn't swapped numbers with every Tom, Dick, and Mary of the media.

TV crews ambushed Darrell outside the building. He mumbled claptrap about cooperating with law enforcement and keeping the firm open for business. He sounded almost as guilty as he looked.

Cash wondered who had tipped the media to the raid. Like a Perry Mason novel, there was no shortage of suspects: cops, agents, state and federal prosecutors, or some combination of the above. The timing of the search, coming so soon after the black-bag job, suggested a powerful figure had coordinated the one-two punch. If not, it was quite a coincidence.

Coincidence or not, the media-saturated search had sealed the law firm's doom. What client would put his fate in the hands of a lawyer whose records were in the hands of Johnny Law?

The next morning, after surveying the full extent of the carnage, Sami and Cash shared the couch in Darrell's office. Darrell slumped behind the big desk. Paler than Rhoden's ghost, he had never seemed less in charge. Though the timing sucked, Cash dropped more bad news on his shell-shocked colleagues. Bad in the form of another expense the firm couldn't afford. "We need to hire counsel."

"Why?" Darrell said.

Leave it to Darrell to ask a dumb question. Cash gave the obvious answer. "The storm troopers aren't fucking around. They didn't toss this place for practice."

"Why can't I represent us?" Darrell's eyes begged Sami to back him up, but she didn't.

"Remember what Lincoln said about a lawyer who represents himself," Cash said.

Darrell scoffed. "That was a hundred years ago."

"Closer to two hundred," Cash said, "but truer words were never spoken."

Sami found her voice. "Carl's right. We need a street fighter. Don't know about you boys, but I don't look good in orange."

Cash knew exactly how he looked in orange. Not bad. Of course, that was then. Now, probably not so good.

She turned to Cash. "Do you have someone in mind?"

Darrell lashed out at her. "Why ask him? He's been in town for what? All of five minutes. I'm the one with contacts here."

Cash set out to steer the representation to Goldy but to do so subtly. Let Darrell exhaust his short and dwindling list of contacts first. After all, it was his firm, even if in name only.

Sami and Cash left Darrell alone to seek a champion to slay not one, not two, but three dragons: the state, the feds, and the shadowy power behind the raid. Two hours later, they gathered in the conference room for Darrell's download.

It hadn't gone well. Darrell ticked off the six lawyers on his wish list, starting alphabetically with Ashby and ending with Webster. Two had hung up after reminding Darrell of unpaid invoices dating from Rhoden's reign.

Three others had cited phantom conflicts. Not actual legal impediments that barred their representation of the firm. More like business considerations that made the engagement undesirable. All but one had been vague about the nature of the alleged conflict. Steve Palmer had been blunter.

"Palmer felt bad about turning us down," Darrell said. "I pressed him on why, and he hemmed and hawed before fessing up. A lawyer from Powell's shop had called, strongly suggesting that he pass on representing us. According to Palmer, other lawyers were getting the same call."

Sami didn't look surprised, cementing Cash's suspicion that she and Darrell were keeping something from him. A secret that pitted Team Powell against Team Pendergass.

"Who at Powell's firm called Palmer?" she asked.

Darrell shook his head. "He wouldn't say. Also said he would deny the whole conversation if I ever brought it up."

"Did Palmer suggest anyone who might be willing to represent us?" Cash said.

"No." Darrell drummed his fingers on the desk. "He ended the call by saying good luck finding anyone in Texas willing to bite the hand that feeds them."

The room fell silent, except for the drumming. Cash processed the turn of events. Powell had the juice to tee up the raid, and his daughter, Jenna, the US attorney in Dallas, had the troops to carry it out.

Moreover, Powell's firm generated millions of dollars in referrals every year—business the mega-firm either didn't want or couldn't take. The castoff clients fell like manna from heaven into the mouths of a host of hungry attorneys, great and small. What lawyers in their right mind would jump off the gravy train?

But why would a patrician like Powell go after a punk like Pendergass? Their two firms occupied different universes. One was soaring. The other, sinking. It was a Godzilla versus Bambi mismatch.

"I take it you found no one to help us." Sami sounded rattled.

"I came close," Darrell said. "Goldstein from San Antonio was tempted, but he's booked in back-to-back murder trials in the Valley. He won't free up for six months."

The mention of Goldstein gave Cash an opening to pitch Goldy. "Glad you brought up Goldstein, because we're getting warmer."

"How so?" Sami said.

"Warmer in the sense of bringing us closer to the right counsel," Cash said. "What about Gary Goldberg?"

Darrell's laughter drowned out the drumming. Sami had the decency not to laugh, but her smile was almost as galling.

"What's so funny?" Cash managed to drain most of the anger from his voice.

"What's the plan here?" Darrell asked. "Are we going to carry the geezer into court on a stretcher? Prop him up at the defense table, like that movie…what was it?"

"*Weekend at Bernie's*," Sami said.

Darrell snapped his fingers. "That's the one. Carl, you're new here and don't know the ins and outs of the local bar. But Goldberg, well, he's on the way out."

Cash bit his tongue. It was hard not to defend Goldy and point out that on his worst day in court, he was twice the lawyer Rhoden had been and a hundred times the lawyer Darrell would ever be. Cash couldn't go there, not without blowing his cover. He kept quiet and waited for Sami to come around.

"On second thought," she said, "maybe we *should* consider Goldberg."

"You're as crazy as he is," Darrell said.

She leaned forward. "Hear me out. There may be only one lawyer in Texas who's not beholden to Powell or scared shitless of him."

Make that two, if I were still practicing law.

She rose. "Get up, fellas."

"Where are we going?" Darrell said.

"We're off to see the wizard."

***

Eva met the three visitors at the reception desk. "Are you here to poach another client from us?" Her voice dripped venom.

"We're here to bring you a client," Sami said.

Eva perked up and escorted them into Goldy's office. Cash estimated two minutes would elapse before she returned to deliver her well-rehearsed lines.

"What can I do for you fine folks?" Folds of skin tugged on Goldy's sunken eyes and sagging jowls. Last year's heart attack had whittled down his body, but his voice remained strong. The rolling bass still shook the rafters.

"We had an unexpected visit from the feds yesterday," Sami said.

Goldy winced. "Saw that on the news last night. Looked like they cleaned out your office."

"We need to get our records back," Darrell said.

Sami added, "And our computers and iPads."

Eva stuck her head into the office and delivered an urgent message from Judge Harlan Robinson. His Honor had to cancel their racquetball game this afternoon.

Cash silently applauded her performance. There had been no call from Robinson. No racquetball game scheduled for today or ever. It was a ploy to convince them that, despite all appearances to the contrary, Goldy had the stamina to square off against a jurist who was thirty years his junior. No spin or subterfuge, however, could erase the ravages of seven decades, two hundred plus trials, six marriages, five divorces, and two heart attacks.

Eva exited, ceding the floor to Goldy. "The feds have a bag full of dirty tricks," he said. "The bastards take everything you need to run a business and slow walk returning your stuff." He offered his guests a drink, but they passed. "Did you bring copies of the search warrant and an inventory of what was seized?"

Sami slid a folder across the desk. "Before we get too deep into the story, we need to be straight with you. It's possible that Stewart Powell and his firm are behind the raid."

Though not completely straight, Cash thought. No need to tell Goldy they were here only after striking out with six competitors.

"Why do you suspect Powell?" Goldy said.

Darrell shared his conversation with Steve Palmer and said, "Does that scare you off?"

Goldy plopped his boots on the desk and leaned back in the chair. “Sonny boy, at my age the only things that scare me are a coven of my exes and losing my car keys.”

Cash smiled. Another line he had heard a thousand times in this office.

CHAPTER TWENTY-ONE

A candlelight vigil in Deep Ellum marked the passage of two years since the discovery of the Dice Cold Killer's first victim. The moniker referred to the dice tattooed on the bottom of the victims' big toes. The dots corresponded to the order of the slayings. A single dot marked the first victim. Snake eyes for number two. The next in line would roll double fours.

Cherry tops barricaded both ends of Hall Street, allowing a crowd in the hundreds to roam the block freely and spill into the alley where DCK had dumped the bodies of numbers one through seven. A rainbow coalition had gathered in memory of the fallen. Black, brown, bronze, white, and fluid across the spectrum of race, gender, and sexuality.

The mourners or celebrants or whatever they were, carried a single rose. The flowers came in all the colors of the Transgender Pride Flag that waved over the makeshift stage.

While Tina waded into the mass of bodies, Cash hung back on the periphery. He recognized former clients in the crowd, as well as someone who could count him as a client. In a white suit, Dr. Katzenbach weaved through the throng. Trans groupies trailed in his wake.

Cash couldn't shake a lingering question. Why had the surgeon hired the late Rocket Rhoden instead of Cash? The question would go unanswered tonight, as Cash steered clear of Katzenbach. The doctor was one of only two people on the planet who knew Carl's identity. If confronted cold, the surgeon might slip and give away their connection.

Besides, Cash was on the lookout for dangerous game tonight. DCK could be here. How could the sick fuck pass on an opportunity to revisit his dumping ground for the bodies and, in the process, taunt the cops? As a bonus, what better time and place to select his next victim?

While Cash scanned for signs of danger, a clear and present one appeared. Skyler Patterson, a slash-and-burn reporter for the *Dallas Morning News*, wore jeans and a "TRANS LIVES MATTER" T-shirt. She looked past Cash. Accustomed as he was becoming to the indignity, the invisibility of old age still stung.

Gamez arrived in an unmarked car and shook hands with every uniformed cop on the block. He went out of his way to avoid Skyler, whose articles had gone from lionizing to lambasting him. Her current crusade was to bully the police chief into picking a new head of the DCK task force.

Cash caught up with Tina, who was leaning against a parked car. Up close, she looked pale and panicky. She struggled to catch her breath.

"Are you okay?" He readied to catch her if she collapsed.

She nodded weakly. "I'll be all right," she whispered.

"Let me take you home."

She shook her head. A hint of color returned to her face. "Wish me luck." She pushed away from the car and disappeared into the crowd. She mounted the stage and led the mourners in "I Will Remember You." It was news to Cash that his roomie could nail the high notes on any night, much less after a bout of stage fright.

During the second verse, DPD Chief Gloria Thomas made her entrance, flanked by two deputy chiefs: Frick and Frack, the Tupper brothers. The brothers, whose real names were Fred and Frank, had joined the force together and picked up the nicknames on day one. They cleared the chief's path to the center of the stage. She had the solid build of a woman who could hold her own in a boardroom or a weight room.

The chief surveyed a crowd that fell silent. The heat index on the block rose, and if there had been a tension index, it would have been off the charts. Glass shattered, sparking a scream. The breaking of more glass prompted uniformed cops to draw their batons. Silence gave way to scattered hissing and catcalls. A shout for the chief to resign echoed down the street.

The night would not end well. Cash's sole goal became getting Tina off the stage and out of harm's way. He motioned for her to come to him, to no avail.

At nearly six feet tall, Chief Thomas was a head taller than Tina. Frick and Frack bookended the women and towered over them. Cash consoled himself with the thought that, at five-six, Tina was the smallest target on stage.

Frick (or was it Frack?) handed a mic to the chief. The crowd stilled. "On behalf of the dedicated men and women of the Dallas Police Department," she said, "we share your sorrow over the slayings that have brought us here tonight, and I want to express our strongest commitment to do everything in our power to catch the person or persons responsible."

"Bullshit!"

Laughter erupted, and not the good-natured kind. Mourners were on the verge of turning into a mob. Undaunted, the chief soldiered on. "We have partnered with the FBI and put our best detectives on a multi-agency task force."

Gamez bulled his way toward the stage. If Cash read the detective right, he would take a bullet for the chief. Cash had to trust that Gamez would do the same for Tina.

Since Tina wouldn't come to Cash, he zigzagged toward the stage, drawing on the instincts honed during his playing days. Block opponents from your path when necessary. Dance around them when possible.

Thomas lost control of the crowd. A chant began as gentle as a breeze but built to gale force: TRANS LIVES MATTER.

Tina calmed the rough seas by taking the mic. Minutes passed before the chant died down. "Chief Thomas, I want to thank you, Detective Gamez, and the other officers for coming tonight, but your presence is not enough. We have a question for you. How many trans men and trans women currently serve in the Dallas Police Department?"

Thomas didn't miss a beat as she took back the mic. "None."

Widespread booing and more shouts of "Bullshit" greeted the response. Calls to resign made a strong comeback.

Again, the chief appeared unfazed. Cash smelled a setup. The exchange of the mic between Tina and Thomas had gone too smoothly, like runners passing a baton on a relay team. Dollars to donuts, the scene had been scripted and choreographed. Cash's mind raced to the worst outcome he could imagine.

Tina allowed the booing to subside before asking, "How do you plan to remedy this lack of inclusion?"

"I'm here not only to mourn with you," the chief said, "but also to celebrate with you. Next week the first trans recruit in the history of the Dallas Police Department will start her thirty-six weeks of training at the police academy."

Cash knew where this was heading and fought harder to reach the stage. His progress through the thicket of bodies came in inches. A good thirty feet still separated him from Tina.

Thomas pulled a badge from her pocket and pinned it on Tina's shirt. When the women clasped hands and lifted their arms in triumph, Thomas nearly yanked Tina off her feet. The crowd erupted into a deafening roar. Cash couldn't tell whether he said "Oh shit" aloud or simply thought it.

***

Focused on spotting a wolf among the sheep, Cash had been slow to notice the Soldiers of Gideon advancing from both ends of the street. Familiar placards filled the air: IF THINE EYE OFFEND THEE, PLUCK IT OUT. The bloody eye painted on the placards added a chilling touch.

Cash redoubled his efforts to reach the stage, but even if he managed to get to Tina, there was no clear path to safety. Gideon's soldiers had seen to that.

Bragg towered over the troops, and he alone carried a sword rather than a placard. Generations of Braggs, beginning with a confederate general, had passed down the sword, which had become the symbol of Gideon's crusade to cleanse the city. Tonight, there was no blood on the blade. Not yet anyway.

Cash couldn't get an accurate count of the enemy. They were coming too fast and on too many fronts. He and Gamez reached the stage at roughly the same time. Frick and Frack had already spirited the chief off stage. The crowd parted for the brass, and Gideon's disciples avoided getting blue blood on their hands.

The cops were holding back. With the chief out of harm's way, it looked as if the thin blue line had decided to watch the bloodbath from afar.

Gideon's disciples descended on the crowd, smiting the unarmed with placards and throwing punches. Screams split the air. Bodies hit pavement. The war of the roses went badly for the trans team.

"We have to get out of here," Cash shouted to Tina.

"I'm not deserting my friends," she shouted back.

Gamez didn't take no for an answer. He heaved Tina over his shoulder and took off, with her kicking and slapping him. The blows didn't slow down the detective.

Cash covered their flank. He had read about the fog of war. How in the madness of mayhem, no one could tell who landed the first blow, who fired the first shot, who started the damned thing.

Tonight, however, Cash saw who fired the first canister. The second. And the third. The police did, and the fog of war became a literal fog. Tear gas dropped both sides to their knees and sent them slithering to safety.

Under heavy cloud cover, Tina, Gamez, and Cash made their escape coughing and hacking. Cash couldn't see six inches ahead or behind. His eyes, throat, nostrils, and chest burned.

During the retreat, Cash picked up a placard on the pavement. Real blood mixed with the painted blood on the eye. The placard should be exhibit number one in the trial of Gideon and his minions for tonight's attack. Perhaps even turn Bragg into a suspect in the seven slayings, given his fixation on plucking the eyes of sinners. Even if Gideon wasn't directly responsible for the murders, he could well have inspired them.

If Gamez couldn't see the connection between Bragg and the seven victims, Cash could use the placard to knock some sense into him.

CHAPTER TWENTY-TWO

Both-sides-ism by the media on last night's melee got Cash's morning off to a bad start. The press predictably and perversely assigned equal blame to the trans-friendly crowd and Gideon's hostile army. The worst offender, Skyler Patterson of the *Dallas Morning News,* praised the police for stopping the carnage but panned them for overreacting.

Skyler's mixed review was probably payback for last night's gas attack. The aftereffects of tear gas kept Cash from risking breakfast. His throat and chest still burned, as if sandpapered from the inside. He settled for black coffee.

Tina shuffled into the kitchen, poured herself a cup, and sat across the table from him. Her bloodshot eyes and don't-fuck-with-me demeanor gave fair warning to let her be. The smart play would have been to heed the warning.

Cash didn't play it smart. "Are you really going through with this?"

"Can we not do this now?" Her voice was raw and ragged. Hard to believe she had channeled Sarah McLachlan twelve hours ago.

"The police chief announced to the world that you're starting the academy on Monday. So, yeah, now's good." The brew tasted bitter. He put down the cup. "By the way, when were you planning to tell me you'd officially signed up?"

"When you learn to respect *my* decisions about *my* life."

"The only reason you're even eligible to join the force is that you finally learned to follow *my* advice." Desperation drove him to dredge up their past. "Who bailed you out of the trans tank? Who got you acquitted in federal court?"

"Oh, do you really want to go there?" She plopped down her cup, sloshing coffee onto the table.

Last chance to do the smart thing and drop it. He didn't. "Just saying. I won't always be around to pull your ass out of a crack."

"Okay, let's get into it." She recaptured the full fury of her feminine pitch. "Who's pulling whose ass out of a sling now, Paw Paw?"

Hard to argue with that, and he didn't try.

Tina wasn't done. "Besides, in the past I followed your *legal* advice. Your instincts as a trial lawyer are spot on. As a so-called friend, they suck." She grabbed her cup and rose.

"Before you leave," he said, "hear me out."

She stopped but remained standing.

"Last night it took a cop with brass balls to rescue you from a beating or worse." He kept his voice steady. "You're what? Five-six and a buck twenty. That you needed saving shows you're not cut out to be a lifeguard."

"I didn't *need* to be saved." Anger amped her voice. "Gamez played Tarzan last night, and he'll hear about that today." She turned to face him. "I can understand Robbie doubting me. He hasn't known me all that long. But you…a real friend would be in my corner."

That shut him up, until she reached the door. "One last point," he said. "DCK's targets have all been high profile. Advocates for this cause or that. Names that pop up in the media. That's his victim type."

"I'm fully aware of that," Tina said.

"By being the first to join the force, you've made yourself the highest profile trans woman in Dallas. Probably in Texas."

"Also aware of that."

"If you're trying to catch the killer by making yourself bait, that's a really bad plan."

"Pardon me for not taking career advice from a lawyer hiding from cartel hitmen." She stormed out, slamming the door behind her.

He called to warn Gamez that Hurricane Tina was barreling toward him. The cop deserved a heads up for saving her last night. God willing, he would be around to do it again next time.

***

Cash's days at Darrell's firm were numbered. No one had said a word to him about packing up, but the looks from his colleagues spoke loud and clear. Darrell's glare rolled out the unwelcome mat. Sami stared past Cash, as if he were already gone.

Law firms exist on a loop that constantly recycles the same question: What have you done for the firm today? For the entire month, Cash had managed to land only one client: Freddy the Forger. A direct relation existed between the money Freddy brought into the firm and the time it bought Cash there.

Both Freddy's money and Cash's time were running out. In addition, Cash's contact with Bettina Biddle had unleashed the wrath of the feds and further eroded his footing at the firm. He had lost the blame game that followed the raid. Nothing short of sheer desperation for work of any kind had kept him around this long.

To make matters worse, Cash's efforts had all been for naught. He hadn't found Marty Biddle's files at the firm, and the widow remained locked inside her gated community and guarded by Powell's goons.

The time at Darrell's shop had taught Cash two things. First, he wasn't alone in looking for Biddle's records. Second, the records weren't hidden at the firm, which had been picked clean. Twice.

Darrell's condo seemed a good place to resume the search for Biddle's files. "I've got a favor to ask," Cash said to Darrell in the breakroom. "My granddaughter and I are getting on each other's nerves. It's past time for me to find my own place. Can I check out your condo? I may want to see what's available in your building."

Darrell didn't look sold on the prospect of having Cash as a neighbor. "Well, I'm booked for—"

"I'll throw in free dinner and drinks."

Darrell cocked his head from side to side, as if weighing the pluses and minuses of killing time with an old man.

Cash closed the deal. "At Fearing's."

"I'm in."

Wednesday after work, Cash and Darrell swung by his condo on the way to dinner. Darrell opened the door, triggering an alarm, and entered the code onto a keypad. Cash looked over the host's shoulder and caught the first two digits. Zero. Six.

Darrell leaned right, and Cash couldn't see the last two. The beeping stopped.

The L-shaped unit on the twentieth floor offered balcony views of both Hall on the north and Cedar Springs to the west, with downtown close but out of sight. Twenty-two hundred square feet. Two bedrooms. Three baths. Tricked out into a player's lair, where all roads led to a master bedroom done in early *American Psycho.*

A four-poster bed dominated the master, perfect for bondage games. A black silk bedspread covered any DNA evidence on the sheets. A theatre size TV took up an entire wall. A painting of a nude sunbather stretched across another.

Next stop on the tour was the study, which looked out of place. Dark wood panels. Leather upholstery. Red velvet drapes. Hardbound books. A six-inch bust of Shakespeare served as a paperweight on a mahogany desk. It sat atop a stack of brochures, the top one for getaways to Thailand.

On the way out, Cash caught the last two digits of the security code. One. Three. The four digits were 0613. He cringed. The sap had it bad. June 13th was Sami's birthday.

CHAPTER TWENTY-THREE

Copying the key to Darrell's condo was a snap. He kept it in the pocket of his coat, which remained hanging in the office when he left for lunch.

Darrell's lunch break gave Cash plenty of time, as duping a key took only minutes. He heated the key with a lighter, until it turned hot to the touch, and pressed it against the sticky side of scotch tape. With the image of the key seared onto the tape, he fixed the tape to a gift card and trimmed the card to the outline of the key. Returned the key to Darrell's coat.

Step one, done.

The second step proved trickier. It involved finding a night and time Darrell would be away from his condo. A decent job of searching the unit and putting everything back in place would take two hours, minimum. The challenge lay not in finding a night the condo would be empty. A dog like Darrell went hunting most nights.

The issue was how long the hound would be gone. Most nights he roamed a rotation of pickup spots until he scored a hookup. Based on Darrell's postmortems of his one-night stands, it could take anywhere from minutes to hours to find a soulmate for the night.

Cash caught a break. At work on Thursday, Darrell boasted about a hot date to a Mavs game the following night. An NBA contest followed by dinner cleared plenty of time to toss the condo.

Friday night, Cash waited until tip-off before arriving at Darrell's building. He wore a Texas Rangers ball cap, its beak shading his forehead, and had latex gloves and paper booties in his pocket.

He hung around outside the building until a brunette appeared in the lobby, a leash to a Yorkipoo in one hand and a phone in the other. Talking nonstop, she struggled with the door, until Cash held it open for her. She smiled at him and continued talking and walking.

He slipped into the building and took the elevator to the twentieth floor. Though not a perfect fit, the homemade key did the trick. He punched in the code, and the beeping stopped.

He froze in the foyer. Something was wrong. The condo was dark. Among Darrell's many annoying habits, a lesser one involved lighting. Upon entering a room, he invariably turned on the lights and left them on when he left. Evidently, no one had taught him that light switches went up and down.

Cash put on the gloves and booties and flipped on lights. He spotted another red flag. The tickets to tonight's Mavs game lay on a table by the door.

Darrell must have changed his plans. Or someone had changed them for him.

Cash's initial instinct was to abort the search and bolt. Darrell could return at any time. Silence settled his nerves, and he decided to make the best of it. He didn't know when, or if, he would get another crack at Darrell's place.

A ringtone of *Sucker for Love* signaled an incoming call. Darrell's recorded voice played on the message machine. "It's truth or Darrell time. At the beep, do your wild thing." Typical Darrell, trying too hard to score.

A pissed-off female left a message. "Lose. My. Number."

Cash pushed deeper into the condo. Away from the light. Toward the dark. He lit up the study and surveyed the damage. Bookcases were down, and hardbacks strewn across the wood floor. Drifts of loose papers made for treacherous footing.

A busted paperweight littered the floor. Cash picked up a shard that had been Shakespeare's skull. A line from a high school production, in which he had played Richard II, came back to him: "The worst is death, and death will have his day."

Cash second-guessed his decision not to flee at the first sign of trouble, the left brain talking. An intruder had beaten him to the condo. What were the odds that Cash would find something the early shift had missed?

Besides, when Darrell returned, Cash couldn't afford to be here. How could he explain what he was doing in the condo? Or how he had gained entry?

The right brain pushed Cash deeper into the darkness, toward the master bedroom. An odor in the hallway unnerved him. After both sides of his brain shut down, his legs carried him to the master. With each step, the stench grew stronger.

At the threshold, he gagged. It was a miracle he didn't vomit and deposit his DNA on the crime scene. Between the blood, piss, and shit on the bed, a forensic team would soon be swimming in the stuff. The mix of bodily excretions had stained the black silk sheets burgundy.

Darrell was tied spread eagle to the four-post bed. He was still. Silent.

When Cash's brain rebooted, the first question that came to mind was whether Darrell's eyes were gone. He moved closer to find out. They weren't. Terror had pried them wide open. Much as Cash wanted to lower the eyelids, he couldn't afford to touch the body, not even with gloves.

Leave everything as is. Don't make the cops' job harder than it will already be.

Even with the eyes intact, the corpse was in worse shape than DCK's victims. The killer had transposed Darrell's penis and tongue. The penis filled the deceased's mouth. The tongue lodged in his carved-out crotch.

Burn marks dotted his arms, torso, legs, and soles. He had been tortured long and hard before the butchery began in earnest. Whatever intel the killer had been after, Cash had to assume Darrell had given up all he knew. And more.

For a nanosecond, Cash considered dialing 911 and leaving an anonymous tip. The nanosecond passed. He couldn't afford for the police to have his voice on tape. Not even Carl's voice.

Cash froze at the sound of gunfire. Or what he thought was gunfire. A single shot.

He looked down, expecting to see blood seeping or spurting from an entry or exit point on his torso. There was no blood. No pain beyond the psychic pain of pure fear. Fear that Darrell's killer had returned.

Or perhaps the shooter had come for Cash. A *sicario* had finally seen through the transformation, tracked Cash to Darrell's condo, and now the two of them would share a death scene.

Cash's paralysis lasted maybe a minute, before he moved slowly, silently to the source of the sound. In the library, books were still surrendering to gravity and falling from the toppled shelves.

The ringing of Darrell's phone shook Cash from his stupor. He rushed from the building and counted on the night air to settle his roiling gut. It didn't. He made it halfway down the block before puking. A twentysomething with a Dallas Stars cap on backwards stopped ten feet from Cash. "Are you all right, old timer?"

Cash nodded toward a seafood restaurant. "Don't order the oysters."

As wet heaves gave way to dry ones, it hit Cash that he had to make a call. He tried Sami on her cell. When she didn't answer right away, he imagined the worst. He had called too late, and the killer had gotten to her.

She finally came on the line. "What do you want, Carl?" She sounded irritated.

"Are you at your place?" he said.

"Yes."

"Get out," he said.

"Why?"

"It's not safe. Check into a hotel, and text me where you're staying. I'll meet you there and explain everything."

"You're scaring me." Her voice betrayed fear. "I'm calling Darrell."

He resorted to the truth as his best chance of spooking her into fleeing. "Darrell's dead, and his killer will be coming for you."

He hung up and waited for her text. In the meantime, he couldn't shake a Bible verse that his grandmother had drilled into him:

"If thy tongue offend thee…."

CHAPTER TWENTY-FOUR

Cash knocked on the door to suite 410 at the Ritz. Sami opened the door. Without a word, she walked to the bed and sat, staring at the TV.

Cash recognized the ten o'clock anchor as a friend with benefits from his past life as a defense lawyer. "Darrell's death won't make this news cycle," he said.

The TV cast the lone light in the suite. Its flickering images in the dark made Sami seem more like a spectral presence than a solid person. Then again, to Cash, she had always been more flash than substance.

A second TV in the living room carried another local station. Dueling newscasts. Same old shit. A drive-by shooting on one channel. A missing SMU coed on the other.

"Why the Ritz?" Cash said.

"The firm has a corporate account here." Her eyes stayed on the TV.

"Pack up," Cash said.

"Why?"

"We're going to a hotel where the firm doesn't have a corporate account."

***

Cash scored another suite for Sami, this one at the Hampton Inn on I-35 at Northwest Highway. The *suite* turned out to be a regular room with modest amenities: a small sitting area with a sofa, a coffee table, and a plate with three slices of cheese and six sad grapes.

She turned on the TV. "From the Ritz to the pits. Am I being punished?"

Cash closed the drapes. "You're being protected."

"From whom?"

"You tell me." He clicked off the TV, shoved her onto the sofa, and sat across from her. He let a minute pass, then another. The silence didn't break her. Ninety-nine percent of the population would be babbling by now.

"Okay," he said, "I'll kick off the conversation. I'm protecting you from the same people who butchered Darrell tonight and who probably killed Rhoden as well."

"Is Darrell really dead?" Her voice broke at the end. The first crack in the shell.

Cash weighed how much detail to share with her. The brutality of Darrell's death had left him shaken. He decided to divulge just enough to scare her into coming clean. "He was tortured for hours before being put out of his misery."

Pale by nature, she turned paler. "Could it have been an S&M scene that went too far?"

"Was Darrell into that?"

"Not that I know of," she said.

"If he'd been a pain freak, you would've picked up on it. The killer went way past kink by slicing off body parts. Darrell was tortured to extract information, and he must've spilled his guts."

Literally and figuratively.

"Wait a second." She leaned forward on the couch. "If there's been nothing on the news, how do you know all this?"

"I saw the body," he said.

"Where?"

"In Darrell's apartment."

Her expression went from shock to fear. "What were you doing there?"

"That's not important."

"It is to me." She glanced at the door.

It didn't take a mind reader to know that Sami was calculating the odds of beating Cash to the exit. He spun a story to allay her fear. "I was thinking of renting a unit in Darrell's building. He offered to show me his pad before the big date tonight. When I got to his room, the door was ajar. I walked in and saw the body."

"Did you report the murder?" she said.

"No. We need to stay clear of the investigation. Tomorrow morning, you'll call the building superintendent and say Darrell didn't show up at work and isn't answering your calls. The super will check on Darrell, discover the body, and report the murder."

She slid to the edge of the couch. "Why do you think I'm in danger?"

"The better question," he said, "is why you know you are."

Sami was good at hiding her emotions but not that good. Fear lines bracketed her mouth. She needed one more push, and Cash obliged. "The cops will write off Darrell's death as a cartel hit."

"Cartel? Why?" Sami asked.

"That's how they cleared Rhoden's death, and the public shrugged. They'll do the same with Darrell."

"You have a cynical view of the police," she said.

"I don't limit my cynicism to cops. We all do what has worked in the past. Chalking up Darrell's death to a cartel kills two birds. First, the police wiggle off the hook to find the killer. They can't be expected to follow the trail south of the border."

"What's the second?" she said.

"It allows the public to chill. The victim got what he deserved. Live by the cartel. Die by the cartel."

The lines around her lips deepened. He tossed a room key onto the table. "You can stay here a week for what a night at the Ritz costs. Hole up here until I give you a green light to go." He walked to the door.

"Wait!" She stood. "Are you leaving me?"

"Sami, I can't fight what I can't see. You and Darrell have been hiding something from me, and I can't figure out what it is." The knob turned in his hand.

He was halfway out the door when she shouted, "Come back. I'll tell you."

He returned to the room and sat across the table from her. He helped himself to a slice of cheese and remembered he hadn't eaten since lunch.

"The first thing you need to understand," she said, "is that Rocket was a brilliant trial lawyer when he wanted to be. But he didn't always play to win."

"You lost me." Cash lied to draw her out.

"Rocket made good money defending clients and monster money *not* defending them."

Cash understood the dirty business model but asked her to explain anyway. He had cast himself in the role of a new character who had never seen Rhoden in action. Or inaction, as the money dictated.

"His biggest scores came from convincing clients not to cooperate. In those cases, he didn't mount a real defense at trial. His job was to sacrifice pawns to spare the kingpin."

"Drug cases?" he asked.

"Mostly drug work, but Martin Biddle was his biggest haul ever."

"How big?"

"A million-five up front. The same at the guilty verdict."

Cash dropped the cheese to the plate, his appetite gone. Biddle had been his cellmate, friend, and client. He had put his life in Cash's hands. Sure, Marty had been guilty of what he had gone down for, but he didn't deserve to take the fall alone. And he sure as hell didn't deserve to die.

"I assume Rhoden pocketed the first payment but got stiffed on the second," Cash said.

"No. He collected the full fee."

"Who paid?"

"Longhorn Investments, under an indemnification clause in the corporate by-laws. All nice and legal."

"Then what's the problem?" Cash said.

"With Rocket, too much was never enough. He always wanted more."

"From Longhorn?" he said.

She shook her head. "From the lawyers who arranged for him to sell out Biddle."

"I need names," Cash said.

"Why? You can't touch them."

"Let me worry about that," Cash said.

She shrugged. "Rocket had a couple of conversations with Stewart Powell, but mostly he dealt with Gerry Freeman. Freeman attended the trial to make sure everything went as planned."

"How much did Rhoden manage to bleed from Powell's firm?"

"Rocket didn't live long enough to collect," she said.

"I don't get it." This time Cash really was lost. Something about her story didn't make sense. "What leverage would Rhoden have? No one would take his word over Powell's." He clammed up, fearful he had already said too much to maintain the fiction of being new in town.

There was a long pause before Sami said, "There are recordings."

CHAPTER TWENTY-FIVE

During Rocket Rhoden's run as the go-to mouthpiece for cartels, a word from him to *el jefe* ended lives. Rhoden's recorded voice threatened more of the same.

Sami leaned back on the couch in her so-called suite at the Hampton Inn. "Because Rocket screwed everyone," she said, "he suspected everyone of being out to screw him."

"Including other lawyers?" Cash knew the answer before asking.

"Especially other lawyers."

He lobbed another softball. "Even pillars of the bar, like Stewart Powell?"

She nodded. "Rocket secretly recorded calls and meetings with Powell and Freeman."

"How many recorded conversations are we talking about?"

"Only a couple with Powell but dozens with Freeman."

"Any calls or meetings with Lou Watson, the Longhorn CEO?" Cash asked.

She shook her head.

Cash scratched his chin. "All the time Rhoden was raking in millions to betray his client Marty Biddle, he was secretly setting up a blackmail scheme."

"That's not how it started," she said. "Originally the recordings were Rocket's insurance against getting stiffed on the back-end fee."

Cash whistled. "Three mil. Not a bad payday for selling out a pawn."

"Only after Longhorn paid in full did Rocket decide to shake down the law firm."

Two characters were missing from her tale of double- and triple-crossing. Namely, Sami and Darrell. Cash let the omission slide. For now. He also didn't mention the obvious. Sami had stuck with Darrell for one reason only: the prospect of FU money from the recordings.

"How much did Rhoden try to squeeze from Powell?" he said.

She scooped up the last two grapes. "Rocket did his homework. Powell's firm grosses over three billion annually, and the name partners take home twenty million in a bad year."

"I get the feeling that you're bracing me for a big-ass blackmail demand."

"One hundred million," she said.

His jaw dropped. He had no words.

"It had to be enough for him to quit law, leave the country, and never come back." She sounded defensive.

Cash checked his watch. Nearly 1:00 a.m. Time to turn up the heat on Sami. Probe her role in the scheme. "Rhoden wasn't leaving you behind, was he? Two can live quite well on a hundred mil." Her blush caught him by surprise. He didn't know she could pull it off.

"I knew nothing about the recordings until after Rocket had received the full trial fee." Sami sounded sincere, but she would be capable of faking sincerity. "Even then, he didn't tell me everything."

"And Darrell?" Cash said.

"He didn't have a clue until I told him everything after Rocket's death."

The puzzle pieces were falling into place. A clearer picture emerged, not only of the murders of two lawyers, separated by a year, but also of the back-to-back searches of Darrell's law firm, forty-eight hours apart. People on every side of the law were desperate to get their hands on the recordings and willing to bathe those hands in blood to do so.

"With Rhoden gone, you and Darrell took over the blackmail scheme."

"It wasn't like that." Her voice shook. "Darrell wasn't greedy. He asked for less."

"How much less?"

"He wanted ten million."

Cash smiled. There she goes again. *He* wanted the payoff. Always minimizing her role in the shakedown. Laying it all on Rhoden first and Darrell later.

He didn't buy it. Darrell being Darrell, whatever damn fool thing he had done, she had pushed him into it. "You've got an interesting concept of greed, Sami. Eight figures, just business as usual, but nine figures…well, *that's* over the line."

Her blush was gone.

"Where are the recordings?" he said.

"They're on a flash drive."

"Where's the drive?"

"I don't know."

He didn't buy that either. If Rhoden had confided to her the existence of the recordings, why wouldn't he also have told her where to find the drive? Then again, Rhoden being Rhoden, perhaps he had trusted her as much as he could ever trust anyone. His faith in the love of his life, or at least the model of the month, had been an inch deep.

Make that skin deep.

On Sami's part, the prospect of a windfall would have kept her close to Rhoden and eager to please him. Not knowing where the flash drive was hidden had removed any temptation for her to cross her lover.

Ain't love grand?

"How were you and Darrell going to get ten million without the drive?"

"The other side doesn't know we don't have it," she said.

That explained why Darrell had suffered, as well as the hell ahead for Sami.

She went on. "We would either find the drive before the payoff or, if we didn't, we would promise to destroy it."

Not a great plan, but the best they could do without the drive. If Sami was lying and they did have the drive, their plan was to bleed ten mil from Powell now and go back later for more. Cash wouldn't put it past her. He defaulted to his standard response to a client's self-serving story. "I don't believe you."

She stiffened, as if stung by his words. Her innocent act would have fooled most men, most of the time. Under the right circumstances, Cash, too, might have swallowed it.

"I really don't know." Her voice broke at the end.

This wasn't the time or place to go soft on her. "It doesn't matter whether *I* believe you. Darrell's killer won't. Not until you've suffered beyond belief and bled out."

"I can't tell you what I don't know." She was either on the verge of tears or damn good at faking it.

Cash bet on the latter. "If you're telling the truth, I assume Darrell didn't know where the drive was either."

"He didn't."

"I'm sure he screamed that over and over, until a sadist with a sharp knife got tired of hearing it and cut out his tongue."

She blanched.

Cash tried every cross-examination trick in the toolbox. Nothing worked. Around 2:00 a.m., he hit a wall. Not out of steam or questions but running low on patience. "Get some sleep," he said, "and come up with better answers in the morning. If not for me, then for the psycho on your trail."

They retreated to separate corners of the room, like boxers between rounds. He ceded the bed to Sami and spent a sleepless night on the sofa.

No matter how hard Cash tried, he couldn't shake the image of Darrell on his death bed. And when he tried counting sheep, every sacrificial lamb had Marty Biddle's face.

***

The alarm woke Sami at seven. Cash had slept fitfully and risen hours ago. She turned on the TV to the local news and shuffled to the bathroom. A click signaled the locking of the bathroom door.

He paid next to no attention to the banter of the news team, all gleaming teeth, fake tans, and blond hair. He had no interest in a story on the top ten items to take to a tailgate party, and Darrell wouldn't make the news cycle until later. Sami had a call to place first.

A familiar name on the tube reeled him toward the TV. As he stared at the screen, his pulse rate quickened. There they stood, side by side: the top cop in Dallas and her pet trans rookie. Chief Thomas introduced Officer Cristina "Tina" Campos to the press corps as the newest member of and spokesperson for the DCK task force.

Tina addressed the reporters for maybe twenty seconds, but Cash didn't process a word she said. Something about her uniform distracted him. It was the padded shoulders, designed to give her the appearance of upper body strength. It didn't fool Cash, and it wouldn't fool DCK.

Sami emerged from the bathroom in jeans and a knit shirt. Her hair was wet and slicked back. No makeup. She looked young, untroubled, and innocent.

The look didn't fool Cash. He remembered the Sami of six hours ago. The hard case who had clammed up on the location of the flash drive. Before calling it a night, he had laid down an ultimatum: fork over the drive or go it alone. Though it still might come to that, he couldn't walk away. Not before taking another shot at wringing the truth from her.

"Ready to go down for breakfast?" She sounded matter of fact, as if last night had never happened.

"Order in."

"Do you intend to keep me here as your prisoner?"

"I intend to keep you alive. That is, if you intend to cooperate. Your safest course is to lie low."

"What do you expect me to do all day?" she said.

"For starters, enjoy a leisurely breakfast. Then call the super in Darrell's building and get the ball rolling on the discovery of his body." He stopped at the door. "The room is in my name and on my credit card."

"Where are you going?" A hint of panic in her voice.

"You're not the only woman I know in danger, and the other one was fool enough to go on TV."

***

Cash tracked down Tina at police headquarters, a glass structure in South Dallas, where land was cheap and life was cheaper. She pulled him outside the building, away from the eyes and ears of passersby, and said, "What are you doing here?"

"I could ask you the same thing," he said. "You're not even close to completing the academy, and yet you land a gig at HQ. What gives?"

"I'm still going through training, but the chief needs me on the task force."

It took all his self-control to keep from calling bullshit. What the chief needed was to get the LGBTQ community off her back, and hiring Tina might accomplish that. For all of five minutes. He held his tongue.

She must have sensed that he was holding back. "What's wrong?" she said.

"If you let the brass fast-track you onto a high-profile assignment, every cop on the force will resent you."

"They already do." She sounded resigned to her fate. "I can live with that."

Cash wasn't so sure. Her voice was ragged. Her eyelids heavy. "Hard night?" he asked.

"It's Robbie. We're going through a rough patch." His silence prompted her to go on. "When we're alone, he's cool with who I am, but he never takes me out. Doesn't introduce me to his friends or family."

Then he's not cool with who you are.

"It might be a cop thing," Cash said.

"You make cop sound like a dirty word." There was more hurt than anger in her tone. "This is my first day on the task force. Big day for me. Thanks for all your support in getting me here." Sarcasm trumped both the hurt and anger in her voice.

"I need a favor," he said.

"Of course you do."

"A murder will be reported this morning. The victim is Darrell Pendergass, the lawyer I've been working for."

"Should I ask how you know this?"

"No."

She sighed. "What's the favor?"

"I need to know whether the cops will work the case or write it off as a cartel hit."

"What makes you think we wouldn't work it?"

We already.

"Because the police spent about five minutes looking into Rhoden's murder before chalking it up to a cartel. The file got buried before he did."

"Are you sure Rhoden wasn't taken out by a cartel?" Tina said.

"No, but I have a friend who might know."

CHAPTER TWENTY-SIX

Alvarez's Hole in the Wall, aka the A-Hole, hadn't changed since Cash's last visit a year earlier. The same toxic brew of feds, locals, and badge groupies. Same stench of sweat, piss, and smoke. The "NO ASSHOLES ALLOWED" sign remained over the door. The sense of *déjà vu* extended to the song playing on the jukebox: "The Bottle Let Me Down" by Merle Haggard. The irony of looping a classic by a felon in a cop bar wasn't lost on Cash.

What had changed was Cash. His earlier visit had been under a different name and with a younger face. The previous name and face had popped up frequently on TV. On the earlier visit, he hadn't lasted at the bar long enough to catch Merle's entire song. In the company of cops, a mouthpiece was as welcome as Rachel Maddow at CPAC.

Anonymity didn't strengthen his desire to tarry in the tinderbox. He was here to see someone. Get that done and skedaddle. With too few women and too many weapons on the premises, the A-Hole rated low on his list of places to kill time.

Carl Meadows mounted a barstool. While Cash could count a hundred enemies and zero allies in the joint, Carl didn't have a friend or foe in sight. He was simply a grizzled stranger, taking life one drink at a time.

At 9:25 p.m., Duane "Leroy" Lee lumbered through a gauntlet of backslapping cops and settled at the bar, two stools down from Cash. The agent wheezed more than breathed. Dollars to donuts, he had come from a happy hour at another bar and was working his way down the drink chain.

Leroy rested his right hand on the bar, cupped palm facing Manny Alvarez, the owner, bouncer, cook, and bartender. Manny pulled a draft Shiner 97 and slid the mug down the bar and into Leroy's waiting hand.

The agent nodded. Manny returned the gesture. Not a word passed between them. The silent transaction spoke volumes about where Leroy spent his off-duty hours.

Since Cash's last sighting of the agent six months ago, Leroy had packed on ten, maybe fifteen pounds. His ass hung over the seat like saddlebags. If his butt widened any more, he would need two barstools.

In a show of solidarity, Leroy elbowed a DEA buddy to his right. Again, no words. He looked to his left at Cash. No hint of recognition. He turned back to the beer at hand.

Cash returned to his beer flight, biding time until Leroy's colleague bailed at 11:05, leaving Cash and Leroy alone at the bar. Cash leaned over and said, "Hey bud, got the time?"

Leroy checked his watch. "Why yes, it's time for another brewski." He belched before giving Cash a straight answer.

"I'll buy," Cash said. "Pick your poison."

Leroy gave Manny the universal sign for another round and moved to the barstool next to Cash's. "Don't recall seeing you before. New here?"

"New to Dallas and to this watering hole."

The Shiners arrived, and the two clinked mugs. Introductions followed. First names only.

"Most of the assholes here are cops or exes," Leroy said, "with a few feds like me thrown in to raise the average IQ. You look like a cop."

Hardly a compliment but exactly what Cash was going for. "Ex," he said. "Carried a badge in Buffalo for twenty-two years." He was careful to pick a city where Leroy hadn't been stationed. "Are you Bureau?"

"Them's fighting words." Leroy put up his dukes but quickly dropped them. "DEA all the way. Twenty-four years, seven months, and fifteen days, but who's counting? Dallas is my fifth and final posting. Figure to settle down here."

"Here in Dallas," Cash said, "or here at the A-Hole?"

Leroy belly laughed. "Hey, that's not a bad idea. Get Manny to rent me a room in back. Save travel time." He took a swig. "How about you? Why the move to Big D?"

"Decided it was time to defrost my blue balls. Also moved in with my granddaughter, at least for the time being."

"Makes sense," Leroy said. "Crashing with family takes a little pressure off your sweet police pension."

"Be even sweeter if I can pick up spare change as a private detective."

"How's that working out for you?" Leroy said. "Must be tough to drum up business in a new town."

"Getting tougher all the time. I had an in with an up-and-coming defense lawyer, but the damn fool went and got himself killed."

Leroy recoiled. "Are you talking about Darrell Pendergass?"

"Yep."

Leroy leaned over and lowered his voice. "I wouldn't mention him here. You don't want your first visit to the A-Hole to be your last."

"Roger that. Besides, given what happened to the kid, it's probably a good thing I wasn't around him all that long. His bad luck might've rubbed off."

"It wasn't bad luck that got the fool killed."

"What did?" Cash said.

Leroy turned back to his beer. "I've already said too much."

The story of Leroy's life, but Cash had a surefire way of priming the pump. He signaled for another round. Two lagers later, it was past midnight, and the crowd had thinned to the dregs. The barflies had fallen like flies. Cash and Leroy were alone at the bar. They might as well have been alone on the planet.

"I get why you can't say more about Darrell's death," Cash said, "since it's an open investigation. Let me throw out a theory, and you react to it."

Leroy shrugged.

Cash took that as a green light. "An S&M scene got out of hand."

"You're cold," Leroy said.

"Theory number two: a cartel took out Darrell."

"Getting warmer."

Cash faked surprise. "Just warmer? I figured to be white hot with that one."

"It might've been a cartel hit," Leroy said, "or staged to look like one."

"Which way are the cops leaning?"

Leroy glanced over his shoulder. Only Cash was within fifteen feet. "The DPD operates under a simple rule: If a homicide can't be solved, hang it on a cartel."

"And you?"

"Let's just say I have my doubts."

"Why?"

Leroy tapped the counter. Seconds later, a fresh mug slid into his palm. "You have to go back to the murder of Darrell's mentor, Rocket Rhoden."

"He was killed before I moved to Dallas, but he was definitely taken out by a cartel, right?"

"If you buy the official report," Leroy said.

"You don't?"

"Like I said, I have doubts."

Cash waited for the reasons. They were slow to come but did.

"Cartels have the loosest lips in the criminal underworld," the agent said.

That's rich, coming from someone with the loosest lips in law enforcement.

Leroy went on. "Cartels love to take credit for their hits, down to posting videos of their kills online. Keeps everyone in tow. Case in point: *Los Lobos* posted word about a contract it has taken out on a sleazy lawyer named Cash McCahill."

Cash bit his lip to keep from saying something he would regret.

Leroy went on. "Terms of the deal are big and bold online. Five mil for proof of death. Enough to draw a swarm of *sicarios* to the streets of Dallas, and when one of them finally cashes in, the cartel will tout the kill online. That is, if *Los Lobos* is still around then. So, why no video of Rhoden's death? Or Darrell's?"

"I can think of one reason," Cash said. "Bragging about offing your lawyers might make other members of the bar antsy about taking cartel cases."

"Riiiiight. Because it's so difficult to find a greedy attorney."

Touché.

"Even if a cartel took out Rhoden," Leroy said, "why go after Pendergass? Cartels generally kill a mouthpiece for one of two reasons. Either he fucked up a case, or he's owed a shit ton of money. At some point it becomes cheaper to kill a lawyer than pay the tab."

"And those reasons don't hold for Darrell?"

"Nope. While Rhoden made a fortune as the go-to lawyer for every cartel in the hemisphere, the bad guys didn't trust Pendergass to handle a parking ticket. The downside for Darrell, no dirty money flowing in. The upside, no reason to snuff him."

"If the DPD pins Darrell's murder on a cartel," Cash said, "which one will get the notch?"

Asking for a friend with a seven-figure price on his head.

"It doesn't matter," the agent said. "All cartels look gray in the night."

CHAPTER TWENTY-SEVEN

Closing time loomed, with Leroy and Cash the last holdouts at the A-Hole. Even Merle on the jukebox had called it a night. Manny the owner was mopping up and muttering under his breath.

Cash steered the conversation back to cartels. "Assuming DPD takes the easy way out—"

Leroy cut him off. "Always a safe assumption."

"Then which lucky cartel gets credit for Darrell's kill?"

Leroy had dodged the question an hour ago and did so again. "Who gives a shit? They're all cut from the same bloody cloth. Butchers who get younger and meaner by the day. Trained to kill and with more firepower than armies on both sides of the border."

Cash knew better. Only one cartel had placed a bounty on his head. Any news about *Los Lobos* bore a direct bearing on his life.

Make that his *lives*.

Leroy looked over his shoulder at Manny, whose grousing had grown louder and more profane. "We're getting the evil eye from the owner." He chugged the beer. "Time to hit the road."

Cash spread six twenties on the bar to cover the tab and tip. Leroy grunted thanks.

"Before shoving off," Cash said, "make an educated guess on which cartel will get the credit or blame for Darrell's death."

"I don't talk shop after hours."

What a load of crap. All Leroy and his lush buddies did was swap war stories. Tales that mangled and mashed up events, real and imagined. A hodgepodge of history and hooey.

Cash tried another tack. "Suppose the SAC asks you to pick a cartel to tag for Darrell's murder. What do you tell him?"

"Put the names of all the cartels in a cap and draw one out."

Leroy slid off the barstool and landed with a thud. His legs went wobbly. He grabbed Cash's arm for balance but quickly let go.

With time running out, Cash resorted to a leading question. "*Los Lobos*?"

"Not them."

"Why not?"

"It has to be a credible threat," Leroy said, "and those bastards are on the ropes."

Cash perked up. "I thought they were the baddest of the bad."

"The turnover at the top is wicked fast. Their soldiers, or what's left of them, are hiding in the mountains and running low on food, ammo, and time. They're on their last legs."

The news got Cash onto his feet and his day off to a good start.

***

Dr. Katzenbach's office opened at 9:00 a.m. on weekdays. Cash started calling at 8:45. Six tries later, the receptionist picked up. He pushed hard but couldn't book an appointment earlier than Friday of the following week.

If *Los Lobos* disappeared, so would the bounty on Cash. He had ten days to tie up loose ends before talking to the surgeon about burying Carl Meadows and resurrecting Cash McCahill. He put on the back burner the issue of when he could return to his old life and moved to the front burner the question of when, if ever, Sami could resume hers.

***

Like a hard-nosed probation officer, Cash checked in on Sami at least once a day and once a night. At the end of week one at the Hampton Inn, a DO NOT DISTURB sign on the door to room 516 gave him pause. He knocked before entering the room with his key.

The sign must have warded off the maid. The room was a mess, with clothes strewn across the unmade bed and damp towels curled on the bathroom floor. No Sami and no note from her. He had told her not to leave the room but to call him if she needed anything.

No surprise that she had flown the coop. A week at the Hampton with no contact to the outside world—other than Cash and hotel staff—must have driven her stir crazy. Hard to blame her for bolting and harder not to assume the worst had befallen her.

The killer of Rhoden and Darrell would see Sami as his final shot at finding the recordings. The flash drive contained grade-A blackmail material, capable of taking down Powell, his firm, and a roster of gold chip clients, including Longhorn Investments.

If the sadist captured Sami, he could prolong her torture for hours or days before death answered her prayers. Even after accepting the hard truth that she didn't know where the drive was, the freak would relish inflicting fresh rounds of suffering.

She had no long-term future. In the short term, there would be pain heaped on more pain. Beyond that, a closed casket in the unlikely event that her body turned up.

Cash rushed to the check-in desk and hit the bell until a middle-aged woman shuffled to the counter. Her nameplate identified her as Jolene. "How may I help you, sir?"

"Jolene, have you seen the woman in room 516 this morning?"

She stared blankly at him. He scrolled to a photo on his phone and showed it to her. "This woman, have you seen her today?"

She shook her head. Cash believed her. She was too listless to lie. He circled the ground floor, hitting the restaurant, exercise room, and gift shop. No dice. He went back to the room and waited. He had a long wait.

***

It was dark when Sami returned. Cash's mood was darker. He didn't rise from the couch. "Where the hell have you been?"

"Good to see you too." She walked to the bedroom and dropped four Neiman-Marcus bags onto the bed. She looked different, starting with her hair. A shorter cut, with an orange streak through the blonde waves. A shade of lipstick he'd never seen on her before.

"Tell me you didn't go to NorthPark," he said.

"I spent a glorious day there."

"And that you didn't pay with credit cards."

She shrugged. He had his answer. If she had ignored his advice on credit cards, she had probably used her phone as well. He directed his anger at himself. He should have confiscated her cards and phone. Failing to do so was like leaving liquor and car keys with a teenage boy.

"Pack up," he said. "We're switching hotels."

He rifled through her purse and pulled out her phone then dropped it to the floor and stomped on it.

"What the fuck!" She lunged for the purse, but he stiff-armed her, holding her at arm's-length with one hand. With the other, he lifted the wallet from the purse.

"My bad, for not cutting up your credit cards. You've got five minutes to pack."

She broke free of his grip. "I'm not going anywhere with you, psycho."

He gave himself ten seconds to calm down. "Every call you made...every charge on a credit card, they can use to track you."

"Who's they?" Her tone said she wasn't buying the threat.

Good question. "The same people who had your law office searched."

"You watch way too many movies," she said.

"In case it has slipped your mind, the office was tossed twice. The first was a private message to you and Darrell to back off. The second, a public show of force to shut down the firm. It takes juice to sic the feds on a lawyer. That requires a green light from DC."

"Do you have a suspect in mind?" she said.

"The same one you do."

CHAPTER TWENTY-EIGHT

Cash broke the news to Tina at the apartment over a dinner of lasagna, garlic bread, and a nice Chianti. "The way the cartel wars are going down south," he said, "Cash McCahill is about to stage a comeback."

She looked more surprised than pleased. Not what he had expected. "What will happen to Carl Meadows?" she said.

"He'll return to the grave in Buffalo, where he was buried two years ago."

"I didn't realize your new life was so bad." A hint of hurt crept into her voice.

"It wasn't bad, but it wasn't real either. I'm a lawyer. That's who I am."

"That's not all you are," she said.

"Pretty damn close."

She downed the wine and poured herself another. "Don't let it go to your head, but you make an okay grandfather. Nosy, overprotective, set in your ways, and stubborn as hell. But all in all, okay."

"If I ever have a real granddaughter," he said, "I hope she's a royal pain in the ass, just like you."

"It was nice having a family for a change." The catch in her voice forecast tears.

"You should be thrilled to get me out of your apartment and out of your hair."

That broke the dam, unleashing her tears. He fought an impulse to rush to her side and gave her time and space to pull herself together. "Hey, you're not rid of me yet." He spoke in the hushed tone reserved for the most fragile clients. "I have to make sure *Los Lobos* is totally gone before Katzenbach reverses the magic time machine."

She dabbed her eyes with a napkin. "This isn't about your leaving. Well, it is, and it isn't."

She had lost Cash, and she hadn't. Her breakdown had been building for some time. Cash's news pushed her over the edge.

"You'll never be rid of me," he said. "When I'm back in the saddle, the first order of business will be reuniting the old gang. Goldy, Eva, and eventually you. Soon as you wise up and quit the cops, you have a standing offer to join the law firm of Goldberg & McCahill as our full-time private investigator. Put those skills to work protecting constitutional rights instead of trampling them."

"While you and I weren't a real family," she said, "it was the closest I've come to having one."

With a decade of highs and lows behind them, Cash knew most of her story. Disowned at fifteen. Living on the streets. In and out of lockup. It was a miracle she had made it to twenty-six.

He also knew what it was like to be without family and shared her pain at the prospect of parting. The bastard son of a con man he had never known and a mother who was dead and gone. Or perhaps just gone. Raised by a grandmother who had died the day before his law school graduation.

"You, Goldy, Eva, and me," he said, "we have each other's backs. That counts as family in my book." He mustered a smile. "However, in the future I will be happy to cede the grandfather role to Goldy."

She folded her napkin and placed it on the table. The tears had stopped, for now. "Good to know that I'll have a job waiting because this cop gig isn't working out. Go ahead and gloat. Say I told you so. Get it over with."

What should have been good news for Cash didn't go down that way. Hard as he had tried to dissuade her from joining the force, why the mixed feelings now?

"What's wrong?" he asked.

"I don't fit in."

He swallowed the I told you so on the tip of his tongue. "Change takes time," he said, "and it's not you who needs to change."

"They look at me like I'm a freak, or worse." She pushed her plate away and pulled the wine glass closer. "Yesterday someone taped my mug shot to my locker."

"Did you report it to HR?"

"That would've made it worse. I'd be a snitch and a freak." She went to a website on her phone, hit play, and handed the phone to Cash. "Then there's this."

Bad lighting of the grainy video, shot at the Dallas County Jail, made it difficult to identify the trembling girl on display to the caged male prisoners. Deputies dragged her by the hair up and down the cellblock and dangled her just outside the long arms of the lawless. The only prisoners not lunging between bars for her were those too busy masturbating.

The prisoners' catcalls nearly drowned out the girl's sobbing. The camera zoomed in on her tear-streaked face. It was Tina, at her most recent arrest. Only last year had she shared with Cash the nightmare that had pushed her to the brink of suicide.

"We can make the website take it down," he said.

"Won't do any good." Her tone took a bitter turn. "It's gone viral."

He deleted it anyway. "Have you talked to Gamez about the harassment?"

That sparked a new round of tears. Whichever way Cash went, he tripped a mine. He left the safety of his seat to offer comfort. He stood behind her, his hands resting on her shoulders. Her tremors coursed through him. He literally felt her pain.

"Robbie's avoiding me." Tears flowed freely. "He's ashamed to be seen with me."

Cash found himself in the strange role of defending a cop. "Give him time. If he's half the man I think he is, he'll come around."

"How long do I have to wait for that? A year? Five? Ten? Until hell freezes over?"

Cash was out of answers.

"I thought he was my friend," she said. "More than a friend."

"Then don't give up."

"On Robbie or the police?"

It was a damn good question, and Cash didn't have an answer.

* * *

The next morning, Tina came to the breakfast table in her police uniform. She was a different person. Her smile projected confidence. "About last night," she said, "I shouldn't have rained on your parade. Great news that you'll be returning to your old life of thwarting justice and freeing the guilty."

Damn, she even sounded like a cop again.

"I'm happy for you," she said.

"Let's hold off on any talk of a parade until we're sure *Los Lobos* is history." He handed her a cup of coffee. "My future is still up in the air. How about yours?"

"I don't know if I can last long term in the department," she said, "but I can't quit until we collar DCK."

He had been afraid of that and prayed that she would catch DCK before he caught her.

"How about you?" she asked. "Ready to help me find a killer?"

"Deal me in," he said, without reminding her that he had two killers on his plate.

CHAPTER TWENTY-NINE

Sami stared at the sunset through the hotel window. "You can't keep me locked up here forever." The days on ice had been hard on her. The nights, harder.

Cash tried to lighten the mood. "We can't leave now, not when we're so close to scoring a free night on Hampton points." That drew no reaction from her. He tried Gamez again. The sixth attempt in two hours went unanswered. He pocketed the phone and said, "You win. We're hitting the town tonight."

"Hot damn!" She sprang from the couch, sprinted to the closet, grabbed an armful of clothes on hangers, and tossed everything onto the bed. "What's the dress?"

"Do you know what formal attire is?"

"Of course."

"The opposite of that."

* * *

As soon as Cash and his dates entered the A-Hole, the cop bar went eerily quiet. Only Merle Haggard on the jukebox broke the silence as he bemoaned a mother's futile efforts to save her outlaw son from a life of crime.

Must be nice to have a mama who tried.

An appearance by Cash McCahill would have enraged the armed and dangerous crowd, but Carl Meadows on his own would pass unnoticed as just another ex-cop. What he couldn't decide was which of his escorts captured more eyes: Tina on his right or Sami to the left. Whichever, it was worth the cover charge of zero dollars to see the patrons drooling like Pavlov's dogs.

After holing up at the Hampton for a week, Sami savored the spotlight. She was accustomed to being best in show, even among a bevy of trophy wives. Tonight, she was one of only six fillies in a stable of steroid stallions and faced no serious competition.

Tina squeezed Cash's arm and whispered, "We have to get the hell out of here."

"One drink and we're off." A promise he had no intention of keeping.

With no Gamez or Leroy in sight, Cash looked for a friendly face and a place to land. He struck out on the former but scored the latter. He dragged Tina to an empty table at the back of the bar. Sami went along willingly. The closer they came to the restrooms, the stronger the stench of piss. For gun nuts who logged mandatory hours at the firing range, the regulars here sure had lousy aim.

Cash sat with his back to the wall and a full view of the bar. If hostiles rushed the table, he would see them coming. It didn't take long. A mountain of a man lumbered to the table and hovered over the seated Sami. "How about a dance, blondie?"

Cash recognized the lug as a patrol officer in the Northwest Division. A fuckup who spent more time in the gym than on the job, with the strong back and weak stats to show for it. Sami was so far out of his league as to make the mismatch laughable.

Without laughing, Sami stood. "Lead the way, big boy."

"Hate to be a buzzkill," Cash said, "but there's no dance floor."

"Don't sweat it, gramps," said the hulk. His hand swallowed Sami's, and off they went. The crowd parted for the couple, creating a tight dance floor. Brooks and Dunn bumped Merle off the jukebox with their cover of "Boot Scootin' Boogie." The crowd whooped and hollered, ringing the dancers and blocking Cash's view of Sami.

He turned back to Tina, certain of three things. Sami's dance card would fill fast. She could take care of herself. And based on the looks toward Tina, she was the one in danger.

"Why are we here?" Tina sounded jumpy.

"Sami was going bonkers, cooped up day and night. What safer venue to blow off steam than a bar crawling with cops?"

"What about me?" Tina said. "This isn't a safe space for me."

"Which is the other reason we're here." Cash looked around the room. Still no sign of Gamez or Leroy. "You're not sitting in the back of the bus any longer."

"Instead, I'm sitting in the back of a bar," she said, "within puking distance of the urinals."

"You have as much right to be here as any of them." He nodded toward the crowd encircling the dancers.

"Didn't your mother ever tell you not to go where you weren't wanted?" she said.

"No."

"Neither did mine, but she should've."

Cash stood. "Hold that thought. I see someone who owes me a drink." He intercepted Leroy on his way to the bar and steered him to the table. Cash introduced his new buddy to his granddaughter, the rookie cop.

"We're not really buddies," the DEA agent told Tina.

Fair enough. She's not really my granddaughter.

"Hold down the table," Cash said, "while I fetch the first round."

No need to twist Leroy's arm. "I'll have a—"

Cash cut him off. "I remember your brand, and I know what my granddaughter drinks." He left for the bar.

When Cash returned to the table, Tina and Leroy were sharing a laugh, no doubt at his expense. As were the drinks: a Chardonnay for Tina, Shiner Bock for Leroy, and Dallas Blonde for himself. He steered the conversation to Leroy's line of work.

"Don't let Leroy's laid-back manner fool you," Cash told Tina. "He's on the front line of the war on drugs, saving us from the cartels."

"You're safe for a few more months anyway." Leroy took a swig and wiped the foam from his lips. "After that, I'm out, and you suckers are on your own."

"What's the latest news from the front?" Cash said.

Everything rode on the agent's answer. The resurrection of Cash McCahill. A reunion with Eva and Goldy. And a return to the courtroom. So much at stake that Cash silently passed the baton to Tina. Let her wring the details from Leroy. That way it wouldn't seem as if an ex-cop from Buffalo had a personal investment in the outcome.

"What's happening south of the border?" she said. "Handicap the winners and…." She clammed up, her eyes ballooning. Cash followed her line of sight to the front door where

Gamez stood. Cash rose, prompting the detective to wheel around and leave the bar. It took Cash half a block to catch him.

Traffic on Commerce Street was light. There were no pedestrians on the sidewalk. Here and there, a homeless person lay burrowed under a mangy blanket or a cardboard sheet.

"Don't let us run you off," Cash said.

Gamez didn't look him in the eye. "I owe you a call. We'll talk tomorrow."

"This won't take long," Cash said. "We can settle it tonight."

Gamez shrugged.

"Tina says you're avoiding her."

The detective continued to dodge eye contact. "I've been busy."

Either Gamez wasn't trying to sell it, or he was a lousy liar. Cash bet on the latter. "You once said something that reminded me of why I'm so damn proud of Tina. You said she had stepped up when no one else would. Called her a game changer."

Gamez finally looked Cash in the eye. "I meant it."

"Then I've got two questions for you. Will you step up for her? And will *you* be a game changer?"

Cash waited for an answer. It took Gamez forever to come up with one. "I'm afraid...I can't love her." It came off as a confession.

"Is that really it?" Cash said. "Or are you afraid that you can?"

Cash returned to the A-Hole and to his seat at the back table. "Why did you run after him?" Tina sounded cross. "What did you hope to accomplish by that?"

"Thought he might be a friend in need," Cash said.

"Well, is he a friend?" she asked.

"I'm not sure." Cash kept his eyes on the entrance. Gamez returned to the bar. "Yeah, it looks like he is."

Tina clutched Cash's hand. "Omigod, we really have to leave now."

"Too late. He's heading our way."

Gamez wound toward the table, shaking hands and slapping backs on the way. Everyone knew everyone at the A-Hole, Carl Meadows and crew excepted. The detective stood behind Sami's empty seat. "Mind if I take this chair?"

"Where are you taking it?" Leroy said.

"You can always count on Leroy," Gamez said, "for a joke a minute and a laugh an hour."

"That seat is taken," Tina said frostily.

"Have a seat," Cash told the detective. "In the unlikely event that Sami tires out, we'll pull up a chair for her."

Gamez sat. Tina wrapped both hands around her wine glass. An awkward silence settled over the table. Cash elbowed Leroy. "Let's go to the bar and leave the young folks alone."

"I'll stay here and keep an eye on Tina," Gamez said.

Cash snickered. "Other way around."

***

From his perch on a barstool, Cash half-listened to Leroy, while keeping one eye on Sami on the dance floor and the other eye on Tina at the table. Sami switched partners with each new song on the jukebox. Tina and Gamez huddled in a world of their own. Every time Cash looked their way, they had scooted closer together. He couldn't hear their conversation but could read their body language.

Gamez jumped to his feet an instant before Tina did. They ran toward the exit. Cash cut them off at the door. "Where are y'all going?"

"They found another body," the detective said.

Cash fished his car keys from his pocket. "I'll go with you."

"Stay here with Sami," Tina said. "We've got this."

CHAPTER THIRTY

The late night at the A-Hole took a toll on Cash. Evidently, on Tina too. It was after eight, and she still hadn't come to the kitchen. Cash fixed breakfast for two and watched hers getting cold.

At 8:45, he knocked on her bedroom door. No answer. He opened the door. No Tina. She must have gone home with Gamez.

Cash took advantage of her absence to spend time in the study. Tina had declared it off-limits to him, which piqued his curiosity.

He flipped on the light and froze. Blowups of trans victims one through seven covered the west wall, arranged in the order of their deaths. Taped to the wall were photos of the victims. A mix of mug and morgue shots. The morgue pics featured close-ups of the soles of their feet with dice tattooed on the pads of the big toes. A single die with one dot for Rosie Perales, the first victim. Snake eyes for number two. And so on.

Plenty of wall space for last night's kill, as well as future victims nine through twelve. The layout projected the cycle of death to end with a roll of double six.

Cash fixated on the mug shots, which captured the rebels in their teens or early twenties. Their expressions ran the gamut: fear, annoyance, resignation, boredom, anger, surliness, and despair. Seven prisoners at booking. Seven different reactions.

The stark expressions of the young rebels reminded Cash of a painting at the Prado in Madrid: Goya's depiction of the execution of Spanish martyrs by Napoleon's army. The emotions etched on the faces of the doomed Spaniards haunted him to this day.

His thoughts turned to Bettina Biddle, a TCU art major who had concentrated her studies on Spanish painters, especially Goya. She, too, haunted him.

The mug shots revealed a link connecting the murders. All victims had a criminal record—mostly juvie busts for prostitution, petty theft, or minor in possession. Though Tina allotted only a single mug shot to each, all but two had racked up several arrests. A record gave the victims something in common with Tina.

And with Cash.

Scores of articles on the Dice Cold Killer papered the east wall. Everything from dry obituaries to lurid tales of the victims' final hellish hours. Neatly arranged on a desk were seven stacks. One per victim. Cash dug into the files, starting with witness statements. Most of the interviewees were johns. None offered much to go on.

Gamez had made repeated runs at Gideon Bragg, founder of the Sword of Gideon, but the cult leader had lawyered up and declined an interview. Probably a wise move, but so much for the biblical claim that the truth would set one free.

Dr. Katzenbach had proven more accommodating, though he, too, had lawyered up for the police interview. With Rhoden at one side and Gerry Freeman of Powell's firm on the other, the doctor had denied knowing three of the seven victims and declined to discuss the other four, citing the federal privacy statute known as HIPAA. Gamez had gotten nowhere with him.

Cash made a mental note that the tag team of Rhoden and Freeman, who had bookended Katzenbach at his interview, had earlier sold Marty Biddle down the river at his criminal trial. Rhoden wouldn't have reached out to Freeman for backup. It had to have been the other way around, with Freeman having brought in Rhoden.

Apparently, whenever Powell, Ingram & Gardner had an especially dirty job, Rhoden got the call over Cash. That still stung.

The files on the desk contained more mug shots, confirming his hunch that arrests had been an occupational hazard for the victims. He couldn't make much sense of the spotty bank records, except that all seven had largely dealt in cash and lived close to the edge.

However, Rosie Perales, victim number one, had been flush at her death. Cash suspected there had been a sugar daddy on the hook.

Likewise, the phone records told Cash little. They showed the numbers placing and receiving calls, but not the names attached to those numbers. Even if he somehow got the names, the phones could turn out to be burners, and the names, aliases. Finally, the records revealed nothing about the content or nature of the calls.

He returned everything to its original stack, moved to the center of the study, and slowly turned a complete circle, taking in a panorama of death.

Tina had brought her work home, committing the cardinal sin for a cop. It was beyond dangerous to allow DCK to dominate her personal life. What had begun as an investigation had become her obsession. Or maybe it was the other way around. Tina's obsession had spawned her investigation.

Either way, Cash feared for her sanity and safety. Cops referred to the unsolved case, the one they couldn't shake, as a whale or a white. Whether in fact or fiction, the quest for the great white whale spelled doom.

Ordinarily, it took years on the force before a whale hooked an officer. It usually ended badly for the cop, who would take the mystery to the grave. Often, to an early one.

***

Cash could shadow only one moving target at a time. Tina now had Gamez to watch her back. Sami had only Cash.

He found Sami in the hotel gift shop and took her to the room. The lack of sun and sleep was taking a toll on her. The bags under her eyes were heavy. Her blue irises, duller.

Time was running out to sweat the truth from her. "Where are the recordings?" he said.

She exhaled loudly. "We've been over this a hundred times. I don't know."

"I don't believe you."

"Go fuck yourself."

"I'm not the one who's about to get fucked." He went to the door and turned back to her. "What the sadist did to Darrell was a love tap compared to the fun he'll have with you." He carried the bluff past the point of leaving the room.

She overtook him at the elevator bank. “If I knew where they were, I’d tell you.” Her eyes welled with tears. “Rocket didn’t trust me. He didn’t trust anybody.”

He fought the temptation to believe her. “Will you take a polygraph?”

“I’ll do anything,” she said.

***

“What’s the girl’s story?” Rich Horton sat behind his desk. He looked like an accountant. Bald. Horn-rimmed glasses. Pasty complexion.

Nothing had changed in Horton’s private office. Cash had spent enough time here to nail the location of every plaque, photo, and puff piece that covered three walls and spanned four decades. The polygrapher had dedicated prime spaces to the plaque bestowed by the Bureau on his retirement and to the *D Magazine* cover hailing his reign as the president of the American Polygraph Association.

Seated in a client chair, Cash stared at Horton’s prized possession. The framed and autographed poster for the TV series *House* featured a head shot of Hugh Laurie, the lead actor, and the greatest tagline in the history of television: EVERYBODY LIES.

Words to live by.

Cash got back on mission. Carl Meadows had never been here and didn’t enjoy the protection accorded an attorney. “Is what I tell you privileged?” Cash asked.

“Are you a lawyer, Mr. Meadows?”

“No, but I work for one.” *Worked* would have been more accurate.

"Do you intend to convey what we say and do here to an attorney, so that he or she can render legal advice?"

Cash nodded.

"Then we can say this conversation is privileged."

Good enough for Cash, who relayed the abridged version to Horton, without naming names. Lawyer A hires Lawyer B to throw a criminal case. B obliges, and the client goes down. B has secretly recorded conversations with A for blackmail. B's assistant, today's test subject, claims not to know the location of the flash drive with the recordings.

"Is that all I need to know?" Horton said.

"For now." Cash omitted the juicy parts. The identities of A and B. The trifecta of grisly murders of Lawyer B, his young associate, and the betrayed client. The danger Sami now faced and, of course, who Carl Meadows really was.

Cash didn't tell Horton the whole story because, well, everybody lies.

***

Cash watched the couple in the testing room from behind a one-way mirror. Sami and Rich Horton were at a table but not across from each other. She faced a blank wall. He sat to her right and slightly behind her. Wires ran from Sami's fingers to a black box on the desk, and three straps banded her torso. Four hours ago, she had seemed nervous but not overly so for a virgin on the box. Now she looked tired and bored.

Cash had forgotten how long the process took. An hour or so for Horton to talk to Sami, to get to know her, and hone the three questions to be tested. A couple of hours to calibrate the machine and get Sami's baseline readings by throwing in random "must lie" questions. Finally, the actual test. The moment of untruth.

Most subjects never went the distance. Cash's clients had usually copped to the crimes before Horton hooked them to the machine. Broken by the mere threat of a test.

Sami didn't break. She barely blinked.

At the five-hour mark, Cash and Horton returned to his private office and sat across the desk from each other. "Interesting woman," Horton said.

"I didn't need a polygraph to tell me that."

"On the issue of whether she knows where the flash drive is," Horton said, "no deception indicated." Which was a roundabout way of saying she was telling the truth.

Cash didn't react to the result, a mix of good news and bad. He stood to leave. "That's what I needed the test to tell me."

"One more thing before you go," Horton said. "She lied about everything else."

CHAPTER THIRTY-ONE

Sami shuddered. "Isn't it dangerous to be here?" The *here* being a law office formerly occupied by not one but two murder victims.

"It's dangerous for you to be anywhere," Cash said.

And for me to be anywhere near you.

He took a stab at settling her nerves. "But since you've been on the lam for a week, the bad guys won't expect you to return to the office."

"Why are we here?" she said.

"To look for the missing flash drive."

"The feds searched and couldn't find it."

"They searched twice," Cash said. "Maybe the third time will be a charm."

The corner office had been dark since Darrell's death. Other than clearing a spot on the wall for his Baylor Law School diploma, Darrell hadn't altered the shrine to his mentor—the patron saint of sleaze.

A wet bar took up an entire wall. A bulletproof window to the world filled another. That left two walls for row after row of framed articles and photos heralding Rhoden's roller-coaster career.

Not even two walls could contain the bounds of the late mouthpiece's ego. A closet overflowed with articles and photos that hadn't made the cut for exhibition.

The two searched from mid-morning to late afternoon, fueled by Red Bulls and Mars Bars. They turned over the desk, emptied the drawers, and sifted through their contents. Took down everything from the walls. Inspected every bottle of booze. Slashed and gutted the chairs and couch. Probed for loose slats in the hardwood floor and tapped the walls for a hidden safe.

They hit one dry hole after another. 6:30 p.m., and only one private office down. Still a second office to go, plus a file space, conference room, and reception area. It was shaping up to be an all-nighter.

They restored Rhoden's office to its prior state as best they could, but the chair and couch were lost causes. At the sound of heavy footsteps outside the closed door, they froze. Sami gripped Cash's arm and whispered, "Do you have a gun?"

He whispered no, without explaining why he couldn't carry.

Wrong answer. Her fingers dug into his bicep. A fear gripped him tighter than her hold. A *sicario* had come to collect the bounty on him, and Sami would be collateral damage. The cartel had seen through his false face. His long-running performance as Carl Meadows neared its end.

"Stay behind me," Cash whispered. He grabbed a bottle of bourbon and moved to the door. She clung to his back. Her hot breath raised a sheen of sweat on his neck.

The door opened slowly, and the nose of a Glock inched into view followed by a hand and an arm. Cash brought the bottle down hard, knocking loose the gun. It skittered across the hardwood floor. He sprang forward for a knockout blow with the bottle, but Sami grabbed his arm.

"Wait!" she shouted. "It's Maury."

A pudgy rent-a-cop staggered into the room, cradling his gun hand. "You almost gave me a fucking heart attack." Heavy wheezing backed up his claim. The nametag identified him as M. Crawford.

"Same," Cash said.

"What are you doing here?" Maury fought for breath between words.

"Maury, it's me. Sami. I work here."

Maury's shaking subsided. "The office has been dark for a week. A tenant on the floor below called to report suspicious noises coming from here."

"Sami lost a ring," Cash said, "and we're searching for it."

"Who are you?" Maury asked Cash.

"I am…was Darrell's investigator."

Maury looked around and keyed on the gutted chairs and couch. "Might've been cheaper to buy a new ring."

"Sentimental value." Sami delivered the lie like a pro. After assuring Maury that everything was fine, she walked him to the door and closed it behind him. She turned to Cash. "On top of nearly getting us killed, this has been a total waste of time."

Cash took a last look around. "We're missing something," he said, more to himself than her.

"Yeah," Sami said, "that would be called lunch and dinner."

He went to the center of the office and slowly turned full circle. Then he did it again. And a third time. "What doesn't belong here?" Again, said more to himself. "What is not like the others?"

He opened the closet and picked up a framed article from 2018. It was a story by Skyler Patterson about an acquitted wife beater who went on to kill his spouse. He put down the article and closed the closet door. "Any lawyer who claims to have won all his trials is a damn liar or has never tried anything tough."

"What's your point?" Sami said.

"Rhoden was good on his feet." It pained Cash to admit this aloud. "But he didn't win them all."

"Take another look around," she said. "He won more trials in fifteen years than most litigators do in a lifetime."

"Exactly, and if there's a common thread to what's hanging on the walls, it's that the gallery showcased his victories. Hell, he had so many wins that there are accounts of acquittals gathering dust in the closet."

"Your point being?"

He walked to the north wall and pointed to a front-page photo of Rhoden and Marty Biddle leaving the courtroom after the guilty verdict. Biddle looked shell-shocked. Rhoden, like he'd just won the lottery. Which, in a way, he had.

"With all those wins on the walls and more crammed in the closet, why would he hang a loss for the world to see?" He removed the photo from the wall. "This is the only defeat on display." He slammed the picture against the desk. Glass shattered. The rectangular frame splintered into four pieces.

"What the hell are you doing?" Sami said.

"What the feds didn't do." He tossed aside the photo and mat, lifted the first leg of the metal frame, and peered through its hollow center. He gripped the section with both hands and said, "Make a wish."

"I wish we'd get something to eat," she said.

Cash snapped the first leg of the frame and shook both pieces. Nothing fell out. He did the same with each section of the frame. He broke the final piece, and a flash drive slid out. It was the size, shape, and color of a cigarette ash.

Like a cig, the flash drive could be hazardous to their health.

CHAPTER THIRTY-TWO

The next day, Cash hotel-hopped again. He moved Sami to a Best Western in Plano, a sprawling suburb in the shadow of Dallas, and took the standard precautions. He put the room on his credit card and in his name—that is, the current one.

Sami looked around the room. "Never thought I'd say this, but I miss the Hampton."

"Sorry to disappoint you, princess, but there was no suite available." The *tough shit* was silent.

Cash sat at the desk, powered on his laptop, and inserted the flash drive into the port. "Take a hike," he said. "Don't leave the hotel and come back to the room in an hour."

She slipped off her shoes and settled onto the bed. He took that as a firm *no*.

He moved the cursor to the menu and clicked. "If you're dreaming of a payoff, don't." He scrolled down the menu. "I'm doing my best to keep you alive. Once you hear what's on the drive, you can't unhear it."

"Same goes for you."

She had him there, but he took another shot at saving her from herself. "Chalk it up to my crazy desire to keep the body count in the low single digits. Two people have already been killed over a scrap of metal that weighs less than an ounce."

"Do you really think the psycho who butchered Darrell will believe I haven't listened to the recordings already?"

She had him again. He continued to scroll and discovered a bonus. In addition to 258 KB of audio files, there were 111 KB of video files.

A feast for the eyes and ears.

***

Cash sampled the recordings, bouncing between audio and video files and jumping back and forth in time. He would track a linear timeline later. For now, he needed a flavor.

The captured conversations ranged wildly in clarity, content, and duration. Words like *cunt* and *cocksucker* came up repeatedly. Most of the exchanges would have earned a hard X rating for language.

Over the course of six months, Rhoden had recorded scores of conversations, ranging from strategy sessions in offices to herky-jerky exchanges in limos. From whispered asides in a courtroom to angry shouting over cell phones. From threats of castration to come-on lines.

During the afternoon, he and Sami barely spoke. Every fifteen minutes or so, she would ask him to play back an excerpt, and he would. She identified the speakers for Cash. She nailed Rhoden and Darrell for sure. With Gerry Freeman of Powell's firm, she approached certainty. Freeman had been Rhoden's handler at the Biddle trial and a frequent visitor to the firm.

The recordings offered not a word from Lou Watson, the CEO of Longhorn. Even Powell proved elusive. There were no video files of him and only a couple of audio files, on both of which he had chosen his few words carefully. He was a master of saying little while laying down the law. The closest he had come to incriminating himself was a threat to Rhoden: "Fuck with me, and the state bar will be the least of your problems."

That had turned out to be true.

In contrast to the tight-lipped Powell, Freeman had bluntly delivered marching orders to Rhoden not to call defense witnesses or put Biddle on the stand. And not to object to the prosecutors' leading questions nor to their jury instructions. From the sidelines, Freeman had micromanaged every detail of the defense.

Or more accurately, the absence of one.

The trial had played out like a fixed fight, in which a crooked manager sends a palooka into the ring with three simple instructions: Don't punch with the right hand. Don't punch with the left. And don't block the opponent's blows.

A nude Sami appeared in a video shot in Rhoden's bedroom. Cash jumped to a new recording, too late to unhear what he had heard and unsee what he had seen.

"About that video of Rocket and me—"

Cash cut her off. "Don't sweat it. We can delete that part."

Rocket being Rocket, there were more sex tapes on the drive, featuring Sami and a bevy of beauties. Bonus footage for the blackmailer.

He shut down the computer, sparing Sami further embarrassment. He had seen and heard enough. Rhoden had gone bug crazy, planting listening devices everywhere. On his phone. In his office, home, and car. Even on his person. Occasionally,

Rhoden had arranged for video to accompany the sound. Like his night with Sami in the sheets.

Cash called room service and ordered dinner. Burgers, fries, and beer for two. While waiting for food to arrive, Sami paced the room. "Well, what do you think?"

"I've heard enough evidence of crimes this afternoon," Cash said, "to fill the entire docket of the Northern District of Texas for the next five years."

She stopped pacing. "We have Powell by the short hairs."

"Before you start packing for your private island, consider one inconvenient fact—Rhoden committed most of the crimes laid out on the drive."

"Like what?"

"For starters, extortion. Rhoden tried to blackmail Powell, which didn't end well for your late boss." *It rarely does for the blackmailer.*

"Old news." She made it sound like extortion was no big deal. "Tell me something I don't know."

Challenge accepted. "This afternoon, we listened to a hundred or so crimes by Rhoden, and there will be hundreds more. The easiest to prove are the illegal recordings. Texas is a one-party consent state."

"What does that mean?" she said.

"Rhoden could legally record phone calls and meetings," he said, "if he remained online or present at the meetings. However, once he left the calls or the room, the recordings flipped from legal to illegal. A felony, good for five years a pop."

She resumed pacing. "Then it's lucky for Rocket that he no longer has to worry about the long arm of the law."

"But *we* do. We could be prosecuted for extortion, assuming we lived long enough to make it to trial."

"Powell is desperate to get his hands on the drive," she said. "We can double what Rocket asked for."

Cash reminded himself that listening to her could get a person killed. Exhibit A: Darrell's mutilated corpse. "Shoot for two hundred million," he said. "That's your plan?"

She nodded.

"If we go down that track," Cash said, "what will double is the body count. The list of the deceased includes Rhoden and Darrell. Add the two of us, and it doubles."

She leaned against the desk. Her perfume was intoxicating. "The drive could set us up for life."

Now it's us. Fat chance. On Cash McCahill's best day, Sami would be a stretch. For Carl Meadows, she was a chimera.

"What's your plan for staying alive?" he said.

"Take the money and run."

What could go wrong?

CHAPTER THIRTY-THREE

That night Cash duped the flash drive of blackmail material and deposited the drives in safety deposit boxes at storage facilities. He left the original drive at It's My Vault and the backup at Whose Vault Is That.

The files were safe, for now. Which was more than he could say for the three women in his life. Bettina lived under house arrest, a wounded bird in a gilded cage. The police department was dangling Tina as bait to catch the Dice Cold Killer. And the sadist who had taken out Darrell, and probably Rhoden as well, was scouring the city for Sami.

Cash stashed Sami at the Best Western and counted on Gamez to protect Tina. Contrary to the gospel according to Meat Loaf, two out of three was bad. He had to find a way to get to Bettina. He didn't have her new phone number and had failed to talk his way past the security guard at Preston Hollow Estates. Whenever she ventured outside the gates, Powell's goons shadowed her.

He hit on a strategy that rested on the safe assumption that people who lived in a gated neighborhood wouldn't stoop to doing their own yard work. In faded jeans, a baggy shirt, and work boots, he parked a half-block from the entrance to Preston Hollow Estates and waited. He didn't have a long wait. Around 7:45 a.m., a flatbed truck loaded with mowers, rakes, hoes, fertilizer, potted plants, and six workers pulled into the enclave.

Now came the extended wait. Four hours later, the flatbed truck left with the men on board but without the tools of their trade. Cash followed the truck to Fernando's, home of the best Tex-Mex in north Dallas.

The six worker bees came in shades of brown and looked to be in their twenties and thirties. They sat outdoors at two tables while the boss took a booth inside. He was older and paler than his charges. Dollars to donuts, his duties consisted of carting the crew around and collecting payments from the landed gentry.

Cash joined the boss in a booth. On closer inspection, he might be in his late forties but prematurely aged by the elements. The sunglasses in his shirt pocket accounted for the white band across his eyes. His right hand rested near a knife on the table. "Do I know you?"

"Not yet." Cash extended his hand. "Carl Meadows. I want to join your crew."

The boss was slow to pull his hand away from the knife to shake. "Harry Beeson, but I don't have an opening. Besides, shouldn't you be looking for something a little less physical?" The at your age was silent but implied.

"I've got a deal for you, Mr. Beeson. I'll work for free this afternoon. Let's see if your boys can keep up with me."

"You're on," Beeson said.

***

Around 12:45 p.m., the flatbed rumbled past the guard at the gate. Cash pulled a straw hat low on his forehead, though it hardly mattered. He couldn't have been more invisible if he had been a real member of the crew.

After hoeing for two hours and raising a crop of blisters, Cash bailed from the job site. Armed with a rake, he wound through the enclave of two dozen high-end homes. According to the billboard on the street, prices for the properties started at six million, which explained why half the inventory remained on the market.

Of the twelve houses that looked lived in, eight had names emblazoned on the mailboxes. Biddle wasn't one of them. That left four houses still in the running. There was no black Escalade in a driveway or girl's bike on a lawn to make it easy on Cash. Nonetheless, he zeroed in on Bettina's place.

Only one residence resembled the Southlake showplace, which had been seized by the feds following Marty's fraud conviction. Both houses shared a Santa Barbara vibe, with white stucco exterior, red tile roof, and palm trees. A style guaranteed to appeal to a TCU art major with a taste for all things Spanish.

Cash tossed aside the rake and rang the bell. Bettina answered the door. For a moment, he lost his breath along with his tongue. It happened every time.

Barefoot and wearing tight shorts and a tank top, she seemed slimmer and shorter. A ponytail and rimless glasses proved to be a good look for her. Then again, what wasn't?

She needed a stern warning not to open the door to strangers. Sure, she lived in a gated community, but a rusty rent-a-cop couldn't be trusted to keep the bad guys at bay. Despite an overwhelming need to protect her, the warning would have to wait.

Fear flashed in her dark eyes. Perhaps she had heard his silent warning. If so, it didn't stick. The fear faded, replaced by puzzlement. "May I help you?" She sounded wary.

"I hope to help you," Cash said.

"Thanks, but we already have a lawn service."

"I came to talk about Marty."

She looked closer. "Hey, you're the one looking into Marty's death. We talked briefly at Seagoville."

"Until your handlers butted in."

"How did you get by Jaime at the gate? He's supposed to call before letting in visitors."

"That's not important. How much time do we have before the guards show up?"

She checked her watch. "About an hour. That's when I pick up the girls from school, with an escort to and from." She didn't drop the name of the pricey, private school.

"May I come in?" he said.

She hesitated before leading him to a living room with high ceilings, a chandelier the size of an SUV, and pockmarked pillars. Everything was in earth tones, including the leather couch. They had barely settled onto the couch when Cash suggested they go outside. Her puzzled look returned. "Why?"

He owed her an explanation. "Your house is probably bugged, top to bottom."

"Bugged?"

"Listening devices, for sure. Cameras, more than likely."

They relocated to the backyard and sat on adjacent deck chairs under the shade of palm trees. A waterfall at one end of the pool and jets along the sides created enough background noise that they barely heard each other.

"You never really explained why you were looking into my husband's death."

"I was hired to look into Rhoden's murder, and that led me to Marty," he lied. The truth was too dangerous for her.

"Who hired you?"

"I can't tell you."

"And you think Rhoden's death is somehow connected to Marty?"

He nodded.

"Why?"

"There's a lot I can't tell you, not now anyway. But if I'm right and your husband didn't commit suicide, the insurance company owes you big time." He surveyed the spacious yard. "Though it doesn't look like you're hurting."

Her eyes narrowed. "I don't own this place."

Cash suspected that Stewart Powell had parked ownership of the property in a shell company, making it untraceable to him or his firm. Jealousy got the better of Cash. "And the Escalade, private school for the twins, security detail, who's footing the bills for all that?"

"I don't have to justify myself to you." Her defensiveness flared.

"No, you don't." Too much of Cash and too little of Carl had surfaced. He dialed down the jealousy. "I'm simply curious as to who's supporting your lifestyle."

"Marty's company is helping us through a difficult time."

He gave her a get-real look.

"What's wrong with that?" Her voice welled with outrage. "You don't think it's possible for one human being to give a shit about another."

"That's not my experience with hedge funds," he said.

That's not anyone's experience with hedge funds.

"Mr. Watson couldn't have been any—"

The pool sweep broke the surface, and a rope of water lashed her. She yelped.

"What is Longhorn getting out of the arrangement?" he said.

She looked away from him. "I accept the suicide ruling on Marty's death and move on."

"For the sake of the girls." He defaulted to defense lawyer mode of mitigation.

She nodded.

"I'm not here to judge you." Another lie.

"Look, if I was sure Marty hadn't killed himself...." She didn't finish the sentence.

In the dark as to his mother's fate, Cash understood the curse of uncertainty and threw her a lifeline. "What you can't do directly, you can do indirectly through me."

"You mean we work together?" she said.

"I can be your eyes and ears outside the gates."

An alert pinged Cash's iPhone. There was breaking news online about Gary Goldberg. Cash's mind went to the worst-case scenario: Goldy had suffered another heart attack, perhaps a fatal one.

Cash cut short the conversation and took off. He read Skyler Patterson's article twice on the run to his parked car. The good news: Goldy was alive. The bad: The old man wouldn't be alive long if Eva or Tina got to him before Cash did.

CHAPTER THIRTY-FOUR

Raised voices carried through the closed door to Goldy's office. Tina dominated the shouting match as the old man struggled to slip in a word edgewise. Cash barged into the office to find Goldy slouched behind his desk. Tina loomed over him while Eva enjoyed the mismatch from the couch.

"You should call the fight," Cash told Eva. "Your boss is getting his ass kicked."

"No way," Eva said. "I'm team Tina."

Goldy glanced at Cash before turning back to Tina. "I see you called in reinforcements."

Tina scoffed. "Does it look like I need help?"

Cash sat next to Eva and said, "I'm late to the party. Catch me up."

"Against my advice," Eva said, "the old fool has agreed to represent the devil."

Cash shrugged. "Isn't that the job description of a criminal defense lawyer?"

"I mean the actual devil in the flesh." More fire in Eva's voice. "Gideon Fucking Bragg."

That confirmed Skyler's scoop. "I side with the gals on this one," Cash said.

Goldy glared at him. "Who gives a hoot? And what the hell are you doing here?"

"As soon as I read online that you were representing Bragg, I figured Tina would rush over to bust your balls. Thought she might need my moral support."

"What she needs," Goldy said, "is a swift kick in the ass."

"How can you defend a serial killer?" Tina said.

Cash put in words what everyone in the room was thinking. "For all we know, Bragg has marked Tina as the next victim."

Goldy managed to make it to his feet. "Y'all have tried and convicted my client before he's even been charged. Has it crossed your mind that he might be innocent?"

"Whether or not he's good for the killings," Tina said, "he's guilty of making life hell for people like me." Her voice crackled with passion. "Check out the videos online of him and his hooligans terrorizing our trans community."

"What happened to innocent until proven guilty?" Goldy said.

"What happened to our rule against representing assholes?" Tina shot back.

Cash bumped on Tina's invocation of a rule that had never existed and could never work. If Goldy weeded out every asshole who walked through the door, they would all starve.

Tina turned to Eva. "Are you buying this bullshit?"

Eva had changed looks again, reverting to her hippie chick days. Loose, flowing locks. No makeup. Granny glasses. "Don't look at me, *chica*," she said. "I warned him against taking on Bragg."

Tina motioned to Cash. "Come on, Paw Paw. Let's get out of here."

As Cash reached the door, Goldy called to him. "Hey Chuck?"

Cash stopped. "It's Carl."

"Whatever. I need an investigator to work with me and my new client. Interested?"

***

Gideon Bragg, Goldy, and Cash sat at a round table in Goldy's office. Bragg sported a sharkskin suit, silk shirt, and Italian loafers. He looked more like a corporate chief than a cult leader.

"Nice threads," Cash said. The tailored job must have set back the Sword of Gideon two thousand dollars. A pittance of the tax-free fortune Bragg and the true believers had amassed.

Bragg pointed to Cash. "Who's the third wheel?"

"His name's Chuck Meadows," Goldy said, "and he's my investigator."

"It's Carl Meadows, and I'm considering it."

Goldy grunted. "Looks more like a Chuck."

Cash didn't shake hands with the client. Not enough sanitizer in the world.

Goldy opened with his standard preamble. "Whatever you say within the confines of this room is protected by the strongest privilege in the common law." Bragg looked bored, confirming Cash's suspicion that he had heard it all before. It wasn't his first brush with the law.

Goldy went on. "If you have something to get off your chest, this is the time and place to do it."

"I do my confessing to God," Bragg said, "not man."

"The Almighty will get around to judging you in the sweet by-and-by," Goldy said. "Right now, I'm more concerned with twelve citizens, good and true, in a jury box."

Bragg leaned forward. "God's judgment is the only one I fear."

Cash rolled his eyes. "Let's leave the big guy out of this for the time being."

"There is no time and no place to leave out God."

"Save the sermon for Sunday," Goldy said, "and shoot straight with us now. What do you know about the murders of the trannies?"

"He means trans women," Cash said.

Goldy kicked Cash under the table. That silenced him briefly.

"I know that God strikes down sinners, and the wicked will burn in hell for eternity." Bragg's voice rose in righteous fury.

"We need to know whether you played a part in carrying out God's judgment." Goldy lowered the decibel level in the room.

"Sinners who fail to repent from their wicked ways doom themselves."

"The good thing about being a deity," Cash said, "is that the Republic of Texas can't charge you with a crime. In contrast, you face the prospect of eight separate indictments. One for each murder." He handed a single page to Bragg and the same page to Goldy.

"What's this?" Bragg said.

"A list of the dates the eight bodies were found," Cash said. "We have to know where you were on each of these dates, what you were doing, who you were with, and who will swear to it under oath."

Bragg looked at the list and shook his head. "I can't remember what I was doing two weeks ago, much less two years ago. I'll have to dig through records."

Cash set a deadline. "You have twenty-four hours."

CHAPTER THIRTY-FIVE

Eva threw open the door to Goldy's office and said, "They're baaaaack."

"Are you ever going to learn to knock before barging in?" Goldy's *faux* outrage carried a zero percent chance of repercussions to the bearer of the tidings, good or bad. "I was in the middle of lecturing Meadows on the finer points of conspiracy law when you so rudely interrupted me."

Eva rolled her eyes. "As if you know any actual law," she said. "Oh, and my random inspections will cease when you stop hiding cigars and booze in here."

Goldy spewed and sputtered but didn't deny the charges.

A seated Cash swiveled toward Eva and said, "Who's back?"

She entered the office and closed the door behind her. "The prick from the Bureau."

Cash had a prime suspect in mind, but there were too many candidates for him to be certain. "Prick doesn't narrow the field much," he said.

Goldy slapped the desk with both palms. "Prick doesn't narrow it at all."

"It's Bowers," she said.

Cash tensed, having seen this movie before and from a front row seat. He had witnessed, at close range, the raid of Darrell Pendergass's office, which had spelled the downfall of Darrell and his firm.

If today followed the script, Bowers would seek Goldy's consent to a search of the office. The old man would tell the agent where to go, at which point Bowers would whip out a warrant authorizing the feds to sweep up everything not nailed down. Tipped off by law enforcement, a swarm of media would publicize the raid and doom the firm.

"How many goons are out there?" Goldy asked.

Eva held up a forefinger. "Just one. Bowers came alone."

Cash did a double take. That wasn't like the Bureau and certainly not like Bowers. For almost every encounter, the feds maneuvered to secure an edge in numbers.

"Guess it's one riot, one ranger," Goldy said.

"Since we're talking about Bowers," Cash said, "it's more like one ambush, one asshole." He looked Goldy in the eye. "You will get pissed off today, probably more than once, but don't do anything rash. Brace yourself to spend the day cooped up in a conference room while agents trash our home away from home." He turned to Eva. "Your number one job is to keep the boss from getting himself arrested for obstruction."

A roll of her eyes. "Wonderful. Another day of babysitting the boss."

"Show the agent in," Cash told her.

On seeing Cash in Goldy's office, Bowers made a hard stop. "For someone new in town, you sure have a penchant for hanging out with the sleaziest lawyers."

Cash held his tongue. Goldy didn't. "The answer is no."

"I haven't asked a question yet," Bowers said.

Goldy shrugged. "Whatever the question is, the answer is no. And don't bother sitting. You won't be here long."

Bowers sat anyway. "I'm looking for Cash McCahill."

Cash tensed but stayed silent. He drew on his ability to remain unruffled while the world crumbled around him. His superpower had salvaged more than one trial on the brink of disaster, and it came in handy now.

"Join the club," Eva said. "We haven't seen or heard from Cash in more than six months. If you're unaware that a cartel has put a contract on his head, you need to talk to your buddies at the DEA."

"We know all about that," Bowers said, "but I suspect that if he's gone underground, one or both of you will know how to reach him."

"We don't," Eva said. "We can't even be sure he's still alive."

Goldy leaned forward. "Why do you want to get hold of Cash?"

Bowers squirmed. It was his turn to fall silent.

"If Cash were to reach out to us," Goldy said, "he'll want to know what you're up to. He won't make a cold call, not to you."

Bowers took a deep breath and slowly exhaled. "We're vetting candidates for an important job."

"Attorney General?" Goldy said.

"I can't say more than that it's a very high position in the executive branch."

Eva looked puzzled. Goldy, more so. "Why in the world would you want to interview Cash about a candidate for AG?" he said.

"He has relevant information about one of the candidates," Bowers said. "Someone he worked with in the past."

"In other words, Cash has dirt on one of the two gals in the running." Goldy clucked his tongue. "Which one are you trying to torpedo?"

Bowers cleared his throat. "I can't identify the candidate for you, but I will do so to Cash. At this point, I'm simply seeking relevant information to provide to the White House." The ASAC made it to the door before turning back. "Tell Cash we know what happened in the Valley. We just need him to confirm it."

"I don't understand," Goldy said.

"Cash will." Bowers handed his business card to Eva on the way out.

Goldy made no effort to hide his skepticism over everything Bowers had said. Cash didn't buy it either. He had never heard of an ASAC with the Bureau stooping to vet candidates, even for the highest positions. That was grunt work for ex-agents looking to score a few extra bucks.

Cash sensed the invisible hand of Stewart Powell pulling the strings. If so, Bowers was scouring for dirt on Regina Delgado, Jenna Powell's rival for the post.

Two decades before, Regina and Cash had worked together on a task force on public corruption in south Texas. Their affair had been inevitable, tempestuous, short-lived, and doomed. Another string of bad decisions haunting Cash.

The affair would embarrass but not disqualify Regina. If affairs were fatal, there would be nobody left in DC to mismanage the government. However, what led to the falling out between the two and to Cash's abrupt departure from the task force could knock her out of contention.

Bowers had drawn a bead on Regina's soft spot. Cash had the goods on her, but he wasn't about to share the dirt with the

ASAC. Not even if he could afford to abandon his alter ego and surface as his true self.

***

Eva and Cash left the office at the same time and boarded the elevator together. "Where are you off to?" He tried to sound casual but wasn't sure it came off that way.

"I'm going to pick up the mail and water the plants at my boss's house," she said. "My former boss."

"Is this the hotshot lawyer who crossed a cartel and disappeared?"

She nodded. "Goldy thinks he's dead and buried where no one will find him. I hope he's halfway around the world and living under a rock."

"Want some company?" He wasn't crazy about the prospect of her spending time alone at his abandoned house. Not with a swarm of *sicarios* trolling the city for a seven-figure payday.

She shrugged. Cash took it as a yes.

Twenty minutes later, he pulled into his driveway for the first time in almost a year. He looked up and down the block. No dark van in sight. Eva unlocked the door and led him inside. Cash almost gagged in the entryway. "What's that smell?"

"I burn incense when I'm here," she said. "I don't know what Cash was smoking, but he must've smoked a ton of them."

Cash reminded himself not to act as if he knew the layout of the house. "Where's the bathroom?" he said.

"Down the hall, first door on the right."

He followed her directions to the bathroom and locked the door. He stared long and hard at the mirror, as if expecting to see the reflection of his old self. No magic tonight.

On the way out, he said to Eva, "Have you had the place checked for bugs?"

She stopped in the doorway. "Why? Did you see a roach or ants?"

"Different kind of bug," he said. "Listening devices. You should have the house swept for them."

***

After dropping off Eva, Cash headed to Tina's apartment. On the drive, he debated the pros and cons of warning Regina about the push by Powell and his FBI flunkies to gut her chances at the AG gig.

The con: He still had hard feelings over how their detail in south Texas had played out, both professionally and personally.

The pro: It was an enemy-of-my-enemy thing.

The pro won out. He bought a burner phone with cash and called Regina's mobile number from the car.

"Who is this?" She sounded groggy.

"You don't know me," Cash said, "and I'm trying to keep it that way."

"Who gave you my cell number?"

"Someone close to you."

"One more evasive answer like that, and I'm hanging up." Her voice had shed the last remnants of sleep. "What do you want?"

"To warn you that Stewart Powell and his friends at the Bureau are digging for dirt on you."

"Tell me something I don't know," she said.

"They're looking for Cash McCahill to supply the dirt."

There was a long silence on the line. “Where is Cash?” A sense of urgency amped her voice.

Cash ignored her question. “The FBI is interested in what happened in south Texas.”

A longer silence followed. When she spoke, it was in a hushed tone. “Why are you telling me this?”

“I may need to call in a chit someday.” He hung up, ditched the burner in White Rock Lake, and made it home in time to watch the Rangers come from behind in the ninth inning.

CHAPTER THIRTY-SIX

Three days later and two days past Cash's artificial deadline, Bragg provided a list of witnesses to corroborate his whereabouts. Eight dates, each marking a murder by the Dice Cold Killer, and Bragg had solid alibis for six of them.

On three dates at issue, the cult leader had been outside Texas at public events, with records of flights, limos, hotels, and restaurants to prove it. For two more, he was in state but hundreds of miles from home base. On one of those nights, he had emceed a fundraiser in Lubbock before a crowd of five hundred. Even for the two occasions when he had been in Big D, a host of witnesses placed him far from Deep Ellum where the bodies had turned up.

For Bragg to bat eight for eight seemed too good to be true and raised suspicions that he and his flock had concocted a seamless web of corroboration. Cash burned three days poring over records and grilling witnesses, trying to bust at least an alibi or two. He found no chink in the armor and no evidence tying Bragg to the DCK killings.

However, he uncovered a few dodgy financial deals that would interest Shafer of the IRS. He copied and kept the evidence of tax fraud. Could come in handy someday.

Time to break the bad news to the boss.

***

Cash knew better than to let Goldy pick the venue for a business meeting. His selections invariably shared three common factors: young women, loud music, and strong liquor. Cash nixed the old man's first choice—a strip club on Harry Hines called The Treasure Chest. The fallback was Mattito's on Oak Lawn, a Tex-Mex restaurant that featured a favorable female-to-male ratio, a shake-the-earth sound system, and multiple margarita machines.

At 7:07 p.m., Cash found Goldy at a table near the bar, working on a basket of chips and a pitcher of frozen margarita. Cash moved them to the backroom, which was quieter but not quiet. He gave the news to Goldy straight. "It looks like our deep-pocket client will dodge his day of reckoning. Your seven-figure trial fee is melting faster than your margarita."

Goldy choked on a chip. "W-w-what? Why?"

"The asshole may be innocent. Well, not guilty of the murders anyway."

Goldy refilled his margarita glass. "Damn. Just my rotten luck to land a flush client, and the sonovabitch lacks the decency to get himself tried."

"Cheer up, old man. Even if Bragg's not a serial killer, he's almost certainly a tax cheat."

"Who are you calling old, Paw Paw?"

Cash clammed up. He had slipped into his prior smartass self. It had been for only two words, but even a single syllable could blow his cover.

Goldy ordered another pitcher of frozen margarita, and Cash breathed easier. The geezer had his priorities straight. Drinks first. Client second. Anything else, like who Carl Meadows really was, a distant third.

"Console yourself with the prospect of representing Bragg on a tax case someday. That is, if the IRS grows the balls to go after his phony church." Cash poured himself a margarita and toasted the one IRS agent with the chops to target a false prophet. "Here's to Marty Shafer, an even bigger asshole than our client."

With Jimmy Buffett's "Margaritaville" blaring over speakers, Cash savored the frozen concoction that would help them hang on. "Now that I've given you the bottom line," he said, "do you want chapter and verse?"

"Save it for the next pitcher." Goldy sounded down.

***

The windowless conference room at police headquarters smelled of disinfectant. Good thing too. Cop hotboxes had a way of triggering tear ducts, sweat glands, and gag reflexes. Several suspects had hurled in front of Cash. A couple had hurled on him.

Detective Gamez cleared his throat. "Well, this is certainly awkward." He sat next to Tina and across the table from Cash and Goldy.

"I should've warned you," Tina told Gamez, "that my grandfather is working with Mr. Goldberg on this case." She didn't try to hide her disgust.

Goldy winked at Tina. “It’s Goldy to an old friend like you.”

Gamez stared hard at Cash. “I get that a lawyer does what lawyers do, which is defend the indefensible. But you, being an ex-cop and all, how do you sleep at night?” He pushed a stack of photos across the table.

Cash treated the question as rhetorical and focused on the top picture: a morgue shot of Rosie Perales, DCK’s first victim. He fought an urge to go through the stack.

“The last time we talked,” Gamez said, “you were all about protecting your precious granddaughter. Now you’re putting her in harm’s way.”

Cash bristled at the charge. “That’s not how I see it, at least not until you convince me that Bragg is good for the murders.”

Gamez turned to Tina. “Are you okay with this? You don’t have to be here.”

“Yes, I do.” She was curt.

Goldy drummed his fingers on the table. “Can we get down to business? Either you’ve got hard evidence on our client or you don’t.”

“We’re still putting the case together,” Gamez said.

Goldy smiled. “Which means you don’t have shit.”

“The killer took a souvenir from each victim,” Tina said. “A tongue, eyes, a hand. If either of you had ever bothered to open a Bible, you’d understand that Bragg is sending a message with the murders. When we find the souvenirs, you’ll be back here, begging for a deal that takes the death penalty off the table.”

“I taught you to bluff better than that,” Cash said to Tina. He turned to Goldy. “Want me to drive a stake through their case?”

The old man nodded.

Cash condensed three days of fieldwork into thirty minutes. He laid out where Bragg had been on the dates of the murders, what he had been doing, and the long list of witnesses who would place him far from the crime scenes. He concluded with the claim that the cops couldn't pin a single murder on Bragg, much less eight killings.

"No one believes Bragg would be fool enough to get his hands bloody," Gamez said. "He has disciples do his dirty work."

"Get back to us after you've cleared the ten thousand or so suspects," Goldy said. "In the meantime, stop feeding Bragg's name to the press."

Gamez's face turned red. "I don't leak."

"And the chief?" Goldy fired back.

The detective repeated, "I. Don't. Leak."

Cash went off script. "You're wasting time on Bragg and his followers."

"What makes you think that?" Tina said.

Goldy kicked Cash under the table. Cash blew past the stop sign and said, "The victims lived every day with the knowledge it could be their last if they went to the wrong place at the wrong time with the wrong person. They were too savvy to let one of Bragg's wingnuts lure them to their deaths. The killer is someone the vics trusted."

"Even if that was true," Gamez said, "how can you work for a hater like Bragg?"

Cash stared back at the detective. "Every minute you spend chasing the wrong man is a minute you don't spend chasing the killer."

Goldy rose, while Cash remained seated. "Are you coming or not?" Goldy said.

"I need to talk to my granddaughter. It's personal."

Gamez nodded to Goldy. “I think we’ve been asked to leave.”

Alone with Tina, Cash said, “What’s wrong? You seem on edge.”

She shrugged. “It’s Robbie. He’s taking me out tonight to Fearing’s.”

“Are you nervous about being seen with him?”

“Other way around,” she said. “I can tell he’s afraid to be seen out with me.”

“He’ll get used to it.”

“I wish I had your confidence.”

Cash laughed. “I wish I had a date.”

CHAPTER THIRTY-SEVEN

Cash claimed the barstool next to Leroy's at the A-Hole and said, "The place is dead tonight." Maybe twenty hard cases had braved a drizzly Monday. Even the jukebox had taken the night off, as had the owner. Alvarez's daughter tended bar. She had inherited her mother's Mediterranean beauty and her father's temper, placing her in the look-but-don't-touch category.

Leroy grunted in what passed in the cop bar as a warm greeting.

"I'm good for the next round," Cash said. "Picked up some work."

"Bully for you." The drug agent didn't sound impressed. "Dope case?"

Cash started to protest that drug work fell outside his wheelhouse but held back. That was Cash's line. He shook his head.

"Then I'll drink with you," the DEA agent said.

As if that was ever in doubt.

"I need to pick your brain," Cash said.

Leroy snorted. "Now you sound like a fucking lawyer. Always with the *quid pro quo*."

"You work for the bastards long enough," Cash said, "and their bad habits rub off on you."

"Who are you working for tonight?"

"I'm not at liberty to divulge the name." Cash worried that he still came off as too lawyerly and braced for Leroy to call him out again. When he didn't, Cash went on. "Who's up and who's down this week in the cartel war south of the border?"

"The same scum who were winning and losing last week."

Cash ordered a round and told the bartender to keep them coming. Based on experience, it would take more than one free drink to loosen Leroy's tongue. "To be more specific, will *Los Lobos* survive?"

Leroy took a closer look at Cash. "I knew a mouthpiece who got on the wrong side of *Los Lobos* and disappeared nearly a year ago. Haven't seen hide nor hair of the damn fool since. He might be dead. Or he might be off the grid." The wheels were turning inside Leroy's dinosaur brain. "Your mystery client, is he Cash McCahill?"

"Still not at liberty to say. This Cash character, is he a friend of yours?"

The agent was slow to answer. "He was a royal pain in the ass."

"But did he grow on you?"

"Yeah, like a fucking fungus." Leroy finished beer number whatever and belched. "Grab a pitcher and meet me at the back booth."

Cash upped the ante by bringing two pitchers to the booth. Leroy refilled his mug and said, "The first thing to understand about my world is that the suits never learn."

"I wouldn't limit that nugget of truth to your world," Cash said.

They clinked mugs in solidarity. Two grunts against the suits.

Leroy continued. "Last year, both governments brokered a peace by backing *Los Lobos* over *La Tigra* and her Sinaloa cartel. They succeeded in stopping the warfare for about six months before a new apex predator appeared."

"*Los Asesinos*?" Cash said.

Leroy nodded. "Bigger, bolder, and more brutal than the competition. Meet the new nightmare."

"So which cartel will come out on top?"

"My money's on *Los Asesinos*," Leroy said. "In cartel warfare, victory goes to the side which places less value on human life. Hard to see anyone beating *Los Asesinos* on that score. They put no value on it."

"When will *Los Lobos* no longer pose a threat?" Cash said.

"A threat to who?"

Good try, Leroy.

"To anyone," Cash said.

"Soon."

Cash rose to leave. "Hey," Leroy said, "we haven't finished the first pitcher yet."

"I'm confident you can handle both."

The agent slid from the booth and stood between Cash and the exit. "You asked a lot of questions tonight. Answer one of mine. Your mystery client, when can you tell me if it's Cash?"

"Soon."

***

With *Los Lobos* on the ropes, Cash showed up at Dr. Katzenbach's office a week before his scheduled appointment. The red-haired receptionist, identified by nameplate as Katya Swenson, was a living billboard for the doctor's wizardry. Her face displayed a beauty not found in nature, all chiseled features, smooth skin, and sharp angles.

Cash made three runs at her. The first broached a simple request for five minutes with Katzenbach, squeezed between appointments. It drew a one-word response: "No."

Between the first and second attempts to storm the gatekeeper, he thumbed through dozens of glossy magazines. Three themes emerged from the reading material in the office: travel, golf, and travel for golf. Based on the principle of one cover one vote, Vegas was the doctor's destination of choice.

Prominently displayed on the wall hung a framed scorecard of Katzenbach's round last spring with Jordan Spieth at the Dallas Country Club. Spieth had shot sixty-nine. Katzenbach, seventy-five. Not bad for the pro or the amateur.

Cash speculated on the backstory behind the round. The doctor must have shelled out big bucks at a charity auction for the privilege of hitting the links with the Dallas-based pro. In return for a winning bid of five or maybe six figures, Katzenbach had bagged the bragging rights to the round of his life and an autographed scorecard.

On his second try, Cash shortened his request to a mere three minutes of the doctor's precious time. Katya's tone turned frosty. Her answer remained the same.

Cash stewed in the waiting room another hour before his final approach. He attempted to engage the receptionist in conversation. "May I call you Katya?"

"I prefer Miss Swenson."

"Miss Swenson, I need a couple of minutes with the doctor. My case is...special."

She sighed loudly. "All patients are special to Dr. Katzenbach."

"No, what I mean..." Cash fell silent, fumbling for a way to describe his situation without divulging too much. "...what he did to me is different from what he does to others."

"Every patient is different," she said, "just as every patient is special."

Getting nowhere with her, he took a last shot. "Will you at least see if there's an opening to move up my appointment?"

"Certainly, Mr. Meadows." She swiveled toward her computer screen and scrolled through the calendar. She filled out an appointment card and handed it to Cash.

The card bore the same date and time as his current appointment. She had written *bye* on the back of the card. He started to object but held his tongue. Courthouse hacks had a saying: A judge can hurt you, but her assistant can kill you. Cash figured the same rule applied here.

He pocketed the card and turned to go. On the way out, he noted that the office closed at noon on Wednesdays. That told him where both he and Katzenbach would be tomorrow afternoon.

***

The next day, Cash climbed the fence and ambushed Katzenbach at the Dallas Country Club between the seventh and eighth holes. Cash banked on the DCC being the doctor's home course, based partly on the framed scorecard in his office, but mostly on the deep pockets who played there. For someone with Katzenbach's skills, the DCC was a bird's nest on manicured grounds.

After three-putting, Katzenbach claimed a bogey five on the seventh hole and cursed all the way to his cart, where Cash waited in the passenger seat. "Who are you?" The doctor's paunch stretched his emerald shirt.

"Don't you recognize me, Doc? I'm your Frankenstein monster. The first and probably last patient to ask you to *add* miles to the odometer."

Katzenbach squinted. "You're the lawyer on the lam. The referral from Tina Campos."

"Bingo."

From across the fairway, a playing partner wearing canary yellow slacks shouted to Katzenbach, "You're down twenty, Doc." The doctor flipped Mellow Yellow the finger.

"Given your lucrative practice," Cash said, "I wouldn't sweat over twenty bucks."

"Twenty *thousand*." Katzenbach turned the key, and the cart lurched forward. "I don't need a distraction like you, but because I have a soft spot for Tina, I'll give you five minutes to clear off the course before I call security."

"Here's my counter," Cash said. "Give me five minutes of your time, and I won't tell your golfing buddies that you shot six and not five on the last hole."

The doctor's brow furrowed. "Here's my counter to your counter. You've got the time it takes me to drive to the next tee box to speak your piece."

Cash could work with that. "The extra years you added to my face, I'm going to need you to roll them back."

The doctor's furrows deepened during the short drive. "It's not that simple. I warned you before the surgeries that reversals are never a sure thing."

"How close can you get to the old me?"

"Close enough to fool your mother," Katzenbach said.

A low bar to the point of being no bar. Cash's mother hadn't seen him since he was eight. More than likely, she had been dead for decades.

"And the reconstruction will be more expensive than the original surgeries."

Cash bumped on the cost projection. The life-saving surgeries had depleted the cash in his go bag. To recapture his lost years, he would have to drain his remaining cash reserves.

"When do you want to schedule the surgeries?" Katzenbach said.

"Soon."

"You know the drill," Katzenbach said. "Payment up front."

Cash laughed. "Hey, that's my line."

***

Finding time alone with Tina proved more difficult than chasing down Katzenbach. Over the last month, she and Gamez had become inseparable, on and off the job. Between her sharp tongue and his slow drawl, their relationship had reached the stage where she routinely completed his sentences.

On Saturday morning, Cash found her alone at the breakfast table and seized the opportunity. "Where's the boy wonder?" he said.

"He's taking a shower."

Cash poured himself coffee and sat at the table with her. "I've got good news for you. I'm pushing up the date to resume my old life. I can move out soon and leave you two alone."

She put down her cup and stared at him. "I don't want you to go."

Cash forced a laugh. "If I left, it would be weeks before you noticed."

"Bullshit."

"You spend ninety percent of your time at Gamez's place, and when you two are here, you spend ninety percent of your time in the bedroom." She started to speak, but he cut her off. "Don't get me wrong. I'm happy you found someone, even if he is a cop."

"Hey," she said, "I'm one too."

"Yeah, well, I'm still hoping that's a phase you'll outgrow." He leaned across the table and filched a slice of toast from her plate. "I talked to Dr. Katzenbach about reversing my surgeries. Soon I will emerge from the cocoon called Carl Meadows and burst forth in all my glory as Cash McCahill."

"Don't get carried away with the caterpillar-to-butterfly analogy," she said. "A snake that sheds its skin is still a snake." She looked up at him. "Will you be safe as your old self?"

"As soon as *Los Lobos* disappears, so does Carl Meadows. For both, their days are numbered."

She pushed her plate away and pulled the cup closer. "It's been nice having a grandfather around."

"Cop or not," he said, "you'll always be family."

Her eyes welled with tears. She tried to speak but gave up.

"I do have a question for you though," Cash said. "Katzenbach charged me an arm and a leg for my original surgeries, and he wants the other arm and leg to reverse the process. How did you afford the work Katzenbach did on you?"

Tina blanched. Gamez's entry into the kitchen gave her a reprieve.

CHAPTER THIRTY-EIGHT

Cash returned to an empty room at the Best Western and mulled over his next move: fight or flight. Freeze was no longer a viable option. A knock on the door startled him. Alone and unarmed, he had no clue who or how many waited outside. Not being able to carry a gun proved damn inconvenient at a time like this.

He grabbed the closest thing to a weapon at hand: the TV remote. Riiiight. If the action turned violent, he could always change the channel. He opened the door an inch or so, sighed in relief, and asked the maid to come back in an hour.

Sami had left a note on the desk, saying she had gone to her apartment to pick up a few things and would be back soon.

Wanna bet?

Cash's call went straight to her voicemail. He searched for her in the hotel, beginning with the workout room and ending at the bar. No sign of Sami, and no one had seen her today. He tried her cell again. Still no answer.

He braced for the worst, expecting to hear that someone had found a body—in one piece or many. More likely, she would never turn up. Either way, it meant more blood on his hands. Another corpse on his conscience.

That Sami had ignored his order to stay put came as no surprise. Nor any comfort. A woman like her could remain cooped up only so long before fleeing the cage. He should never have left her alone and unguarded.

After the third call went to voicemail, he drove to her apartment near downtown. He had confiscated the keys to her place and car, but she would have backup keys for an emergency and an Uber account for transport. He might have slowed her down but hadn't clipped her wings.

Cash entered Sami's apartment and surveyed the damage. Broken glass and busted furniture littered every room. A search team had ripped up carpets and slashed upholstery. Books with broken spines lay strewn across the floor.

The searchers hadn't found the flash drive, but Cash doubted they had left empty-handed. They had Sami now, and she wouldn't stand up to torture, not for long anyway. She would spill everything she knew, starting with where to find Cash.

He couldn't shake an image of Darrell's butchered body in his ransacked apartment. The two toss jobs bore the same fingerprints—not that a forensic team would find any prints of the wrecking crew at either crime scene.

The sadists would take pains to keep Sami conscious while they sliced and diced her. She couldn't placate her captors by turning over the booty they demanded. But there was booty, and there was booty. Though the barbarians wouldn't get their bloody hands on the blackmail material, they could amuse themselves for hours or days with their new plaything.

Death had taken its sweet, sadistic time before freeing Darrell from pain beyond imagination. Even had he been able to surrender the flash drive, it wouldn't have saved his life. At best, it might have cut short the suffering and made for a more presentable corpse. Perhaps even allowed for an open casket ceremony.

Cash climbed from the pit of despair. There was a small chance Sami was still alive. The convergence of her and the search team at the same place and time would not have been a coincidence. The captors must have staked out her apartment complex and waited for her return.

Cash calculated the over and under on how long Sami could withstand torture before giving him up. Thirty minutes max, if the sadists started below her neck. A minute or less if they went straight to the face.

He had a choice of action or inaction. Sit back and wait for the killers to come for him. Or take the fight to Powell and count on the element of surprise. He was halfway to the lawyer's downtown office, when Goldy's excited call sent him speeding in the opposite direction.

The line was bad, and it was hard to understand the old man, but three words came through clearly: Dice. Cold. Killer.

***

A semicircle of cop cars filled the driveway in front of Gideon Bragg's ranch house outside Aledo, Texas, an hour's drive west of Dallas. Inside the ring of cherry tops, crime tape cordoned off the porch. The tape was more symbolic than successful. Cops trooped to and from the house freely.

Parked helter-skelter on the paved road leading to the ranch were a dozen SUVs belonging to the DPD, FBI, DEA, and IRS, along with an equal number of TV trucks bearing station call letters, all starting with K or W.

Cops kept civilians outside the yellow tape but couldn't block TV cameras from shooting footage of the simultaneous searches of the house and barn. Nor could they stop reporters from shouting questions that went unanswered.

Cash recognized most of the media mob by sight and a few by voice. He couldn't see Skyler Patterson among the scrum, but her shrill tone cut through the cacophony.

An acne-scarred cop confronted Cash at the porch. "Set foot inside the tape," Officer Acne said, "and I'll bust you for obstruction." Cash moved back for a wider view of the action. Streams of cops and agents in windbreakers flowed to and from the house and barn, entering with empty boxes and leaving with full ones.

A tragedy of biblical proportions was unfolding before Cash's eyes. A plague of locusts had descended upon Bragg's property. Likely the first of many plagues to befall the hell-fire-and-brimstone preacher.

Cash shouted to Gamez, who was directing foot traffic from the porch. The detective mouthed, Go away. Cash waved at him to come over. Gamez trudged toward him. The two stood on opposite sides of the tape and on different planes, with the detective a step above. "If you get arrested out here," he said, "don't count on me to spring you."

Cash nodded toward the house. "Is Tina inside?"

"She's at HQ, prepping the chief for a press conference at the top of the hour."

"What's up?" Cash said. "I mean, besides the usual trampling of a citizen's constitutional rights." He immediately regretted the crack, which sounded too lawyerly and not at all like a retired cop.

Gamez ignored the remark and lifted the crime tape, not to let Cash in but to allow Bragg out. With his hands cuffed behind his back and a uniformed officer on each arm, the prisoner passed by Cash, whose criminal defense instincts kicked in. "Don't say a word until Goldy gets to the station."

Bragg stopped abruptly, turned toward the familiar voice, and nodded.

"Keep him moving," Gamez told the arresting officers.

Bragg and his escorts weaved through a gauntlet of reporters shouting questions and shooting footage. The prisoner kept mum but didn't shy from the cameras. Far from it. At six-six, he swaggered past the media mob as if he were leading a parade.

The officers loaded Bragg into a cop car, forgoing the ritual of butting the arrestee's head against the roof. Too many cameras around for that old trick. The cherry top fought for every inch, until it broke free of the logjam and took off toward Dallas. The search went on.

Cash turned to Gamez. "What the hell?"

"We got him." The taciturn detective sounded almost giddy. "We caught the Dice Cold Killer. It's Bragg."

Cash shook his head in disbelief. "No fucking way. We showed you the records. He was nowhere near any of the crime scenes."

"No one ever thought Bragg did his own dirty work," Gamez said. "He targeted the trans women, and his followers grabbed them. Maybe his foot soldiers killed the vics, but that doesn't absolve Bragg of the ultimate responsibility for the murders. The blood is on his hands."

"How do you figure on proving that?"

"The missing body parts are no longer missing. Bragg kept souvenirs, and we found them."

CHAPTER THIRTY-NINE

It was past midnight when Goldy, Cash, and Eva gathered in the conference room to go over the search warrant and the inventory of items seized. The raid had stretched to sundown, and cops had slow-walked Bragg's booking, pushing the bail hearing to tomorrow and guaranteeing him at least one night behind bars.

"This damn warrant doesn't tell me jack." Goldy's voice was raspy. "I need to see the supporting affidavit by the agent."

Eva checked the docket online and said, "It's under seal."

"It will remain under wraps for a while," Cash said. In law enforcement, like life, knowledge was power. Sealing the affidavit withheld key information from the defense, such as who or what had sent the cops to Bragg's ranch to search for evidence.

"The warrant did tell us one thing," Goldy said. "It was signed by Randolph Scott. That prick would sign a grocery list if a prosecutor put one on his desk."

Whenever Scott's signature appeared on a warrant, Cash suspected the feds of gaming the "random" assignment wheel to land before the one judge in the courtroom who would rubber-stamp anything from the government. The weaker the evidence of probable cause to justify a search, the stronger the motive to seek out Scott. Also, the more reason to keep the agent's affidavit under seal.

Justice wasn't blind in Scott's court. She just didn't bother to read the fine print.

"The inventory doesn't tell us much either," Cash said. "The cops carted off everything that wasn't nailed down. Phones, computers, papers, ledgers."

"What about this last entry?" Eva said. "I've never seen *human remains* on an inventory before."

Goldy flipped to the last page. "What does that even mean?"

"According to Gamez," Cash said, "they found body parts in a freezer in the barn, presumably kept by the killer as souvenirs. Eyeballs, tongues, ears, hands. Even a penis or two. Whatever was missing from corpses one through eight turned up at Bragg's ranch."

Goldy went from pale to paler. "Then why didn't the sonsabitches write it up like that? Put down four eyeballs, three tongues, two ears, and a penis in a pear tree."

"To the cops," Cash said, "parts are parts." He rose and headed to the door.

"Where do you think you're going?" Goldy's tone warned Cash not to take another step.

Cash said, "Home."

The old man slapped both palms on the desk. "Like hell you are. It's all-hands-on-deck time. We've got to prepare for Bragg's bail hearing tomorrow…uh…today."

Cash smiled. "Good luck finding a judge who'll spring an accused serial killer who has a collection of body parts at his place and shitloads of cash stashed away."

Eva beat Cash to the door and got in his face. "What do you have that's more important than the bail hearing?"

Leave it to the Latina to put Cash on the spot. He was about to embark on the suicide mission that Goldy had interrupted by dispatching him to Bragg's ranch. No way would he involve Eva or Goldy. "I've got a meeting this morning with a big shot attorney who has a deep pocket client in trouble." Cash's every word was true, without coming close to the truth.

"Then by all means, go chase the almighty dollar." Her voice registered equal parts disgust and disappointment. "By the way, you were right about the bugs. We hired an ex-agent, and he found a half-dozen devices planted all over Cash's house."

Cash stopped in the doorway. "Debug these offices too."

"For someone new in town, you sure seem to know a lot." She sounded beyond suspicious. "Are you sure you've never met Cash?"

Cash shook his head. "I don't know him, but I know a little about cartels."

What he didn't know was whether the bugs had been planted by *Los Lobos* or the feds.

***

Cash thought through the timing and site of the ambush of Stewart Powell. On timing, it had to be today. The sooner, the better. If Sami was still alive, her odds of staying so worsened by the minute.

As for the locale, Powell would be untouchable in his Highland Park fortress, protected as it was by the latest in sensors, alarms, and cameras. Mini drones patrolled the gated estate from the heavens. Powell's workplace would be worse. A security force of ex-cops guarded the Bank of America Tower and its tenants, making his penthouse office more impregnable than his mansion.

With home and work sites off the table, Cash had two brief windows of opportunity: at the start or end of Powell's morning commute. He ruled out the former because of the ubiquitous Highland Park Police Department. The HPPD buzzed over and around the stately mansions on Beverly Drive, like bees drawn to honey. Trying to snatch the blue-chip lawyer in or near his home base guaranteed a police response time of a minute or less.

Cash went with the better of two bad options. The fifteen-story parking lot, appended by an underground tunnel to the office tower, offered reserved spaces on level one for VIPs. Cash would bet his law license that Powell had scored a plum spot.

Cash parked on Commerce Street at 6:00 a.m., walked a block to the parking lot, and waited on level one. An hour passed before he sighted the target. Sure enough, Powell had *the* reserved space. His silver Benz pulled into slot number one, the closest space to the elevator bank.

Powell opened the driver's door and got halfway out. A charcoal suit meshed nicely with his salt-and-pepper hair. Cash pushed him back onto the seat and held a pistol to his temple. Or what passed as a pistol anyway.

For a felon like Cash, possession of a firearm carried a five-year sentence. However, Carl Meadows had a clean record, at least until today, and the federal felony didn't apply to a toy Colt M1911 that retailed for $14.95 and fired sponge bullets.

Powell didn't blink. Nor did he call out Cash on the counterfeit Colt. Then again, with the barrel pressed to his head, it would've been tough to get a good look at the gun.

"Who are you?" Powell said.

"My name's not important."

"No, who are you really?" Powell sounded maddeningly calm. "I know who you *claim* to be. I also know that you're not who you claim to be."

No surprise that the lawyer had dug into the background of the ex-cop from Buffalo, whose name and life story Cash had exhumed from the grave. Cash wondered whether Powell had hired private detectives to do the digging or assigned the work to the FBI.

"All you need to know," Cash said, "is that I'm the one holding a gun to your head."

"What do you want?"

"Before we go on a short drive, hand over your phone."

The lawyer hesitated before doing so. Cash removed the sim card and tossed it. He slid onto the back seat and tapped Powell's shoulder with the barrel, a signal to start the car.

Powell keyed the ignition. "Where are we going?"

"To the top floor of the garage."

The Mercedes climbed from G-1 to the roof. Open to the elements, the top level represented the last refuge for tenants and visitors in search of parking. This early in the day, the Mercedes had the entire level to itself. Powell parked in the space closest to the elevator bank and killed the engine. "What now?"

"Hand me the keys," Cash said, "and get out of the car."

Powell complied. They stood alone on the roof, fifteen floors above streets that were coming alive with traffic. A gray haze enveloped downtown. The lot vibrated as a parade of cars corkscrewed to open spaces, the garage filling level by level. Cash gave himself fifteen minutes, maybe less, before they would have company on the roof.

"Where's Sami?" Cash said.

"I don't know who—"

Cash cut him off. "We don't have time for your bullshit."

"You're right about that. Very soon there will be witnesses to what you're doing." Powell sounded sure of himself, as if he had charge of the situation.

Cash injected fear into the dynamic, by pointing the pistol at Powell's gut. "This is your two-minute warning." He checked his watch. "At exactly 7:05, you will do a perfect swan dive off the roof."

"Why would I do that?"

"You were overcome with guilt," Cash said.

"Over what?"

Cash hadn't expected a smidgen of remorse from Powell, but there was too little fear in his voice. "Over what you did to Marty Biddle, for starters. Then to Rocket Rhoden and Darrell Pendergass. Perhaps Sami, too, depending on the shape she's in."

"You don't really expect me to incriminate myself, do you?"

"No. I've listened to Rhoden's recordings. You were careful in what you said. Unfortunately for you, Freeman wasn't. He dropped himself and you in the grease."

There it was. A flicker of fear flashed in Powell's eyes. Time to get down to business. "You have something I want," Cash said, "and I have something you want."

"Sounds like the basis of a trade."

"More like a standoff," Cash said.

"My daughter is about to become the attorney general of the United States, where she will be in a position to make or break you."

"Not if Regina Delgado has anything to say about it."

"She doesn't," Powell said.

"Even with Regina out of the picture, the recordings can take down you, your daughter, and your entire firm. If you release Sami unharmed and leave her and me alone, no one other than me will ever listen to them."

"If it's too late for the girl," Powell said, "what if we agree to leave you alone?"

"If any harm has come to Sami, the recordings go to the *Dallas Morning News*."

Powell's icy façade returned. "That won't prove to be a problem for me."

"And the *New York Times*," Cash added.

Powell frowned.

"I'll throw in CNN for good measure."

The frown deepened.

"I'm going to the Best Western in Plano now," Cash said. "When I arrive, Sami had better be there, no worse for wear." He slid onto the driver's seat of Powell's Mercedes.

"You're adding carjacking to the kidnapping charge?" Powell said.

"Your car will be parked in its regular space." Cash started the Benz and spiraled downward. Lower and lower.

CHAPTER FORTY

Cash returned to an empty room at the Best Western. No Sami and no reason to believe she would ever show at the hotel. Or turn up anywhere. Powell had called his bluff, meaning Sami would be tortured first for info and later for fun.

Cash was packing Sami's clothes when a tapping on the door startled him. He braced for whatever awaited and slowly opened the door. Sami fell into his arms, zonked out of her mind. Eyes glassy. Babbling unintelligibly. Limbs rubbery.

He carried her to the bed and assessed the damage. The torturers had spared her face, but bruises and burn marks covered the bare soles of her feet. Stiff jeans swallowed her slender frame, and a knit shirt hung loosely. Attached to the pants and shirt were Walmart price tags. Raw tracks of tears ran from her bloodshot eyes to her hollow cheeks. Other than her feet, there were no visible wounds, but the invisible ones would last a lifetime.

He let her sleep. Two hours later, he roused her. "Do you want to talk about it?" he said. She shook her head. Just as well.

Wringing the details from Sami would be a challenge for a shrink. Or possibly a job for a sob sister like Eva or Tina.

Much as Sami needed a shower and more sleep, Cash had to relocate them to a new hotel. Powell might have second thoughts about the standoff. "Freshen up," he said, "while I finish packing."

He pulled her to her feet and led her to the bathroom. She winced with every step. He left the bathroom door open in case she cried out or fell.

This time, he would be sure to catch her.

***

Cash upgraded Sami to a junior suite at the Adolphus Hotel in downtown Dallas and told her not to set foot outside the room under any circumstances. The historic hotel was two blocks from Cash's next stop: Goldy's office at Founders' Square.

He found the old man slumped behind his desk and Eva on the couch. Their expressions told Cash that the bail hearing hadn't gone well. No surprise there.

"Hope you had better luck this morning than we did," Eva said. "Any good news?"

"I'm still alive," Cash said.

Goldy snorted. "What's that supposed to mean?"

Cash had already said too much. Determined not to drag them into his death match with Powell, he changed the subject. "Did you get the agent's affidavit?"

"That ain't happening," Goldy said, "not any time soon."

"If you have any bright ideas," Eva said to Cash, "now's the time to share them."

He came up with two but kept them to himself.

* * *

Cash went to Gamez's house and found Tina there. Signs of her touches were cropping up in what had previously been a spartan living room. A crystal vase with fresh-cut flowers had her fingerprints all over it. Same for a lavender scented candle. Could a glass menagerie on the mantle and frilly curtains be far behind?

Gamez fidgeted in a high-back chair and made stabs at small talk with Cash. Clichés about the fickleness of Texas weather, another disappointing season for the Cowboys, the latest cockup at City Hall. He finally gave up and said, "Tina will join us soon."

Cash smiled. "Wanna bet?"

Evidently, Gamez didn't. Good thing too. Another nine minutes passed before she padded into the living room. She wore a black silk robe that stopped short of her knees. Wet hair. No makeup. No shoes. No apology.

Gamez stood. Tina took the chair abandoned by her lover and spoke to Cash. "What are you doing here?"

"Funny," Cash said, "but I was about to ask you two the same question. Shouldn't you be out fighting crime?"

Gamez rested a hand on Tina's shoulder. "The past weeks have been hell. We're taking a day off."

"With the chief's blessing," Tina said. "She's funny that way. We catch a serial killer, and she's cool with us taking a little R and R."

"Only you didn't catch the killer," Cash said.

That brought Tina to her feet. "Save it for the jury."

Cash remained seated. "Hear me out."

"Sure." Tina sounded wary. "Because the way we want to spend our free day is listening to your bullshit defense theory."

"The killer has to be someone the victims knew and trusted," Cash said.

"We've heard all this before," Gamez said, "but here's something you haven't heard. We've got hours and hours of Bragg's recorded sermons, where he repeatedly incites his flock to cleanse the filth from the streets of Dallas."

"One guess as to who your client is calling filth," Tina said.

"If hate speech counts as proof of murder," Cash said, "then you have thousands of suspects to weed through. And that's just starting with your own department."

"We don't have the time or energy to play games with you." The detective's tone signaled a wrap to the conversation. "When you get around to explaining how those body parts turned up in Bragg's barn, we'll talk further."

"Give me the search warrant affidavit," Cash said, "and I'll blow holes in it."

Tina and Gamez exchanged a look. His said no. Hers, hell no.

Cash bid against himself. "If you're afraid to give me a copy, let me read it. No one will know."

"I'll know," Gamez said.

Tina walked to the couch and loomed over Cash. "You're asking us to break the law."

"And risk our jobs," Gamez said.

Cash stood. "I'm asking you to *do* your jobs. If Bragg turns out to be guilty, I'll be the first to throw a parade for you. But if he's not, the real killer's still out there."

Tina and Gamez exchanged another look. This time, their faces mirrored indecision.

Cash cut his ask to the bone. "At least tell me who tipped you to search Bragg's property."

A long silence worked in Cash's favor. He liked his odds that one of the pair would crack, and Gamez did. "An anonymous source phoned it in."

Cash erupted in laughter. "How the hell did you snow a judge into relying on an anonymous tip to issue a warrant?"

The detective's face turned red. "The tip was very specific."

"I'm sure it was," Cash said, "almost as if the tipster had planted the evidence there himself."

CHAPTER FORTY-ONE

Cash gave up on trying to catch Tina alone and off the clock. Once she and Gamez were no longer on the down-low, they had become inseparable. Two sides of the same cop.

Monday morning, Cash ambushed her at police headquarters. "Why are you avoiding me?"

Her frown warned that he had picked the wrong time and place for a confrontation. Civilians packed the lobby. A female officer comforted a crying mother. A baby in a stroller squalled, while two tykes played tag.

"We can't talk here," Tina said.

Cash stood his ground. "We talk here and now. Well, now anyway."

She punched the down elevator button, rather than heading up to her office on the top floor.

Must not be bring-your-grandfather-to-work day.

In the basement, she led him to a windowless room that reeked of ammonia. Except for a calendar from Ace Hardware, the walls were bare. No one had bothered to flip the calendar to the current month or year. They sat across from each other on metal chairs at a metal table.

"Don't show up at my workplace," Tina said, "not while you're on Bragg's team. People will get the wrong idea."

"You haven't answered my question. Why are you avoiding me?"

"After going to the dark side," she said, "don't expect me to roll out the red carpet."

Cash shook his head. "No, that's not it."

"I've been busy." The bags under her eyes backed up the claim.

"Never be too busy for family."

"Spoken like someone who's never had one," she said.

Ouch. Cash had no comeback for that.

Her eyes sought forgiveness before her lips did. "Sorry. I shouldn't have said that, and it's not true."

True enough that the words stung. "You make choices in life," he said, "and live with them." He let her wallow in guilt for a few seconds. "While we're on the subject of life-changing choices, I need to know how you met Katzenbach and, more importantly, how you afforded him."

She went pale. "That was long ago, in a different life."

"It was ten years ago," he said. "You were sixteen and homeless, living hand-to-mouth on the streets of Dallas." Literally hand-to-mouth, he thought, given that picking pockets and giving head had kept her alive.

She stared at the table. "It's a period I'm not proud of."

"Which is it? So long ago you can't remember or so painful you can't forget?"

"The latter," she said.

Cash 's hand covered hers. She didn't flinch or pull away. "I wouldn't force you down memory lane," he said, "if it wasn't important."

"How much do you need to know?" Her voice faltered.

"Everything." From defending her for a decade, he could recite her rap sheet in his sleep, beginning with her first juvie bust at fourteen. He had been at her side for the touchpoints where society had chosen correction over compassion, punishment over protection, the cane over the carrot.

"I'm waiting," he said.

"I paid Katzenbach the same way I paid you. A little here and there."

"I don't buy it. I know what I billed you." He didn't mention that her invoices had long since been written off. "And I know how much Katzenbach charges. His fees have put me in a hole."

"I'm not lying." Her eyes met his, briefly. "Katzenbach got paid over a period of years. Not directly by me but indirectly."

"You lost me." Not really, but he needed to draw her out.

"I didn't find Katzenbach, so much as he found me. Well, a friend of his did."

"Who's the friend?"

"Benny," she said.

"Last name?"

She shook her head. "He was always called Benny from Vegas. I met him only once, but he paid for my operations."

"Why would he do that?" Cash asked as if he didn't know.

"Benny has a thing for trans teens. The younger, the better. Bonus points if there was no family around to interfere."

"How does a predator like Benny find prey in Dallas?"

"That's where Katzenbach comes in. He and Benny are running buddies. Katzenbach is a high roller in Vegas. What the casinos call a whale."

The connection between Katzenbach and Benny became clearer but triggered more questions. "How did you get on Katzenbach's radar?" Cash asked.

"Through Brandi," Tina said.

Like Tina, Brandi Foxx had been a repeat client of Cash's and more of a charity case than a cash cow. The last time he had seen Brandi, she lay on a slab at the morgue with double deuces tattooed on her big toes, marking her as victim number four of the Dice Cold Killer.

"Brandi was the most beautiful thing I'd ever seen," Tina said. "Katzenbach had done the work on her. I pressed her on how she had afforded the surgeries. For the longest time, she dodged the question. Finally, I wore her down. Looking back on it now, I think she was trying to protect me."

Tina teared up. "Anyway, she introduced me to Katzenbach, who introduced me to Benny."

Based on Cash's knowledge of the flesh trade gleaned from two decades of representing prostitutes of all stripes, there would be a pimp in the mix. "How does Benny in Vegas keep track of working girls like you and Brandi in Dallas?"

"For starters, it wasn't just me and Brandi in Dallas. Benny had lots of boys and girls in dozens of cities. From time to time, he sent me and Brandi to work other states and brought in subs to backfill for us here."

None of which surprised Cash. Sex traffickers played a shell game, moving tricks around to con customers into thinking today's menu featured fresh meat.

"And Katzenbach worked on all of these girls?" he said.

"Not sure about that, but he did the surgeries on me, Brandi, and several more I could name."

"I still have the same question. Who looked after you and Brandi in Dallas? Certainly not a busy doctor like Katzenbach."

She shook her head. "That's where Rocky came in."

"Your piece of shit pimp," Cash said.

"Not the term he would use."

"It's what I'd call him to his face." Cash drew the line at pimps. Rocky hadn't been the first or last pimp to try to hire Cash. *Never going to happen.*

Over the years, Tina had rejected every sweet plea deal Cash had presented to her and always for the same reason. The deals would have required her to turn on Rocky. Cash chalked up her refusal to loyalty, fear, or a healthy mix of the two. "Didn't he dump you when you turned twenty?"

"I was nineteen, but who's counting?" She smiled.

Cash didn't.

Tina continued. "Benny caters to a clientele that shares his taste for trans teens. Katzenbach makes sure that Benny has a full stable, cut to his specs."

Cash shook his head. "Why would a successful surgeon like Katzenbach get involved with a sex trafficking ring? I'm sure Benny pays top dollar, but so do the doc's legit patients."

"I don't know," Tina said, "but Katzenbach and Benny go back a long way. I got the sense that Benny had something on Katzenbach."

"Could you pick Benny out of a lineup?"

"I think so," she said. "I went to Vegas with Katzenbach once, and that was the only time I met Benny. He was inspecting the merch."

"Did Benny ever…?" Cash didn't finish the sentence.

Tina shook her head.

"Katzenbach?"

"Lord no. As far as I know, Katzenbach never touched any of us girls outside the operating room."

Cash was skeptical. "Not even on the trip to Vegas?"

"Definitely not there. He was too busy gambling."

"The doc's a big gambler?"

"More like an addict," she said. "I watched him play blackjack at Caesar's. OMG. He took over a table and played all five hands at the same time, five thousand dollars a hand. In thirty minutes, he dropped a half mil."

Suddenly Katzenbach's willingness to join a criminal conspiracy didn't seem so far-fetched. If Benny held markers, he had the doc by the balls. The image of Katzenbach's crown jewels in Benny's hand reminded Cash of the body parts found in Bragg's barn. Among them were a pair of testicles.

The balls were now in Cash's court.

CHAPTER FORTY-TWO

In Cash's recurring nightmare, he held a stick of dynamite in each hand, the fuses lit. To survive, he had to toss both sticks as far as he could and run like hell the other way. Try as he might, the deadly devices stuck to his palms.

He woke in a sweat. His eyes were slow to adjust to the dark. His mind, slower to process his surroundings. It dawned on him that he was in Tina's apartment. Alone. Her absence had become the rule and not the exception, now that she and Gamez were a couple.

The nightmare reflected Cash's new reality. In one hand, he possessed recordings so explosive they could destroy Stewart Powell, his law firm, and a roster of blue-chip clients, including Longhorn Investments. In the other, he had the goods on Katzenbach and his sex trafficking partner, Benny from Vegas.

Two smoking guns in his grasp, and he didn't know what to do with either. There was only one certainty. At any second, both could blow up in his face.

At 3:17 a.m., Cash gave up on sleep and trudged to Tina's study, which he had converted to his war room. He flipped on the lights and passed through a gauntlet of ghosts on the right and left. The eyes of the dead bore down on him.

Photos and articles about Marty Biddle and his death in prison plastered the east wall. The collection featured shots of the chief suspects, including Big Black, Warden Stockman, Lou Watson, Gerry Freeman, Stewart Powell, and his daughter Jenna. Everyone on the wall of shame had the motive, means, or opportunity to silence Biddle permanently. A few hit the trifecta by having all three.

Except for Big Black, the suspects on the east wall weren't the type to get their hands dirty, but they could pull strings to make a murder look like a suicide. Cash reserved a blank space on the wall for the lowest rung on the conspiracy ladder: the inmate or guard who had slipped the noose around Biddle's neck.

The gallery on the west wall still featured the mug and morgue shots of the eight victims of the Dice Cold Killer that Tina had arranged. Interspersed among the pictures were articles on the slayings, most written by Skyler Patterson of the *Dallas Morning News*. According to rumor, she had inked a six-figure deal for a true crime book on DCK, with the contract contingent upon the killer's conviction or death.

East or west, right or left, up or down…all roads led to the unlikely pairing of Rocket Rhoden and Stewart Powell. The murdered mouthpiece and the pillar of the bar were the common link between the investigations, the bridge between the walls. Both lawyers had sold out Biddle, and both had represented Katzenbach.

Two festering injustices pulled Cash in different directions. One reality tipped the balance toward the west and the DCK investigation. Changing the ruling on Marty's death certificate from suicide to homicide would mean the world to Bettina and the twins, but it wouldn't bring back Biddle.

Sure, Sami Priest lived in fear of Powell and his henchmen, but she had brought the danger upon herself. Greed had gotten her into this jam, and she counted on beauty to bail her out.

Not this time, girl.

In contrast, the victims of the Dice Cold Killer were innocents, at least in a relative sense. Cash would make book that the cops had lived down to expectations by nabbing the wrong man, putting more trans women at risk. Maybe even Tina.

DCK wouldn't stop at eight. He would roll the dice again.

***

Cash held off until 6:15 a.m. before ringing Gamez's doorbell. Early hour be damned, this was an emergency. Besides, no cop on day shift should sleep past six.

Gamez came to the door, wearing a sweat-stained Aggie T-shirt and gym shorts. "It's way too early."

"I need to talk to you and Tina. Now," Cash said.

Tina appeared at the door. She wore an A&M jersey that fit her like a mini-dress and held a coffee cup with both hands. "Don't make us call the cops," she said.

"You are the cops." Cash barged into the house. "Start acting like it."

Instead of like horny teenagers playing hooky.

Cash settled onto the sofa, a sign he planned to stay a while. Tina and Gamez followed him into the living room. Both remained standing. Clearly, they didn't share his plan.

"Make yourself at home," she said, with sarcasm to spare.

"No time to beat around the bush," Cash said, "not with a killer on the loose."

Gamez sighed and took a seat. "I don't know how things worked in Buffalo, but on any given day in Dallas, there are probably a dozen killers roaming the streets. We'll get around to catching most of the bad guys sooner or later."

"DCK is still out there," Cash said, "and he'll strike again."

Tina rolled her eyes. "OMG. This is like that movie *Groundhog Day*. Every morning you pop out of your hole and spout the same lines, and every day we clobber you."

"That's more like whack-a-mole," Cash said.

"Whatever game you're playing," she said, "just stop."

Cash slid to the edge of the sofa. "Today is different. I know who the Dice Cold Killer is."

"Let me take a wild guess." Gamez took Tina's sarcasm to a new level. "It's not Gideon Bragg."

"It's Dr. Katzenbach."

Stunned silence greeted Cash's revelation. The reaction from the cops came in stages. First, Tina and Gamez turned slowly toward each other, eyes wide and mouths agape. Next, the detective mouthed *WOW*. Finally, Tina burst into laughter.

"It's exactly like *Groundhog Day*," she said. "A comedy."

"It's a tragedy," Cash said, "and we have a duty to end it."

"Take my advice," she said, "and don't repeat your crank theory outside this room. Accusing someone of a crime is textbook defamation. If you make those accusations publicly, Katzenbach will own you."

He already does.

"It's not defamation," Cash said, "if it's true."

"Another word of advice," she said. "Think twice before attacking that particular doctor."

She didn't say more but had said enough. Katzenbach was about to take a scalpel to Cash's face, as Tina knew but Gamez didn't.

"This sounds like a family problem," Gamez said. "You two carry on, while I tackle my third set of reps." He kissed Tina and left the room.

Tina moved to the sofa and sat next to Cash. "Now that we're alone, it's time for a reality check. You do realize that you're only *playing* my grandfather, right?"

"Not the first time you've used that line," he said.

"And probably not the last."

"Give me thirty minutes," Cash said, "to lay out my case against Katzenbach."

"You have fifteen, before Robbie and I hit the shower."

It was his turn to roll his eyes. "TMI."

"I needed to drive home the point that you're not really *mi abuelo*."

CHAPTER FORTY-THREE

Cash and Tina sat on deck chairs by the small pool in Gamez's backyard. He pitched the case against Katzenbach in twenty minutes. She spiked it in two.

"Let me get this straight." Her voice toggled between amusement and astonishment. "Your theory is that Katzenbach made the victims beautiful to exploit them in the sex trade and later killed them when the risk of exposure became too great."

"Something like that," Cash said. "Maybe he feared the law. Maybe he feared his fellow traffickers. Either way, the theory fits Brandi Foxx like a glove."

"But not the others."

"We have to subpoena Katzenbach's records," he said. "Medical files, financial documents, travel receipts, tax filings, phone bills, texts, emails, everything."

"Where do you get *we*? Just like you're not really my grandfather, you're not really an ex-cop either."

"But—"

"But nothing." Her tone took a sharp turn toward annoyance. "Don't you realize that Robbie is every bit as haunted by the killings as you and I are? Even more so. He has dug into the victims' backgrounds from birth to death, looking for connections, for anything that links them. He's interviewed friends and family."

"Has he explored the Katzenbach angle?"

"He's exhausted every angle."

"How many of the victims had been Katzenbach's patients?" His question came off as a challenge.

"Four."

Cash was taken aback. It wasn't the answer he expected. Not even close. "Well, how many worked in Rocky's stable?"

"Three."

Again, her response came too quickly to challenge. Cash recalibrated his goal. As a defense lawyer, he won cases by knowing more than the government did. Here, he clearly knew less. Winning her over was a lost cause, but he worked to keep her talking and glean as much intel as he could.

"Seems your side has done some spadework." He sounded chastened, without really feeling so. "Did you know that Katzenbach hired both Rhoden and Gerry Freeman of Powell's firm?"

"For what?" she asked.

Cash shrugged.

"Could've been for anything," she said. "Taxes, a DUI, whatever."

"Both Rhoden and Freeman were at the surgeon's side during Gamez's interview early in the investigation," he said, "before you joined the force."

She rolled her eyes. "Omigod! I get it now. Katzenbach wounded your fragile ego by hiring Rhoden instead of you, and that makes him a serial killer."

"You're way off base," he said. "Katzenbach didn't hire me because of my connection to you."

"You really need to get over yourself." She left the chair, sat on the edge of the pool, and circled her feet in the water. "FYI, early in the investigation, an anonymous donor put up a hundred thousand dollars for information leading to the arrest of the Dice Cold Killer."

"And the anonymous donor is?" he asked.

"Remaining anonymous."

Bingo. She had divulged information he could use. By all but outing Katzenbach as the donor, she had put him back in play. Sick fucks had a history of worming their way into the investigation of their crimes. That not only allowed them to monitor the progress of the police but also fed their sense of superiority to the world.

"Stick to being a defense lawyer," she said, "where you can play fast and loose with the facts. Leave the discovery of what really happened to us."

Cash left Gamez's house with confidence in his theory shaken but not shattered. One stop down, two to go.

***

Cash timed the second stop of the day for noon, when he could be certain of catching Goldy and Eva at the office. Wednesday was chili rice day at the firm. Every hump day, Eva picked up lunch at a hole-in-the-wall called Hanoi Henry's, a block from the federal courthouse and 8,417 miles from Hanoi.

Henry was a Vietnam vet who had mastered the art of cuisine at a POW camp. His takeout shop had only three items on the menu: chili rice for $5.95, more chili rice for $7.95, and even more chili rice at $9.95. The customer base consisted mostly of courthouse hacks.

Eva placed lunch on the conference room table. Chili rice for her. More chili rice for Goldy. Even more chili rice for Cash. Heartburn as the second course for all three.

Goldy belched before getting down to business. "Meadows, you damn well better have some good news for us. Every day that Bragg rots in jail is another day he threatens to fire us and hire new lawyers. We're hanging on by a thread."

Cash figured as much. Cutthroat was the kindest term for the competition. With a client in the tank bleeding money, sharks were circling.

"We've been getting a lot of good press on this case," Goldy said.

Well, press anyway.

"I'd sure as hell hate to piss away the PR bonanza by getting ourselves shitcanned," Goldy said.

Cash stirred the bowl of chili rice until the ribbons of grease on the surface swirled into the mix. "I've got great news. I found a better suspect for the slayings."

He spent ten minutes laying out the case against Katzenbach. The jury of two perked up three times. First, when Cash pointed out that the surgeon had done work on four of the victims. Again, upon disclosing the six-figure reward for tips. Finally, upon learning that Katzenbach had hired Rhoden and Freeman for his defense.

Each positive reaction from the pair, however, sparked pushback of equal or greater force. "That leaves four victims who were *not* Katzenbach's patients," Goldy said.

Eva piled on. "And five with no known connection to Tina's pimp or the mysterious Benny from Vegas."

"Even if your wild-ass theory about Katzenbach held water," Goldy said, "what's his motive for killing the ones who weren't his patients?"

"I'm still tying up loose ends." Cash sounded defensive.

Goldy belched again. "Your theory gave me heartburn."

"That's the chili rice talking," Cash said.

They finished lunch in silence. Two bases touched. On to the third stop of the day before heading home.

***

Despite sentencing Sami to solitary confinement in her suite at the Adolphus Hotel, Cash didn't expect to find her there. He didn't. Instead, she turned up at the first place he looked: the shoe department of the downtown Neiman Marcus, a few blocks from the hotel.

Red soles flashed the Louboutin brand. Her red face copped to going AWOL.

"Buy sneakers instead," he said. "You'll need them to run for your life."

She lifted a leg and twirled her ankle, modeling a shoe for him. "Like them?" The stiletto heel looked like a weapon.

"Let's go," he said.

"After we enjoy an early dinner at the Zodiac Room. I'm sick of room service."

"Do you know why baserunners get picked off?"

She had a blank look. "What sport are we talking about?"

"Baseball."

"No clue," she said.

"They get cocky and careless. A runner starts by taking a safe lead off the bag. The pitcher throws over, but the runner returns to the base in plenty of time. The runner gains confidence and extends his lead. Another throw. Another safe return. Each time the runner drifts farther from base. Until wham. A pickoff catches him between bags, and he's tagged out."

"There's a shorter way to tell me not to leave my hotel room," she said.

"Okay, don't leave your hotel room."

"After our dinner at the Zodiac."

Cash relented. Though there were only a handful of early diners, he took the most secluded booth and the lookout post, facing the entrance.

"To what do I owe the rare pleasure of your company?" Her voice had an edge.

"We have a decision to make," he said. "We can't go on hiding forever."

A waiter took their orders. Greek salad and iced tea for her. Falafel and black coffee for him. Popovers and strawberry butter for the table.

"The only thing we need to decide," Sami said, "is how much to demand from Powell in return for the flash drive. We need enough to set us up for life."

We? Us?

Cash lost his appetite. She hadn't learned a fucking thing from being kidnapped and nearly killed, much less from the fates of Rhoden and Darrell. He lay four twenties on the table and walked out, without taking a bite.

***

With three stops of the day behind him, Cash returned to Tina's dark apartment. As soon as he opened the door, the smell of smoke set off an internal alarm. He wasn't a smoker. Neither was Tina or Gamez.

A smoker had invaded the apartment and left behind a lingering odor. There were other signs of an intrusion. Magazines, books, and reading glasses were slightly off-kilter. Not by much but enough to send a message.

He went through the apartment, room by room, closet by closet. Nothing missing, but something had been added. In the study, a new photo joined the gallery of the Dice Cold Killer's victims. A picture of Tina in her police uniform filled position number nine in the hit parade.

CHAPTER FORTY-FOUR

Alone in Tina's apartment, Cash took stock of his limited options over a breakfast of burnt toast and black coffee. He faced grim facts and hard choices. For starters, Sami was a lost cause, gripped by a fatal case of greed. Her fixation on the blackmail scheme doomed her.

Let the dead bury the dead.

He alone knew the location of the thumb drives. It had to be that way. The recordings had already taken out two lawyers, with Sami on deck. He wouldn't risk the lives of Eva, Tina, or Goldy, even if it meant Powell skated on three murders.

Still, the current standoff couldn't hold forever. Powell hadn't stayed on top by leaving loose ends. The goon squad would come for Cash. Maybe not today or tomorrow, but soon. When they did, he would suffer torture beyond bearing. If he coughed up the location of the drives, those would be his last words. If he held out, it would be the silence before his last breath.

That left him with no trusted ally to call on and two options for beating Powell to the punch: law enforcement or the press. One option was bad. The other, worse.

Skyler Patterson of the *Dallas Morning News* was the poster child for bad options. It wasn't Skyler he distrusted as much as the higher-ups. Skyler would trash her mother for a byline. Dirt on Powell and Katzenbach would be gold to her, but both stories would be hard sales to her chickenshit editors, despite the corroboration provided by the recordings.

Perhaps Skyler could sway the suits. In addition to the lure of serial bylines, profit would push her to go to the mat. With a book deal on the Dice Cold Killer already in the bag, a political scandal embroiling Powell and his Fortune 500 clientele could net her another contract. In a publish-or-perish world, two books were better than one.

Regardless of how the internal politics of the paper played out, both Powell and Katzenbach would soon learn that Cash had gone to the media. The press leaked worse than the police, and the prosecutors, worst of all.

The Skyler option was bad, but the law enforcement route would be worse. Jenna Powell's position as the US attorney in Dallas and attorney general-in-waiting cinched that. She had the juice to protect her father and punish his enemies.

Two options before him. Both sucked, but the choice was clear.

***

Cash vetoed Skyler Patterson's first three suggestions for a meeting place and time: Mattito's, Gloria's, or Mesero. All three venues would be rocking during happy hour, which meant too many eyes on the odd couple.

She couldn't break free to meet until 5:00 p.m., when the tax fraud trial she was covering adjourned for the day. That gave Cash time to tie up a loose end.

He knew where and when to find Gamez without Tina at his side. The detective emerged from the men's steam room at the downtown YMCA gym, naked except for a towel wrapped around his waist. "Are you stalking me?" Gamez said.

Cash had stripped down to a towel as well. "Go back in the sauna. We need to talk."

"Sorry, but I don't have time." Gamez didn't sound sorry. "Tina and I have an early dinner date, and she hates it when I'm late."

"Give me ten minutes." Cash held open the sauna door. "It's about Tina."

As Gamez entered the sauna, Cash noticed the Marine tattoo on his right shoulder. *Semper Fi* in red, white, and blue ink. Always faithful. Cash was counting on that.

They were alone in the steam room, which was roughly the size of a large closet. A lone overhead bulb glowed orange. Hanging on the cedar walls were a digital clock that flashed 4:31 and a temperature control that read 148 degrees.

The cop ladled water onto a bucket of heated stones. The stones hissed, and steam shimmied to the ceiling. The men slumped on benches across from each other, sweating like punched out boxers. Wispy clouds made Gamez seem more like a ghostly presence than an actual person. The concern in his voice cut through the fog. "What about Tina?"

"You need to get her out of Dallas," Cash said. "Out of the state would be better, and in a faraway country, best of all."

As steam clouds thickened, even the ghost of Gamez disappeared. The silence proved more oppressive than the heat.

Gamez broke the silence, not the heat. "What makes you think she'll listen to me?"

"Because she loves you." Cash surprised himself by saying it aloud. Accepting it as the new normal came as a bigger surprise.

"I think I love her too." The cop sounded shaky. No surprise. It was a big step for him. He had to be taking shit from the force and his family. Probably even questioning what the attraction to her said about him.

Cash told Gamez about the break-in at Tina's apartment. The intruder had taken nothing but had taped Tina's picture to the west wall of the study in the spot reserved for victim number nine of the Dice Cold Killer.

The news shook Gamez, as evidenced by the catch in his voice. "If this is some kind of trick to help Bragg beat the rap—"

Cash cut him off. "It isn't. I'm trying to keep Tina alive."

"We have the Dice Cold Killer behind bars."

"Are you willing to bet Tina's life on that?"

A long silence proved Gamez wasn't. "Tina won't accept that she needs protection."

"All the more reason we have to protect her," Cash said.

The detective ladled more water onto the rocks. "Where could we send her?" A finger snap echoed like gunfire. "Hey, I've got an idea. You're from Buffalo, right? Maybe you've got a friend there, a cop or an ex who will put her up for a while."

"I was thinking more along the lines of Europe or South America. And I hear Australia is nice this time of year."

"She'd never go," Gamez said.

"Unless it was pitched to her as a romantic vacation for two." Sweat beaded Cash's brow. "She wouldn't turn down a getaway to the Gold Coast with the man she loves."

Gamez scoffed. "Like two cops could afford that."

"You keep her out of the country for two or three weeks," Cash said, "and I'll spring for plane tickets, hotels, meals, and all the beer you kids can drink."

By Cash's rough calculations, that would deplete his cash reserves well below the up-front money needed for his surgery. To keep Tina safe, he would put off the operation for months, even years.

"What's the catch?" Gamez said.

"No catch but two conditions. Don't tell Tina who's picking up the tab, and don't make her feel like a second-class citizen. If you can't handle the shit you're catching from so-called friends or the looks you'll get from strangers, let her find someone who can."

***

Cash had settled into the darkest booth at Lee Harvey's Bar and Grill south of downtown when a text from Skyler Patterson pinged his iPhone:

Sorry to no show but pulling an all-nighter. Read about it tomorrow.

Cash shook his head. It had damn well better be Pulitzer material, because she could kiss goodbye two monster stories.

CHAPTER FORTY-FIVE

The headline hooked Cash:

PROMINENT LAWYER FACES
FRAUD CHARGES.

He scrolled the article to make sure Skyler hadn't skewered him, which was like checking the obits to confirm he was still alive. On further reflection, the headline alone should have assured Cash that the story wasn't about him. Skyler had called him many things in person and print: colorful, controversial, embattled, disgraced, felon.

But prominent? Never.

Still, the headline brought back the second worst day of Cash's life: his arrest on a bogus jury tampering charge. Every harrowing second of the night replayed in his mind in slow motion. The storming of the Ritz by federal agents. The hard takedown by Bureau bullies. The perp walk through a gauntlet of reporters, which led to his lockup for two years and the loss of his law license for three.

Since his release from Club Fed five years ago, he had regained the license. The Bureau retained a stat for his arrest and conviction. He kept the felony on his record, along with the scars on his psyche.

The prospect of Stewart Powell's fall from the pinnacle to prison lifted Cash's spirits. Surely just desserts awaited his nemesis. After all, who better fit the billing than Powell? Who was more prominent than he?

A spoiler alert in the first paragraph dashed Cash's dream that justice would be done. Gerry Freeman emerged as the butt of the story. Stewart Powell's name appeared nowhere, and the firm name surfaced only once, in connection with a written statement from a shill.

The statement read: "In serving our clients and the public, the attorneys at Powell, Ingram & Gardner adhere to the highest standards of ethics and enjoy an international reputation for professionalism and integrity. We are deeply saddened and disappointed that a former partner has fallen short of our lofty standards."

The release said nothing and yet said it all. Describing Freeman as a former partner pegged him as the fall guy for the fraud. The firm had branded Freeman a rogue, canned him, and served him up to the feds.

On a second read, Cash noted less what the article said than what it didn't. While Skyler got the byline, her editors' fingerprints were all over the piece. Her standard MO was to go for the jugular. The final version delivered paper cuts to everyone but Freeman.

The night before, Cash had planned to turn over the recordings to Skyler, deeming her a better bad option than Johnny Law. Now, however, it seemed as if there had never been a real choice. Powell, the press, the police, and the prosecutors all merged into a single enemy camp.

Without a plan C, Cash clung to the original strategy: Skyler or bust. He didn't believe for a second that Freeman had gone rogue and trusted that Skyler wouldn't either. Cash's license, liberty, even his life depended on it.

He called the reporter at 6:36 a.m. She was slow to answer. "Who are you, and what do you want?" She sounded groggy.

Cash introduced himself as Carl Meadows and reminded her that she had canceled their meeting the previous evening. "Did I wake you?" he said.

"Not for long." Her tone sharpened from groggy to cranky. "You have ten seconds to tell me why you're calling before I hang up."

"I read your story this morning," Cash said.

"I'll send you a gold star."

Good sign. Her sarcastic side had surfaced. "You missed the big picture," he said.

"Send a letter to the editor."

"Should I also send your editor the recordings between Rhoden and Gerry Freeman? How about the ones between Rhoden and Stewart Powell?"

"You have recordings?" Her voice shed the last remnants of sleep.

"If you want to hear them, be at my apartment in an hour. If you're not here by then, I'll call the next reporter on the list." With no next reporter and no list, he gave Skyler the address of Tina's apartment and hung up.

***

Thirty minutes later, Skyler arrived at Tina's apartment wearing red sneakers, mismatched socks, faded jeans, and a purple TCU sweatshirt. No makeup. Wild, frizzy hair. They sat at the kitchen table, each armed with a cup of coffee. She got down to business. "Who are you?"

Cash gave his alias and fake occupation. "We have met before." He didn't specify when, where, or why.

She didn't ask or act as if she gave a shit. "Who are you working for?"

"That's confidential."

"Are you trying to take down Powell or derail his daughter's rise to AG?" she asked.

"They're not mutually exclusive."

Her green-gray eyes narrowed. "Why did you reach out to me?"

"You and I are pursuing the same story," Cash said, "but from different angles. The recordings are too hot for me to sit on any longer. They've already gotten two lawyers killed. The more people who listen to them, the safer I'll be."

"If all you want is a broader audience," she said, "why not put them online?"

"They need context, which is where you come in."

"Then let me hear them."

"If I turn over the flash drive to you, how do I know you won't bury it?"

"If I can confirm the recordings are the real deal and not doctored, I'll milk them for stories from now until the cows come home."

That was good enough for Cash. She had spun lesser scandals into series that ran for months and even years. He left the kitchen and returned with a thumb drive and a laptop. "We don't have time to listen to everything." He slipped the drive into the port. "Here's a sample to whet your appetite."

"I'll need to take the drive with me," she said.

"Patience, grasshopper."

He hit play and made it through three conversations, two between Rhoden and Freeman and one between Rhoden and Powell, before the barbarians breached the gate.

CHAPTER FORTY-SIX

A loud bang brought Cash to his feet. A beat later, Skyler rose. The pounding of boots on a hardwood floor echoed down the hallway. Shouts of "FBI" split the air. Agents in SWAT gear with guns drawn executed what the Bureau euphemistically called a "dynamic entry." The rest of the world called it a raid.

Without a word passing between them, Cash and Skyler executed a perfect play. He tossed her the drive and powered down the computer. She slipped her hand under her jeans and put the drive where it wouldn't be found.

Not without a cavity search anyway.

FBI agents flooded the kitchen and fanned out, with enough firepower to take down a terrorist cell. They cleared a path for Stanley Bowers, the Assistant Special Agent in Charge of the Dallas office. He swaggered to the center of the room. His porcine lips twisted into a smirk.

Cash's blood pressure spiked. He had a history with the prick Bowers. Fortunately, Carl Meadows didn't and hoped to keep it that way.

Bowers's role in the raid made sense. Powell needed a flunky to do his dirty work. With designs on the director's job in DC, Bowers would play ball with a power broker who bankrolled scores of senators.

"Is this your apartment?" Bowers asked Cash.

Cash shook his head. "I'm a guest here." So far, no false statement to the feds, which meant he hadn't committed a felony. Today. Yet. He pressed his luck by adding, "Neither of us can consent to a search of this apartment." That sounded lawyerly, and he vowed to dumb it down.

"Then it's a good thing we don't need your consent." Bowers slapped a document on the table. Cash picked it up and flipped through the pages. The heading and signature line were all he needed to read. Judge Ferguson had signed a search warrant that green-lit the goons to tear the place apart.

"There's a nicer way to do this," Cash told Bowers. "You knock on the door. I open it. You hand me the warrant. I step aside to let you in. Saves wear and tear on the place, and you don't need an army to do a two-person job."

Bowers snickered. "If either of you so much as breathes in my direction, I'll haul your sorry asses to jail and lose the paperwork." He turned to the agent on his right, identified by her nametag as R. Martinez and recognized by Cash as Rosa. "Put these two in separate rooms," Bowers told her. "Don't let them leave or make a call."

"Hate to be a stickler for the rules," Cash said, "but we're entitled to call an attorney."

"You can call your mouthpiece," Bowers said, "when I get around to booking you, which shouldn't be long."

"I don't need a lawyer," Skyler said, "but I should call my editor at the *Dallas Morning News*. She's waiting to hear from me, and boy, do I have a story for her."

That wiped the smirk from Bowers's face. Even with a patron like Powell, he couldn't afford to piss off the hometown paper. Skyler played her ace: the work badge with her name, address, and picture. Her credentials trumped the search warrant.

Bowers stared at the badge before looking up at Skyler. "Miss Patterson, you're free to leave." He turned to Cash. "And who the hell are you?"

Cash pulled out his wallet and tendered the fake driver's license. *That* counted as a false statement to a fed and was thereby a felony, but it seemed like a lesser offense than if he had said the alias aloud.

Bowers handed back the license. "Meadows, you stay."

After Skyler departed, Cash enjoyed the escalating frustration of the agents. The search team burned hours looking for an item that had left the building, right under their noses.

* * *

Except for breaks to shit, piss, or drink, Cash remained a prisoner in the study, under the eye and thumb of a minder. Agent Rosa Martinez didn't have to say a word to signal her displeasure at drawing guard duty. Cash tried to break the ice by extending his hand to shake and got a glare in return. He lowered the hand and his expectations.

It was going to be a long day.

Cash could hear but not see the calculated wreckage visited by agents on a mission. Rosa would be the face of the search for him, and it wasn't a bad face to study. Dark eyes. Proud cheeks.

Mocha skin. Full lips pressed together so tightly that it would take a crowbar to pry them apart.

Cash tried again to spark a conversation. "What are they looking for?"

"Evidence of a crime," she said.

"If you tell me what they're after, maybe we can speed up the process."

"If I tell you, I'll have to kill you." It didn't come off as a joke.

Still, he took those few words as a sign of a slow thaw. Every hour or so, he tried to kick-start a conversation. His efforts went nowhere.

Around lunch, an agent swung by the study and said, "Is this asshole giving you trouble, Rosa?"

"Like he could." Gruffness didn't come naturally to her. It was an act for her fellow agents and not a particularly good one.

Marty Shafer of the IRS walked past the open study door, whistling a familiar tune. Even after he was out of sight, the song lingered. Seven years ago, he had whistled the same song while cuffing Cash in the Ritz lobby: "Folsom Prison Blues."

Cash kept a poker face as his world threatened to fall apart. He had given Bowers a fake driver's license and an alias. The feds could bust him for that, giving Shafer the pleasure of slapping on the cuffs again.

"Why is the IRS crashing the Bureau's party?" Cash said.

"Every now and then," Rosa said, "we let the paper pushers tag along on searches and pretend to be real agents."

"There has to be more to it than that," Cash said.

She stood and stretched her legs. The SWAT gear had her sweating. "To the tax man, everything looks like a tax crime."

"What's the Bureau investigating here?"

"I don't know and wouldn't tell you if I did."

"Mind if I ask the tax man?"

"Knock yourself out," she said.

***

When Shafer spelled Rosa on guard duty, she couldn't flee the study fast enough. With the arrival of the IRS agent, a whiff of Old Spice wafted into the room. He barely glanced at Cash and stared at the morgue shots on the west wall: the gallery of the Dice Cold Killer's victims.

Shafer was long in the tooth to play second banana to the Bureau on a shit detail. His contemporaries at the IRS's Criminal Investigation Division, CID for short, were supervisors. They sat behind desks and shuffled papers. Thirty years in, Shafer was still a grunt.

That told Cash one of two things: Either Shafer was very bad at his job, or he had been too good at it. Either he had royally fucked up a case, or he had undertaken a righteous investigation of an untouchable target.

As a defense lawyer, Cash had tangled twice with Shafer, and their record stood at one and one. Not bad for either side. Shafer knew how to build a tax case, and he wouldn't be the first agent punished for aggravated competence.

"You're looking at the wrong wall," Cash said.

"Not if I'm looking to solve seven murders," Shafer said.

"Eight."

The agent turned away from the wall and toward Cash. "You seem to be obsessed with serial killings. Do you get off on blood and gore?"

"My granddaughter is with the DPD, and she's working the DCK investigation. Like the victims, she's a trans woman, so I have a strong interest in seeing the killer caught."

"He has been caught," Shafer said.

"I don't think so." Cash changed the subject. "By the way, this is her apartment that you guys are trashing. Mind telling me what you're looking for?"

"That's above my pay grade."

Cash bought that. The Bureau didn't have a reputation for sharing. "Look at the other wall. That's where you'll find your tax case."

Rosa's return to the study killed the conversation. On the way out, Shafer handed Cash a business card. "Any time you want to report a tax crime, give me a call."

Cash pocketed the card. "I may do that."

Shafer stopped at the door. "And if you happen to be the tax cheat, we'll work something out."

CHAPTER FORTY-SEVEN

Dusk descended on Dallas before the search team left Tina's apartment. They didn't take Cash's computer or cell phone, having imaged both during the day.

No sweat. Cash hadn't downloaded the recordings on either device.

Cash's call to Tina went unanswered. He left her a message that he was on his way to Gamez's house and called Goldy from the car. "Remember an agent named Marty Shafer?"

"Sure," Goldy said. "Mean as an ex-wife and works the criminal side of the Service."

"What's the book on him?" Cash had a vague recollection that the agent had stepped on the wrong toes. "Specifically, how does someone spend thirty years in a bureaucracy like the IRS and never rise above field agent?"

"Another case of good deeds never going unpunished," Goldy said. "Before you miraculously passed the bar, the IRS transferred Shafer from Detroit to Dallas. He hit the town like a tornado, targeting rich tax cheats. It was a field day for us defense counsel, but it made him a slew of powerful enemies.

Shafer didn't give a shit on either count. He was on a mission, and his supervisor at the time had his back."

Goldy succumbed to a coughing fit. He went on with a raspy voice. "The tax cheats took their beefs and their checkbooks to DC, where the chickenshits in Congress did what they always do. They taught the agency a lesson by slashing its budget. The IRS got the message: Leave the big boys alone, or we'll cut your funding to the bone."

Cash recalled a saying that agents lived and died by: Small cases mean small problems. Big cases, big problems.

"Either Shafer didn't get the message," Goldy said, "or he's a slow learner. He went after an oil magnate who happened to be the biggest contributor to the Texas governor at the time. That brought Shafer's career to a screeching halt. The oil man and the crooked guv, well, they're doing just fine."

"I'm surprised Shafer didn't get his ass fired," Cash said.

"That would've been doing him a favor. Fire a flamethrower, and he becomes a loose cannon, or worse, a whistleblower. Keep him buried in a basement counting paper clips, and the brass can muzzle him."

Cash thanked Goldy for the history lesson and hung up. He had found a place to unload one big case, maybe two, and in the process, saddle Shafer with one big problem, maybe two.

* * *

Tina came to the door in a black robe. She flipped on the porch light but didn't invite Cash in. "What is it now?" Her tone toggled between annoyance and anger.

"Are you going to let me in?" he said.

"Do I have a choice?" She didn't wait for an answer before stepping aside.

"I sure as hell didn't," Cash said, "not when the FBI broke down the door to the apartment this morning." He handed her the search warrant. "An early Valentine from your boyfriend's asshole buddies at the Bureau."

She never made it past the first page. "This is *my* apartment." Her voice shook in anger.

"I know. I was there."

"What were they looking for?"

"They wouldn't say."

"What did they take?" she said.

"If you believe the inventory signed by Bowers, they took nothing."

"I don't believe him," she said.

Oddly enough, Cash did, at least this once.

She sighed in surrender. "You'd better come in."

He followed her to the living room. The lights were low. An incense candle on the mantle flickered. "Robbie," she called out, "come here, honey."

Gamez lumbered into the living room and nodded to Cash. The detective wore pajama bottoms and no top. His washboard abs glistened with sweat. Tina handed him the warrant. As he flipped through it, his brow furrowed. He asked Cash the same two questions she had: What were they searching for and what did they take?

Cash had a good idea what the agents were after but didn't share it with them. It was too dangerous to expose the couple to the deadly flash drive. "Whatever they were looking for," he said, "apparently they didn't find it."

"You should've called me." Tina sounded upset.

"They took my phone and computer to image and kept them all day."

"What do we do now?" Tina said.

"Nothing," Cash said. "Until we figure out what's going on, you two lie low and steer clear of Tina's apartment."

And of me.

"Want me to put out feelers to friends in the Bureau," Gamez said, "to see if I can find out what they were after?"

Cash shook his head. "You have bigger fish to fry. There's a serial killer on the loose. Stay focused on catching him."

"We'll agree to disagree on DCK," Gamez said. "As far as the DPD is concerned, we've got our killer in a cage."

Cash wouldn't get anywhere with Gamez, so he took another tack. Divide and conquer. "I need to speak to my granddaughter…alone."

"Whatever you want to say to me," Tina said, "you can tell us both."

Gamez pulled her closer. "Hear him out and then show him out." He kissed her cheek and left the room.

"Let's go outside," Cash said.

She followed him to the backyard. The pool lights cast the water in a shimmering turquoise glow. Tina and Cash sat on deck chairs. Crickets chirped, and wind whistled through magnolia trees.

"Do you know why innocent folks get convicted?" Cash launched into a lesson that Goldy had hammered into him a hundred times. He ignored her eye roll and went on. "Tunnel vision. Cops focus their investigation too early on one suspect. They magnify every detail that points to his guilt and dismiss everything that doesn't."

"Robbie knows what he's doing." Her voice had an edge.

"He's young and under tremendous pressure to pin the murders on Bragg."

"We found the missing body parts in your client's barn," she said.

"Based on an anonymous tip. Pretty damn convenient."

"We've been through all this." She sounded exasperated.

"You're right," he said, "and it's not why I came tonight. Given what went down at your apartment today, Carl Meadows needs to disappear soon and clear the way for Cash's comeback."

"Is that safe?" she said.

"Safer than the alternative. *Los Lobos* is on its last legs, and living in Carl's skin gets more dangerous by the day."

"Do you want me to line up Katzenbach?" she said.

Cash locked eyes with her. "I want you to stay a million miles away from him."

"How do you plan to recapture your lost youth without him?"

He had been asking himself the same question for two days and still had no answer.

CHAPTER FORTY-EIGHT

Cash set out to track down a pair of agents as different as night and day: let-it-slide Leroy and stick-up-the-ass Shafer. He started at the A-Hole. Good odds that one or both would gravitate to a bar that bled red, white, and blue. But mostly blue.

Rosa Martinez hovered over the jukebox. She had been Cash's babysitter during the raid on Tina's apartment. Shedding her SWAT gear in favor of a black T-shirt and jeans made her seem smaller, slimmer, and sexier.

Cash hesitated at the door of the cop bar, but Rosa's selection of "Friends in Low Places" lured him inside. Nobody walked out on Garth.

A black bodybuilder grabbed Rosa from behind, wrapping his massive arms around her small waist. He lifted her off her feet and carried her to the center of the room. He moved around tables to make space for a dance floor.

The brute twirled Rosa like a rag doll. When the song ended, she clutched the arm of the closest bystander to steady herself.

Her anchor turned out to be Cash. "Sorry, mister, but…." She pushed away from him. "Meadows, you've got some nerve showing your face here."

"Or maybe I've got nothing to hide," Cash said.

"More likely, you're still trying to find out what we were after."

Wrong, but he was willing to let her think so. "Whatever. I'm ready to bury the hatchet." He extended his hand to shake.

She slapped away his hand and walked to the jukebox for her next pick: "Hit the Road, Jack." Cash ignored the invitation to leave and settled on a barstool.

Based upon past visits to the A-Hole, tonight's crowd was atypical in two respects. There were more feds than cops, and DEA agents outnumbered their Bureau counterparts.

Dozens of drug agents had gathered to celebrate the guilty verdict of a GHB kingpin in Ferguson's court. Given the defendant's connection to several rapes and at least two deaths, he was a lock for a life sentence.

Cash nursed a lager and bided his time. Backslappers plied Leroy with drinks and toasted his late career success as the lead agent in a press-worthy case. Already sloppy drunk, Leroy would nod off soon, at a table or on the floor.

Three stools to Cash's left, Shafer drank alone at the bar. A twinge of sympathy for the solitary soul passed quickly. There is no lonelier person on the planet than a tax agent at a party.

Cash pondered who to approach first. While Shafer would likely bail from the bar earlier, Leroy might pass out at any moment. Shafer's proximity tipped the scales. Cash slid to the stool next to him and said, "Congrats on the GHB verdict. The DEA always drafts you guys to trace the money trail. You get the grunt work with no glory."

"Story of my life." Shafer sounded more resigned than bitter. He took a hard look at Cash. "Takes balls to walk into a cop bar the same day we tossed your place."

"Like I mentioned a dozen times today," Cash said, "it wasn't my apartment. You ransacked a cop's crib. That's got to be bad karma."

"Not if he's a dirty cop."

"*She* is my granddaughter," Cash said, "who couldn't be cleaner."

"And you? How clean are you?" Shafer turned away from Cash.

"Squeaky, but I can point you in the direction of someone who isn't."

"I'm all ears," the agent said.

"He's one of the highest paid doctors in Dallas."

Shafer snickered. "Do you know what we call a doctor who cheats on his taxes?"

Cash shook his head.

"A doctor," Shafer said.

"Do you know what we call an agent who can't see a crime committed under his nose?" Cash said.

It was Shafer's turn to shake his head.

"An agent."

"You seem to have forgotten where you are." Shafer smiled. "You're surrounded by dozens of federal agents, all armed, liquored up, and looking for trouble. Any one of these hotheads would be more than happy to kick your ass."

"I'm counting on you to get off your ass and investigate a surgeon who's taking money under the table. Big money."

Shafer put down his mug and faced Cash. "Doctors who cheat on their taxes are a dime a dozen. There's no way my supervisors will authorize me to open a file on a prominent doctor, certainly not on your word."

"What if the surgeon is in bed with sex traffickers?" Cash said.

Shafer's jaw slacked. He had swallowed the hook.

CHAPTER FORTY-NINE

An hour ticked by in Katzenbach's reception area, bringing Carl Meadows that much closer to his second death and Cash McCahill to his resurrection. Cash felt out of place among the pampered patients, who skewed female, lily white, and dressed to kill. It looked like a casting call for *The Real Housewives of Dallas.*

Second thoughts dogged Cash. Why would a surgeon with a Midas touch sully his hands with dirty money from sex traffickers? What if there was no link between the trafficking ring and the DCK killings? What if Tina and Gamez were right, and the cops had the killer behind bars? With Bragg in lockup, the DCK killings *had* stopped.

Katya, the receptionist, made the wait tolerable, not by saying or doing anything but simply by being there. She defied age and could be anywhere from thirty to fifty. Sculpted features like hers didn't occur naturally, at least not in Cash's experience. The pale redhead was proof of a god whose name was Katzenbach.

At the seventy-minute mark and counting, Cash tried for the third time to strike up a conversation with Katya. "Is Katzenbach always this busy?"

Her condescending smile chastised him for the lame opening line. For Carl Meadows, a retired cop from Buffalo and a grandfather to boot, the odds of engaging Katya on a personal level were less than zero. Even for Cash McCahill, a single attorney a generation younger than Carl, the odds were daunting.

"Please take a seat, Mr. Meadows, and I'll call you when Dr. Katzenbach is ready to see you."

When Cash's time came, Katya ushered him into the doctor's private office and left the men alone. Katzenbach pressed a button on the desk. The door locked with a click.

The office hadn't changed since Cash's last visit a year before. To his right, a Warhol self-portrait reflected the doctor's expensive taste in art. On the opposite wall, two diplomas touted his educational pedigree: Brown undergrad and Harvard Med. A loop of classical music over the sound system added to the air of culture.

Seated across the desk from Katzenbach, Cash experienced a crisis of confidence and conscience. His second thoughts spawned third thoughts. He had concocted an image of the doctor as an evil mastermind. In the flesh, he looked grandfatherly and harmless. White, wavy hair. Trim beard. Ruddy complexion.

The notion that Katzenbach would conspire with sex traffickers seemed farfetched, even foolish. Guilt over unleashing a bulldog like Shafer on the skilled surgeon gripped Cash.

"How may I help you, Mr. Meadows?"

"When we're alone like this," Cash said, "you can drop the alias. I miss the sound of my real name, and you're one of only two people who know who I am." An afterthought hit him. "Are you recording this conversation?"

Katzenbach answered "No" without hesitation. Cash didn't believe him. "Does your receptionist know who I am?"

Katzenbach hesitated this time. "She knows everything that goes on here, and she can be trusted."

Cash bought the first half of his answer but not the second. "How do you know my secret is safe with her?"

"Because I created her."

Cash resisted the temptation to slap the smug smile from the doctor's face. "You're not a god," he said.

Katzenbach's smile spread from smug to galling. "Ask Katya about that or, better yet, Tina. And if you still have doubts, look in the mirror."

He had Cash there. Carl Meadows was so different in age and appearance from Cash as to be a new person. Probably the same held true for Katya.

If Katzenbach was truly godlike, he had the power to create and destroy. The prospect of going under a knife wielded by someone Cash had flagged to the IRS set off alarms. If the doctor were to find out....

It wouldn't take long for Shafer to contact Katzenbach. Given that, the sooner Cash underwent the surgery, the better. He even toyed with the idea of asking Shafer to hold back for a month or two but worried the odd request might backfire and prod the agent to accelerate the investigation.

Cash played the odds that he still had a window before Shafer sprang into action. "It's time to roll back the odometer," he said, "and raise Cash McCahill from the dead."

"Is it safe to revert to your old self?" Katzenbach sounded more curious than concerned.

"The question," Cash said, "is whether Carl is in greater danger now than Cash would be, and the answer is yes." Whatever harm a dying cartel could do to Cash paled compared to the hellfire that Powell could inflict on Carl.

Katzenbach ordered Cash to stand. He hesitated but stood.

"Empty your pockets," the doctor said.

Cash balked. "What's going on?"

Katzenbach repeated the command, and Cash complied. He dumped onto the desk an iPhone, wallet, car keys, and seventy-two cents in change.

"Now what?" Cash said.

Katzenbach opened a desk drawer and pulled out a hand-held metal detector, the size and shape of a pickleball paddle. He walked over to Cash and waved the detector over every inch of Cash's six-foot frame.

Katzenbach clicked off the detector. Cash had passed the screening.

"Put the items back in your pocket and sit." Katzenbach returned to his chair behind the desk. "You know what the surgery costs and how to make the payment."

Cash nodded. One hundred thousand dollars in cash. Full amount up front. Terms so incriminating as to be the stuff of Shafer's dreams.

"And you can make the new me as good as the old me?" Cash said.

"Better. As a bonus, I'll shave five years from your face."

"Do you still operate on Thursdays and Fridays at Forest Park?" Cash said.

Katzenbach put the wand back in the drawer. "I won't be performing your surgery there. I'll do it here Saturday morning."

Cash started to protest but held his tongue. In the end, Katzenbach held the scalpel and the leverage. Cash's face and fate were in the doctor's hands.

CHAPTER FIFTY

Skyler Patterson had one tell for a lie and another for bad news. The former triggered rapid blinking. The latter, a head cock to the right. The tilt of Skyler's head braced Cash for a bummer.

Angela's Café served home cooking by an aged staff to a more aged clientele. The comfort food came with a side order of sass. In a back booth, Skyler and Cash kept their heads low and voices down. She finished a cup of coffee before dropping the bombshell. "You don't have Powell."

Cash lost his appetite for the breakfast burrito and hash browns on his plate. "But the recordings…."

She shook her head. "I've gone over them twice, as have my editors."

"I can identify Powell's voice, if that's the issue." Desperation ratcheted his voice higher and louder.

"The evidence on him is too thin," she said. "Rhoden recorded scores of conversations, but only two with Powell. Both were short, cryptic, and not all that incriminating."

"You have to put Powell's conversations in context." Cash dialed down the desperation. "He was the mastermind of the conspiracy to keep Biddle from flipping. If that's not obstruction, I don't know what is."

Skyler's fingers drummed a file folder next to her plate of *huevos con chorizo*. She stopped drumming, pulled a document from the folder, and slid it toward Cash.

He skimmed the factual resume, which recited the *facts* underlying Gerry Freeman's guilty plea. The pleading, signed by Freeman and his lawyer, was too long to read at the table. Besides, the first two pages gave the gist. Freeman was taking a fall for the firm, his partners, and their clients.

"Can I have this copy?" Cash said.

She shook her head. "It's still under seal."

"How did you get it?" Cash didn't expect an answer and didn't get one.

Her forefinger tapped the document. "This pleading is the other reason Powell will skate. Freeman swears under oath that the scheme to sacrifice Biddle was his idea and he executed it alone, without the knowledge or participation of anyone else at the firm. This is Powell's get-out-of-jail-free card."

"And that doesn't stink to you?"

"Of course it does," she said, "but with no smoking-gun recording and no witness to nail Powell, you don't have the goods on him."

Cash asked the waiter to package his untouched burrito for takeaway. His appetite might return by lunch, though he wouldn't bet on it. "What's Freeman looking at?"

"As a payoff from the firm," she said, "or a sentence from the court?"

"Both."

"On the sentencing side, the plea deal caps his exposure at five years, which is good news for him. The bad news—of the eight judges in the federal courthouse, he drew Fergy. I'm betting on the full nickel."

"And his windfall from the firm?"

"When Freeman rolls out of the joint in roughly three years," she said, "his share of the partnership will set him up nicely for life. *If* he can manage to stay alive inside."

"I doubt Freeman will survive a year behind bars," said Cash, who had done two. Without the protection of Big Black, Cash never would have made it out alive.

"Freeman will know to keep his mouth shut," Skyler said.

Cash slid the factual resume back to her. "Or maybe his mouth will set him free."

* * *

The burrito survived the lunch hour by the skin of its tortilla. Cash had placed it in the microwave when Marty Shafer of the IRS called. Cash skipped lunch to speed to the seventh floor of the federal courthouse.

Shafer's digs looked more like a storage room than an office, with cardboard boxes stacked floor to ceiling against two walls. The other walls were bare, except for a framed, black-and-white photograph of Frank J. Wilson, the treasury agent who had taken down Capone and the patron saint of grunts like Shafer.

Allergic to paperwork, Cash sneezed all the way to his seat. "You really should go electronic, Shafer, and give yourself a little room to breathe."

The agent scoffed. "I'm old school."

In more ways than one.

The longer Cash stared at Shafer, the more closely he resembled Wilson in the photo. Both were balding, wore wire-rimmed glasses, and had long, lined faces. Both looked as if it pained them to smile.

"Your tip on Dr. Katzenbach didn't pan out." The agent sounded matter-of-fact, as if he had expected the outcome.

Cash slumped. The day kept getting better and better.

"Are you saying Katzenbach's returns included the money from Vegas?" Cash sounded incredulous.

"I can't answer that."

"Because you don't know or won't say?"

"Because I *can't* say."

"Let me see his returns," Cash said.

Shafer shook his head. "That would violate Title 26 of the United States Code, Section 7213, and land me smack dab in prison."

It was Cash's turn to shake his head. "Damn. I would've bet my license that the money from Vegas flowed under the table."

"What license would that be?" the agent asked.

Cash covered the slip. "My private investigator's license."

"Much as I'd love to pull your meal ticket for sending me on this snipe hunt," Shafer said, "I can't in good conscience take the bet, because I have inside dope." He stroked his chin. "I can tell you this much without breaking the law. Katzenbach passed a full audit five years ago."

"Can you tell me who represented Katzenbach in the audit?" Cash said.

Shafer nodded. "He had two lawyers. The late Rob Rhoden and prison-bound Gerry Freeman."

Cash smelled a bribe. "Maybe Katzenbach's lawyers got to the auditor."

"No way," Shafer said. "I've known the revenue agent for twenty years, and he's a Boy Scout. Any hint of a bribe, and Katzenbach would already be behind bars. It was a clean audit. Every dollar made in the clinic reported. Offset by every dollar blown in bad investments."

Cash made it to the door before turning around. "What can you tell me about the bad investments?"

"I'm sure you've heard the expression 'doctor deals'."

"Sure," Cash said. "Being easy marks, doctors can't wait to pour good money into sinkholes."

"P.T. Barnum should've said there's a doctor born every minute." Shafer almost managed to smile at his own witticism. "Katzenbach poured millions into an investment based on his own patent. He even went public with the startup. The venture tanked, giving him a carryover loss for years."

The intel reeled Cash back into the office, where he noticed something eerie about Frank J. Wilson's photo. Wherever Cash went, Wilson's eyes followed him.

Shafer's eyes likewise tracked Cash the whole time.

CHAPTER FIFTY-ONE

Cash lay awake at night, inventorying Katzenbach's office from memory. Every detail reinforced the image of a paragon of knowledge, achievement, wealth, and taste. The Warhol self-portrait, Ivy League diplomas, classical music, flawless receptionist. All fed by and feeding the doctor's insatiable ego.

After taking stock of what had been on display, Cash considered what had not. Most puzzling was the absence of any trace of the patent or the public company mentioned by Shafer. No certificate, plaque, or press release. Nothing to celebrate the breakthrough and the startup it had spawned.

It was out of character for an egomaniac like Katzenbach not to showcase his achievements. In that respect, he reminded Cash of Rocket Rhoden, whose office walls exhibited his history of acquittals.

Only one explanation made sense. The path to fame and fortune promised by the patent and public company had gone off the rails. The hit to the bottom line must have been hard. The blow to the surgeon's ego, harder.

Inventions flop. Startups sink. Happens all the time. There had to be more to the story than a simple setback in business. Perhaps the ill-fated patent still dogged the doctor.

What Cash knew about intellectual property could fit into a thimble, with room left for the fingertip. He needed a patent lawyer and knew where to find one. During his final semester at law school, he had enrolled in an IP class but dropped out after the first lecture. The technical jargon reminded him of the lone tax class he had suffered through. He had no desire to revisit that misery.

More off-putting than the subject matter had been his classmates. Couldn't throw a textbook in the class without hitting an engineer. Chemical. Mechanical. Electrical. Every type of engineer except the train kind. The prospect of competing against the Mensa mob had sent Cash flying out the door.

There was a reason Hollywood didn't make movies about patent lawyers.

* * *

The next morning, Cash ambushed Winthrop Putnam III on the steps of SMU's Underwood Law Library. The stooped professor didn't look a day older than ninety. Then again, he hadn't looked a day older than ninety when Cash had been a third-year law student, twenty years ago.

Horn-rimmed glasses swallowed Putnam's peanut-shaped face and magnified his leaky eyes. Liver spots dotted the hand that gripped the stair rail.

"Did you take my class, young man?" The pipes were shockingly strong, reminding Cash of Goldy's rolling baritone. For both lions in winter, the roar would be the last thing to go.

Cash smiled at "young man." It would be a stretch to call Cash McCahill young, and it bordered on crazy to describe Carl Meadows that way. Thick as Putnam's glasses were, he might need a stronger prescription.

"No sir. I'm an investigator, not a lawyer. I have a few questions about a patent, and they say you're the dean of the patent bar."

"Do you want to apply for one?"

"No. My questions concern a particular patent from about a decade back."

"Fire away," the professor said.

Cash gave him a bare bones background, divulging only the name of the patentee and the approximate year of the application. Not that Cash knew more. The professor asked about the nature of the invention, but Cash had no clue.

"What is it you want to know?" Putnam asked.

"Everything you can dig up. Whether a patent was granted and if so, the rest of the story. The history of competing patents, lawsuits, licensing, whatever."

The prof stroked his flaccid chin. "Give me a thousand dollars and two days, and I'll have your answer."

"If I make it two thousand, can I get my answer tomorrow?"

***

Cash kept the conversation light and loose while sampling an appetizer of Greek meatballs and feta cheese. Eva savored a second glass of the house red and vetoed Goldy's third attempt to order ouzo.

"You're not the boss of me," Goldy groused.

"Guess again." Her no-nonsense tone chased away the waiter.

Cash had reserved a private dining room at the Greek Isles in case things got out of hand. Colorful scenes of Mediterranean beaches plastered the walls, and the pungent odor of garlic triggered Cash's taste buds.

"If you're trying to wine and dine me for more work," Goldy told Cash, "you'd better get Miss Buzzkill to back off and fetch me a real drink."

Cash stayed silent. He would wait until Eva had consumed more wine before springing the news on her.

"I'm not sure what I'm doing here," she said, "other than babysitting Goldy."

Cash raised his wine glass. "Let's toast to new and old friends."

Eva lifted her glass. She wore biker chick black. Lots of leather. No lace. She elbowed Goldy. He grumbled but raised his water glass.

"Are you familiar with a DEA agent named Leroy Lee?" Cash said.

Goldy snorted. "Laziest slug this side of the border."

"That's the one," Cash said. "Leroy delivered some good news recently. *Los Lobos* is on its last legs. Give it a month or so, and they'll be another cautionary tale in cartel history. The next season of *Narcos*."

"Why are we talking about this?" Eva asked.

"Indulge me," Cash said.

She shrugged.

"What always happens to cartels," Cash said, "is that they learn too late the lethal lesson of life and death in the drug world. Hard as it is to rise to the top of the heap, it's a hundred times harder to stay there."

Eva's eyes lit up. "Wait, if *Los Lobos* goes away, then—"

Cash finished her sentence. "Cash can come back."

“Assuming he’s still alive.” Goldy sounded morose.

“Now look who’s the buzzkill,” Cash said. “I have it on good authority that he’s very much alive, rested, and ready to return to the fold.”

Eva’s eyes narrowed. “Are you?” She looked closer. “Who are you?”

“My toast gave you a clue.”

“To new and old friends,” she said.

Cash raised his glass again. “Allow me to reintroduce myself, as your new *and* old friend.”

Eva caught on before Goldy did and unleashed a string of obscenities before throwing her glass at Cash. Fortunately, her aim was not as sharp as her tongue. He dodged, and glass shattered against the wall.

A day that had begun with bad news and progressed to worse news ended with a death threat. Cash took it in stride, confident that Eva might hurt him but would never kill him.

Besides, he had been living under a death sentence for almost a year.

CHAPTER FIFTY-TWO

Cash spent another sleepless night replaying Eva's parting shot as she stormed from the restaurant. The pain in her eyes haunted him more than her words.

The next morning at breakfast, he updated Tina on the timing of the operation. "It's too soon," she said. "As long as *Los Lobos* shows any signs of life, you should put off the surgery."

"In addition to talking to Leroy, I've done my own research. *Los Lobos* is down to a few holdouts hiding in the mountains. The only question is whether the *federales* or *Los Asesinos* get to them first. Either way, they'll be extinct soon."

"Wait until then," she said.

"We're not talking about a simple nip tuck job here. I'm about to undergo a whole series of operations. It was harder than you'd imagine to age thirty years and will be harder still to reverse the process."

Cash didn't share the real reason for rushing the surgeries. He had put Katzenbach on Shafer's shit list, which meant the doctor might go down before the cartel did.

"As pigheaded and overprotective as you've been," she said, "I've gotten used to having you around. Never had a real father in my life before."

"Grandfather," Cash said.

"Never had one of those either."

Cash resorted to the truth. "Since you moved in with Gamez, I've gotten used to *not* having you around."

"When are you going to drop the bombshell on Eva and Goldy?" she said. "If Cash just shows up out of nowhere, Goldy will have another heart attack."

"I gave both of them the news last night."

"How did they take it?"

He winced. "Not well."

"They'll get over it," she said.

"Hope I live long enough to witness that."

Tina lifted the cup with both hands. "I'll stay with you during the surgeries and recovery."

"That won't be necessary," he said, while thinking it might well be. That is, if he planned to survive the operations. Given his suspicions about Katzenbach, however, Tina needed to steer clear of the doctor at all times, but especially while Cash was unconscious.

***

Winthrop Putnam's office was a refuge within a refuge within a refuge. Only the most persevering students braved the trek to Putnam's door on the top floor of Storey Hall, a preserve for tenured law professors. Storey nestled snugly in the bosom of SMU. The private university took shelter in the Park Cities, an enclave of wealth, power, and privilege that had all but dug a moat to keep out the Dallas riffraff.

Crammed bookshelves wrapped around three walls in Putnam's office. Dings and nicks on the mahogany desk testified to the many moves that had marked a forty-year run at the law school. A tobacco pipe rested in the grooved rim of an ashtray. A woody aroma indicated the pipe was more than decorative.

Putnam slid a slim document across the desk. "My report on the patent you asked about."

Cash skimmed the executive summary on page one. "Spell out the key findings in twenty-five words or less." A tall order, given Putnam's profession. The lecturer probably couldn't say hello in twenty-five words or less.

Putnam cleared his throat. "To begin with, a public company called Gemini LLC owned the patent, which covered a formula for an antidepressant. Dr. Katzenbach was Gemini's founder and CEO."

"It was a drug?" Cash said.

Putnam nodded. "Dr. Katzenbach applied for the patent twelve years ago. One of my former students at Powell, Ingram & Gardner handled the legal work, not only in forming Gemini but also in filing the patent application."

The firm name didn't surprise Cash. Every step he took, he bumped into Powell.

The professor went on. "A competitor filed an application for a similar formula at roughly the same time, and the race was on. Both sides threatened to sue, but neither filed suit. Both camps conducted parallel clinical tests. Two years later, Gemini suspended testing and abandoned its patent. The competitor got to the market first and cashed in."

"Why did Katzenbach throw in the towel?"

Putnam shook his head. "You'd have to ask him, his lawyer, or the FDA."

"Would the feds tell me?" Cash asked.

"Doubtful."

"What's your best guess as to why he folded?"

"A couple of thoughts come to mind. Sometimes one patentee buys out the other, but that didn't happen here. If it had, the competitor would've purchased all rights to Gemini's patent, on the theory that two patents are better than one."

"What's the other reason?" Cash said.

"The test results might've doomed Gemini."

"There has to be a way for me to find out what happened."

Putnam filled the pipe with tobacco and lit up, ignoring the raft of no smoking signs posted across the campus. Cash didn't call him on it. After all, he had broken a rule or two in his day.

"Do you know anyone in the drug world?" The professor spoke between puffs on the pipe.

"Quite a few people actually," Cash said.

***

Cash lured DEA agent Leroy Lee to lunch with an offer to pick up the tab. A draft Corona awaited the agent at Dunston's Steakhouse on Harry Hines Boulevard. Harry Hines was the closest Dallas came to a red-light district, with its string of strip clubs, massage parlors, rent-by-the-hour motels, and sleazy bars.

Undercover for most of his inglorious career, Leroy knew the menu by heart and the waiters by name. He ordered the sirloin strip charred to hockey puck hardness, an overbaked potato, and the limitless salad bar.

Cash held his request until Leroy overloaded a salad plate and plopped down at the table. "I need info from the FDA. Do you have a contact there?"

"What kind of information?" Leroy asked.

Cash took that as a yes. "A decade ago, a formula for an antidepressant underwent testing. I need to know the results of those tests."

Leroy snorted. "The feds will never tell you that."

"But will they tell you?"

Leroy licked the creamy salad dressing from his lips. "Spot me another brew, and we'll see."

***

Better than one fed pulling strings was two feds doing so. On the way home, Cash swung by Shafer's office at the courthouse. "I haven't forgotten about your dirty doctor." The tax agent sounded testy. "Give me time, but don't get your hopes up. Like I said before, the doc aced his last audit."

Cash told Shafer about the aborted testing of Gemini's antidepressant formula and the need for details from the FDA. He suggested the agent put the FDA inquiry on the front burner and postpone any interview of Katzenbach for a month or so.

Cash took to heart the agent's warning to keep his expectations low. In a race between the DEA and IRS, it wasn't so much a rematch of the tortoise versus the hare. More like, a slog between the tortoise and the terrapin.

CHAPTER FIFTY-THREE

After Shafer and Leroy struck out with the FDA, Cash called Professor Putnam. "My friends with badges couldn't help. Any suggestions on a backup plan to get the test results?"

Putnam stopped puffing on a pipe and cleared his throat. "You could file a request under the Freedom of Information Act."

Cash had already dismissed that idea. FOIA took too long and usually hit a dry hole. "I don't have the time."

"You could contact the successful patentee," the professor said, "the one whose invention went to market. He might know why Katzenbach folded."

***

He turned out to be she. Before visiting Dr. A. Bell in Houston, Cash did his homework. For starters, the A stood for Angela. She had racked up three degrees from Texas A&M: an undergrad major in chemistry, a masters in the same subject, and a PhD in chemical engineering.

The slim, ponytailed redhead wore a maroon and white warmup that blended seamlessly into her surroundings. She sat on a maroon chair behind a maroon desk. Autographed photos of Aggie sports stars dominated the walls. Not a single picture of a politician of any stripe in sight.

Cash warmed to her instantly. He nodded toward a cluster of patents on the west wall. "You've put your science background to good use."

"I can't take credit for the whole lot." Her drawl hinted at West Texas roots. "Not full credit anyway. I'm the CEO of the Reveille Group. While some of those patents are my babies, we partnered with the inventors on most of them."

"Who's we?" Cash said.

"Reveille is an incubator, funded by a consortium of Aggie angels. Inventors from all over the world bring ideas to us. We pick the most promising and invest whatever it takes to turn their idea into a patent and the patent into a product."

"For a cut of the profits, I presume."

She nodded.

"I need to ask you about a patent application submitted by a company called Gemini about a decade ago." Cash handed her Putnam's report.

Bell didn't read past the first page. She pointed to a framed certificate to her right. "We developed a formula for an antidepressant and took it through multiple rounds of testing. As soon as the FDA approved it, we sold our rights to Johnson & Johnson. The pill is marketed under the brand name of Paxiprofrin and has been available by prescription for five…six years now."

"I'm less interested in the success of your patent," Cash said, "than in the failure of a competitor. What can you tell me about Dr. Solomon Katzenbach or his company Gemini?"

She frowned. "Not much, I'm afraid. Developing a new drug is always a race to the patent office, followed by a race to the market. Early in my career, I realized I could spend my time in the lab or the courtroom. I decided to leave the legal wrangling to Manny Quinn. He's been my attorney for twenty-plus years."

"Mad Dog" Quinn had a reputation as a scorched-earth litigator, a pit bull who would sue a paraplegic for her last penny. "Mind if I talk to Quinn?"

"He won't be able to add much," she said. "As I recall, he sent the competitor's attorney a demand letter, and they immediately dropped their patent application. Wish all Manny's legal bills were that light."

"What does that tell you?" Cash asked.

"My lawyer could beat up their lawyer."

CHAPTER FIFTY-FOUR

A midnight call woke Cash from what had promised to be his first good sleep in a week. "Is Tina there?" Gamez sounded panicky, and he didn't spook easily.

"I assumed she was with you," Cash said.

Because she always is.

"I haven't seen her since she left for work this morning. She called at three and left a message that she'd be late for dinner. Didn't say why." The normally slow-talking detective spoke at a rapid clip. "No word since then. I've called her six times. All went straight to voicemail. This isn't like her."

Cash's mind defaulted to the worst-case scenario. Occupational hazard of a lawyer who had seen the evil that men do, generally to women.

Whatever had befallen Tina, Cash blamed himself. He had rattled too many cages. In the past week alone, he had shared his suspicions about Dr. Katzenbach with a widening circle. That circle must have expanded to the breaking point.

If Katzenbach sensed the authorities were closing in, he would do whatever it took to slip the noose. If he traced his troubles to Cash, everyone in his world would be in danger, starting with Tina.

"I should never have let the suits make her the sacrificial lamb." Gamez's voice welled with regret. "I should've stopped her from joining the force."

"No one could've stopped her," Cash said. "Lord knows I tried. Besides, Tina is no lamb." He had run out of words of comfort, for Gamez and himself. "Have you notified the department?"

"No."

"Call the chief," Cash said. "Tell her Tina is missing and at risk. The blue wave needs to flood the streets."

"What are you going to do?"

"I'll call the hospitals." True, but not the whole truth. Cash didn't mention the first call he would make.

***

Cash phoned the county morgue. A deputy coroner told him that cops had dropped off a trans Jane Doe around midnight. Cash sped to the morgue, fearing the worst. He paced the reception area for fifteen minutes before Tommy Cochoran showed up to escort him to the display room.

Fifteen minutes felt like an eternity. The walk down the corridor, like the last mile to the gallows.

The pot-bellied public servant was in spitting distance of retirement. A tobacco wad bulged his right cheek. As they walked down the hall, Cash fought a sense of foreboding by making small talk. "Busy night?"

"I wouldn't be on graveyard if we weren't slammed day and night, with the cops putting a rush on every job." Cochoran stopped by the body. "Well, not every job."

Case in point. The lonely corpse lay on a gurney, a sheet shrouding her. The outline of the frame was short, slender. Tina's size. Cash's hands shook as he reached for the sheet. Cochoran grabbed his arm and said, "That's my job."

"Shouldn't there be a cop here for an ID?" Cash said.

"If you recognize her, we'll call a patrol officer to take your statement. If not, why waste their time?" Cochoran uncovered her face.

A rush of relief overwhelmed Cash. It wasn't Tina. Not even close. Still, somebody's daughter had ended up as a Jane Doe.

The light-skinned black teen looked small for her age, whatever it was. Her crimson hair fanned out, like a pool of blood. Rope burns ringed her neck, and her eyes were bloodshot.

Cash pointed to her neck. He couldn't speak, not yet.

"Yeah," Cochoran said, "the bloodshot eyes and ligature marks make this an easy call. Homicide. Death by strangulation." He whipped off the sheet, revealing rope burns on her wrists and ankles. "She was bound, but no signs of a struggle. No defensive wounds. No skin or blood under her fingernails. Looks like the bondage part was consensual."

"Was she…?" Cash didn't finish the sentence.

"Semen was found in her mouth and anus. Can't tell yet whether it was pre- or postmortem."

The preliminary findings cleared the Dice Cold Killer for this vic. She didn't fit DCK's demographic: white, a few years older, and with more surgeries under her belt. Above her belt too.

There were also no signs of prolonged torture, no dice tattoos on her big toes, and no missing body parts. Serial killers often took souvenirs, and DCK was no exception. Eyes, tongues, hands, even penises. The sick fuck had harvested them all and hidden them in a safe place.

Well, safe until an anonymous tip led the police to a freezer in Gideon Bragg's barn. The discovery of body parts there proved one of two things. Either Bragg was the serial killer or the target of a tight frame.

The strangling of the black teen would go down as a typical trans killing in Texas. It didn't take much cynicism on Cash's part to predict the slaying would sink to the bottom of a bottomless barrel of unsolved cases. There would be no press conference and no task force in the wake of Jane Doe's death. Not much more than a token follow-up by the police and a passing story by the press.

"Sorry I couldn't help," Cash said.

Cochoran shifted the tobacco wad to his left cheek. "Me too. We need the vic's name to notify her next of kin." He draped the corpse. "Otherwise, she goes down as a Jane Doe for eternity."

While Cash was paying his last respects, Gamez called from the car and shouted over a wailing siren. The detective was hauling ass to the emergency room at Baylor Hospital, where an ambulance had taken Tina.

Beyond that, Gamez knew nothing.

* * *

Cash shuddered every time he entered Baylor Hospital. Twenty years before, his grandmother had died on the third floor. That extinguished his last link to blood family, assuming his mother was gone for good.

Cash found Gamez on the third floor, pacing the waiting room and accosting every doctor and nurse who had the misfortune of crossing his path. He ran to Cash and gripped both arms. "They won't let me see her. Said I'm not family."

"Close enough," Cash said. "I'll talk to the receptionist."

The receptionist stuck to her guns on Gamez but allowed Cash, as the grandfather, to see the patient. A nurse escorted him to a private room and gave him five minutes.

Tina lay awake on the bed. She looked pale and, without makeup, younger than her twenty-six years. "Get me out of here." She sounded groggy. "The nurses wake me every hour for a pill, a test, or a shot. This is torture."

"I think they call it treatment."

"Call Robbie," she said. "He'll come get me."

"Your boyfriend is having a meltdown in the lobby because they won't let him see you. There's a good chance he'll be tased tonight."

Cash sat on the edge of the bed. "What happened?"

"Nothing. I just got a little dizzy. No big deal."

"It's a big deal if it happened while you were driving. Did it?"

She shrugged. He took that as a yes.

"The doctors are overreacting," she said.

"Thanks, Dr. Campos, but I'll want a second opinion on that."

"Don't be a dick," she said.

He smiled. "Funny, you said the same thing to me at our first meeting, more than a decade ago. You were trying to convince me to handle your juvie case, and I was trying to refer you out."

"I won the argument then," she said.

A dark-haired, dark-eyed woman entered the room. She didn't look much older than Tina. Sunita Singh introduced herself as Tina's doctor. "I understand you're the grandfather."

Cash nodded.

"May we have a word outside?" the doctor said.

Tina struggled to sit up. “Whatever you want to tell him, you can say to me.”

Cash kissed Tina on the cheek and turned to Singh. “Let’s step outside. Less background noise.”

Once outside the hospital room, Cash said, “Her fiancé is freaking out in the waiting room. Can we deal him into our conversation?” Describing Gamez as her fiancé stretched the truth, but it gave the boyfriend a shot at entrance.

Singh nodded. She and Cash found Gamez pacing the hall, and the three of them entered a private office appended to the waiting room. Wadded tissues filled the trash basket.

“What’s wrong with Tina?” Gamez beat Cash to the obvious question.

“We have more questions than answers now.” The doc had a faint Indian accent that gave her voice a soothing lilt. “She suffered heart palpitations while driving. Fortunately, she pulled over and dialed 911 before passing out. When she arrived here, her heart rate had elevated to a dangerous level.”

“Is she okay now?” Cash said.

“Her heart rate is almost back to normal,” she said, “but we don’t know what caused the condition. Has this happened before?”

“No,” the detective said. “She’s as fit as—”

Cash cut him off. “Yes. Recently, but I chalked it up to an anxiety attack.”

Gamez stiffened. His lips parted, but no sound came out.

“It might be more serious than that,” Singh said. “We need to run tests.”

“What kind of doctor are you?” Cash asked.

“I’m a heart specialist,” she said.

“Whoever and whatever Tina needs,” Cash said, “I’ll cover it.”

Carl Meadows's go bag was about to go bust. Another reason for Carl, who didn't have a bank account to his name, to morph back into Cash.

CHAPTER FIFTY-FIVE

Gamez caught up with Cash in the hospital parking lot. 2:16 a.m. found them alone on the fourth floor. The gray cloud from decades of car exhaust stung Cash's eyes, throat, and chest.

"How long have you known something was wrong with Tina?" Gamez's tone was accusatory.

Since the meeting with Dr. Singh, Cash had been wrestling with the same question. The answer turned on the meaning of the word "known."

"Do you remember the night Bragg's bullies crashed the vigil in Deep Ellum?" Cash said.

"How could I forget?" Gamez said. "We barely escaped with our skins."

"Before Tina went on stage, she was hyperventilating and had to lean against a car to keep from collapsing. The episode came and went in a flash, and I wrote it off as stage fright. Now I'm not so sure."

"You should've had her tested back then."

A wounded Cash went on offense. "You've been living on and off with her for months. A detective is supposed to notice things like a bad ticker. Or were you too busy fucking her in the short term to give a shit about the long term?"

"Fuck you." Gamez's words echoed in the garage.

The echo stole Cash's thunder and gave him no need to respond in kind. He cooled off. "Tomorrow, we'll get the doc to run every test under the sun. Then we'll have her run them again."

"Roger that." The detective sounded as if he had already bailed from the conversation.

"But while Tina's undergoing tests," Cash said, "I've got a job for you."

"So now I'm working for you?"

"You're working *with* me." Cash let the novel concept sink in. "Do you have the autopsy reports on DCK's victims?"

"I've got access to them," Gamez said.

"I need hard copies tomorrow…I mean, today."

"Why? What is it you expect to find?"

"It's what I expect *not* to find."

***

Cash arrived at the federal courthouse on three hours' sleep and squeezed into the back row of Judge Ferguson's packed courtroom. Gerry Freeman sat at the defense table for his arraignment, with a young attorney at his side. Cash didn't recognize the defense counsel, which was a bad sign for Freeman.

Fergy hadn't taken the bench, and the crowd was buzzing. It wasn't every day a white-shoe attorney shed his Brioni pinstripe for an orange jumpsuit.

The press, including Skyler Patterson, filled the front row. She scanned the room until her gaze fixed on Cash. They nodded to each other. A wry smile from her failed to draw one from him. At least two people in the courtroom were aware that a travesty of justice was about to unfold.

Stewart Powell no-showed, but Paula Marshall, his law partner and Eva's ex, arrived to witness Freeman's fall from grace. Cash didn't recognize anyone else from Powell's firm in attendance.

That was cold.

Arraignments generally take five to ten minutes if the defendant is pleading not guilty but closer to thirty minutes for a guilty plea. Fergy took the bench and started the internal clock ticking. After presiding over thousands of these proceedings, he could recite the script in his sleep.

The judge swore in Freeman and launched into a litany of rights a defendant forfeited by pleading guilty. Rights to a trial, a jury of his peers, to call witnesses on his behalf, and to confront adverse witnesses. Freeman surrendered them all.

The prosecutor filed a signed plea agreement that capped the defendant's sentence at five years, and the judge confirmed the absence of any side deals. Fergy prompted Freeman to state on the record that he was pleading guilty because he was guilty.

Then came the kicker. The prosecutor read into the record a factual resume and filed it with the court. The language tracked the document Skyler had shown Cash at Angela's Café. She had secured the sealed pleading through a source in the prosecution or defense camp. With leakers on both sides, it could have been both.

In the signed statement, Freeman swore under oath that he and Rhoden had conceived and carried out the conspiracy alone and without the participation, approval, or knowledge of others. That got Powell and his firm off the hook. Ditto for Longhorn Investments, Powell's biggest client and the late Martin Biddle's employer.

Cash didn't buy a word of it. Nor would Fergy. However, the judge would go along with the fiction for two reasons. First, the guilty plea wiped a case from his crowded docket. Judges, like prosecutors and defense counsel, played a role in the kabuki theater.

More important, His Honor had an eye on an open seat on the Fifth Circuit Court of Appeals. Powell had scores of US senators by the short hairs and could deliver an appellate bench to a judge who played ball.

Fergy accepted the guilty plea, ending Freeman's last chance to avoid prison and spiking Cash's best shot at solving the mystery of Biddle's death.

* * *

In the afternoon, Cash found Tina roaming the hospital halls. "Shouldn't you be resting in bed?" he said.

She didn't miss a beat or a step. "Shouldn't you mind your own business?"

He kept pace with her. "We need to talk."

"Say what you came to say and shove off."

"In private."

She returned to her room. He closed the door behind them and patted the bed, suggesting she lie down.

"I'll stand," she said.

"The reason I'm here—"

She cut him off. "I don't need you or Robbie sticking your nose in my business. I'm a big girl."

He spoke without thinking. "That's open to debate."

Her eyes flashed and nostrils flared.

"The word big, that what's open to debate." *Not the girl part.* He got back on topic. "Brandi Foxx, we've never really talked about her."

Tina leaned against the door. "Not an hour goes by that I don't think of her. She was my best friend, my roommate, my rock. I wouldn't be alive but for her."

"Brandi introduced you to Katzenbach, right?"

She nodded.

"There's something I've never understood," he said. "You and Brandi were street kids, cut off from family, scrounging for food and shelter. How did you two get on Katzenbach's radar, or how did he get on yours?"

"I told you about Benny from Vegas."

Cash sensed there was more to it. "How much do you know about Brandi's life before she transitioned?"

"Not much. She rarely talked about her upbringing in Oklahoma. There had been a lot of pain, not many good memories."

"When DCK killed Brandi, what did you do with her personal belongings? Did you send them to her family?"

"*I* was her family." A flash of anger jolted Tina's voice. "The clothes, I sent to Goodwill. The rest I put in a storage locker at the apartment complex."

Cash left the hospital to chase another ghost.

CHAPTER FIFTY-SIX

Cash spent hump day connecting the dots. Gamez had given him copies of the files on DCK's victims, including autopsy reports, phone and bank records. The building super had pocketed a big tip by moving the trunk of Brandi's belongings from the basement to Tina's apartment.

In the morning, Cash pored over the victims' files. Among the eight victims were scores of phone numbers and thousands of entries. Page after page of the numbers on both ends of the calls. None of which told Cash anything, except that the women were popular.

The bank records were scant. Most of the vics had accounts from time to time, but the accounts generally remained drained or dormant. Only one account had been flush at the victim's death. For the six months prior to Rosie Perales's murder, seven to eight K a month had been deposited into her account. The cash deposits always varied, but they remained under ten thousand, thereby avoiding an IRS reporting requirement by the bank.

He confirmed that Rosie had been victim number one of the Dice Cold Killer and smelled one of two scenarios: Either she had found a sugar daddy or a blackmail mark.

Cash saved the worst for last. He studied the eight autopsy reports in the chronological order of the killings. The surface similarities among the victims had been widely reported. All had been young, white, trans women.

Likewise, word had gotten out that the corpses were missing a body part, though the missing parts varied. Eyes, tongues, hands, and penises rounded out DCK's souvenir collection, as found in Bragg's barn. The killer had gone Old Testament in meting out punishment.

All this Cash had known before. What he learned from the autopsy reports was that, in addition to a missing body part, all eight corpses were short the same organ. DCK had stolen their hearts.

Literally.

It was as if a doctor had performed heart transplant surgery but forgotten to install a new ticker. After removing the organ, DCK had closed the incision with surgical thread, leaving a crimson X to mark the spot where a heart had been. In death, the vics shared the same scarlet letter.

As far as Cash knew, the hearts were still missing. None had turned up in Bragg's barn. The revelation stoked Cash's fury and fear. He was furious that Gamez and Tina had held back from him a crucial piece of the puzzle. He was terrified that DCK hungered for a fresh heart.

***

Cash skipped lunch and turned his attention to Brandi's trunk. He didn't have a key to the lock, but a crowbar solved that problem. He pried open the rusty lid, and the trunk exhaled a blast of stale air.

Inside were the remains of a life cut short. Make that two lives: Brandi before and after her transition. A stack of report cards traced the regression of Brad Fisher from a stellar student in grade school to a middling one in junior high, and a high school dropout.

Around the age of sixteen, Brandi emerged as who she had always been. Goodbye, Ada, Oklahoma. Hello, Dallas, Texas.

Cash dug through the wreckage of Brandi's dodgy subsistence on the streets of Big D. The trunk bulged with costume jewelry, rainbow-colored wigs, and stuffed animals, but it mostly contained papers. Receipts, court records, flyers, coupons, and photos.

There were hundreds of photos, many with Tina at her side. Shots of the besties posing, vamping, or goofing off. A professional portfolio featured Brandi at her most seductive, seventeen going on thirty-seven. The portfolio revealed her fully clothed, nude, and everything in between.

The photos of Tina took Cash back to their first meeting and the first words she had said to him. He had been visiting another prisoner at the county jail when a scruffy street kid had called out, "Hey, dude, spring me, and I'll blow you."

"Here's my counter," he said. "If I get you out, you agree to stop blowing strangers."

He had called in a chit and arranged her release. She hadn't stopped servicing johns immediately, but she got there.

He left memory lane and searched for a diary or some other shortcut to Brandi's innermost thoughts. No dice. He crammed everything back in the trunk and was about to close it when an epiphany struck. Something didn't add up.

He pulled the birth certificate in Brad's name and the driver's license in Brandi's and placed them side by side. A match on the month and day, but Brandi Foxx was two years older than Brad Fisher.

Who does that? Who adds miles to the odometer?

Other than Cash, of course, but he had a good reason—the desire to keep breathing. Tina had some explaining to do, but Cash had two stops first.

***

Cash found Freddy the Forger at his office, otherwise known as the back booth at Rosita's on Maple Avenue. Freddy barely looked up from his *huevos con chorizo*. He didn't seem happy to see Cash, despite his status as a paying customer. "If you've got a problem with the documents, take it up with the manufacturer. I'm simply the middleman."

Cash didn't call Freddy on the obvious lie. He remained standing and dropped Brandi's license on the table. "Recognize the girl?"

Freddy shook his head.

"How about the license?" Cash said. "Is it your work?"

Freddy picked up the license and held it to his eyes. Flipped it over and back several times. "Good quality but not up to my standards."

"Know who made it?" Cash said.

Freddy shook his head. A less obvious lie.

***

The only person on the planet more predictable than Freddy was Gamez. Cash found the detective in Tina's hospital room. As soon as Cash entered the room, their conversation stopped. Tina looked guilty. Gamez, guilty as hell.

On a scale of one to ten, Cash's pent-up rage flared to an eleven. He didn't care which of the two took fire first, but he wanted to confront them separately. Less chance that way for the pair to get their stories straight.

Cash led Gamez to a coffee shop on the ground floor and said, "Stop holding out on me."

"I don't know what you're talking about." The detective sounded 100 percent defensive and zero percent persuasive.

"When were you going to tell me about the hearts?"

Gamez never stammered, except now. "I g-g-gave you the autopsy reports. You can read, can't you?"

Cash slapped the table. "I can read between the lines too. You and Tina have been hiding the ball from me for the entire investigation."

"How so?"

"You should've told me about the missing hearts," Cash said.

"That intel is strictly embargoed. Only six people in the department know about it. We always hold back something to weed out false confessions."

"Two of the six in the know being you and Tina."

The veins on the cop's temples throbbed. "Besides, what does it tell you about DCK that you didn't already know? That he's a sick fuck? The whole world knows that. That he took body parts? Again, everyone knows."

"Removing the hearts involves a whole new level of depravity." Mid-sentence, a counter argument came to Cash. "Or maybe it doesn't. Perhaps the killer had a reason to take the hearts. Some motive more devious than depraved."

"My hunch is that we didn't find them in Bragg's barn," Gamez said, "because he ate them."

Cash shuddered. He had read about drug cartels that forced initiates to eat the heart of an enemy. *Los Lobos*, the cartel with a contract on him, had posted videos of the initiation rite.

The waiter brought menus to the booth. Cash had lost his appetite. He handed back the menu and ordered coffee. The detective did likewise.

***

"How old are you?" Cash said to Tina.

She pressed a remote control, and the hospital bed jackknifed her into a seated position. "That's not something a gentleman asks a—"

"Cut the crap and give me a straight answer."

She looked flustered. "Where's Robbie?"

"I told him to take a hike." He repeated the question.

"You know how old I am. Twenty-six."

"That's what it says on your driver's license, but how old are you really?" She glanced at the closed door. Cash shook his head. "He's not coming back until I leave, and that won't happen until you shoot straight with me."

"Twenty-four," she whispered.

"Why lie about your age, and why add years?"

"It goes back to a question you asked in the past, about how I afforded Katzenbach. Brandi and I were desperate to do the surgeries, but we couldn't come close to affording them, not even when we worked for Rocky. We found a way to pay for them."

"How?"

"We became test subjects for a new drug Katzenbach had developed. The tests ran for six months, and the payments covered our surgeries. Brandi and I went through the tests and the operations together."

Cash saw where this was going. "And being sixteen at the time, you two needed parental consent to participate in the study."

"Not just to the study," she said, "but to the surgeries as well. There's no way in hell that her parents or mine would've consented to either."

"By claiming to be eighteen, you two cut your parents out of the loop."

She nodded.

Cash dropped Brandi's driver's license in Tina's lap. "Who made the fake licenses for you and Brandi?"

"Dr. Katzenbach's assistant took care of all that."

***

Back at the apartment, Cash rummaged through Brandi's trunk again and found what he was looking for. An authorization signed by her to be a subject of a drug study by Gemini Labs.

CHAPTER FIFTY-SEVEN

Photos on the walls of Dr. Sunita Singh's private office at Baylor Hospital captured her parasailing, surfing, scuba diving, kayaking, and rock climbing. A woman for all seasons.

Seated behind a desk, she looked even younger than she had on the hospital floor. The dates on her diplomas gave Cash some comfort that she had the experience to treat Tina: a BS *summa cum laude* from Princeton fifteen years ago and an MD *magna cum laude* from Johns Hopkins a decade ago.

The doctor got down to business. "Your granddaughter shows signs of atrial fibrillation."

"Give it to me in English, Doc."

"She has an irregular heartbeat."

He winced. "How serious is that?"

"We take all cases of AFib seriously, but we have more tests to run before making a final diagnosis."

"My job involves reading people," Cash said, "and I'm pretty good at it. When I look at you, I see someone who's holding back."

Her dark eyes narrowed. “My job entails gathering the necessary data, and I’m pretty good at mine too.”

He didn’t doubt it. “Call me when you’re ready to share more.” He rose and placed a business card on her desk. If things went as planned, the card would soon be obsolete. Come Saturday, the name and number would vanish, along with Carl Meadows.

“Please sit, Mr. Meadows.”

He did.

“I read people too,” she said, “and my take is that as soon as you leave here, you’ll google atrial fibrillation and become an instant expert on the subject.”

His shrug copped to the charge.

“Why did I bother with medical school and residency, when all I needed was an app?” Her smile proved contagious.

A doctor with a sense of humor. What’s next? A politician with a sense of honor?

“Let me save you the trouble,” she said. “The biggest risk from AFib is that it can lead to stroke and heart failure.”

The words *stroke* and *heart failure* wiped the smile from his face. “Did she have a stroke?”

“There’s no indication of that,” the cardiologist said.

“Can it be treated?”

She nodded. “By medication, blood thinners, and in some cases, surgery.”

“Tina’s no stranger to surgery,” he said. “If that’s what it takes, don’t sweat the cost. What insurance won’t cover, I will.”

Even if it means my surgeries must wait.

Singh held up both palms in the universal stop sign. “Don’t get ahead of the science, Mr. Meadows. I’m not suggesting surgery at this stage. More than likely, Tina will learn to live with her condition by taking regular meds. In addition, she may need to make lifestyle adjustments. All that, however, should await the lab results."

"Are you suggesting she quit the police force? I've been urging her to resign for months, but she won't listen to me. Maybe you can convince her."

"You're doing it again, sir. Getting ahead of the tests. We'll discuss the treatment plan after we know more."

"Have you shared all this with Tina?" he said.

"Yes, and she authorized me to disclose her condition to you. Otherwise, HIPAA would prevent me from doing so."

"What about Detective Gamez? Does he know?"

"No. Tina signed a HIPAA waiver for you, but not him." She leaned forward and rested her forearms on the desk. "I asked you to meet because I need your help."

"Like I said, Doc, whatever you need. Cost is no concern."

"What I need is more information about Tina. Things like the meds she's on now and those she has taken in the past. Her history with drugs, alcohol, and tobacco. The list of surgeries performed on her, including the when, where, and by whom. In short, I want to know everything she has put into her body or done to it."

"Hasn't Tina told you all this?"

Her forehead furrowed. "I don't think she has told me everything."

"Did she tell you about a drug study she participated in a decade ago?"

Singh shook her head.

"She probably doesn't know what the testing did to her." He pushed the business card closer to her fingertips. "But I know someone who does."

***

Cash brought a peace offering to Goldy's office: two pizzas from Cane Rosso. The Truff Daddy and the Honey Bastard. The aroma of garlic filled the conference room, where Eva and Cash salivated like Pavlov's dogs.

Goldy showed up fifteen minutes late for lunch. He looked more pleased than surprised by the pies but more surprised than pleased by the bearer. "Where the hell have you been the past three days?" He grabbed a slice and talked between bites. "Remind me whose side you're on. I keep forgetting."

"You also seem to have forgotten who brought home the bacon," Cash said.

Goldy stopped chewing. "Is there bacon on one of these?"

"The Honey Bastard," Cash said.

Goldy reached for a slice of the Bastard.

"Is there a business portion to this working meal?" Eva's tone was curt.

"This is more of a celebration," Cash said.

She looked puzzled. "What are we celebrating?"

Cash dropped a stack of documents on the table. "These are the autopsy reports on DCK's victims. You should finish eating before reading them."

"Give me the G-rated version." Goldy spoke with a mouthful of dough.

"These documents free Bragg and point a finger at the serial killer."

Eva took her first slice of pizza, already two slices behind her boss. "We need a little more detail than that," she said.

"I've been troubled all along by the idea that savvy trans women, with a sixth sense of the dangers they face every day, would let down their guard around Bragg or his minions. That scenario never made sense." Cash paused to let his point sink in.

"We've argued that to the cops and prosecutors," Goldy said, "and they dismissed it."

"We need to keep hammering it home. The killer is someone the women trusted. Someone like their doctor."

Eva and Goldy looked at each other. He frowned. She smiled. As if both knew where Cash was heading.

"The autopsy reports detail what all the victims are missing," Cash said.

Goldy grabbed another slice. "Everyone knows the killer took a body part."

"He also took their hearts."

Goldy stopped chewing. Eva put down her first and likely last slice. "It's still a leap to go from that to accusing a prominent surgeon," she said.

"The hearts were removed with surgical precision," Cash said, "and then the corpse was stitched up, leaving a scarlet X where the heart had been."

"Do you think we're dealing with a Hannibal Lecter copycat?" she said.

Cash shook his head. "We're dealing with someone who wants us to think the killer is a Hannibal Lecter copycat."

CHAPTER FIFTY-EIGHT

Cash set aside the day before his surgery to tie up loose ends. He was having second thoughts about undergoing the operation and third thoughts about letting Katzenbach do the cutting.

Fridays were Katzenbach's operating days, which could be why Cash's calls to the doctor's cellphone went straight to voicemail. It didn't, however, explain why Katya didn't pick up the office line.

More troubling still, Cash's calls to Tina went unanswered. For all he knew, she might be drugged and helpless in a hospital where Katzenbach enjoyed privileges. A big swinging dick doctor like him could waltz in and out of her private room at will.

Cash's alarm over Tina swung wildly between scared and scared shitless, all the while reserving a healthy dose of fear for himself. Going under the knife tomorrow would be scary in a five-star hospital, but submitting to surgery at Katzenbach's office, after-hours and off the books, shook him to the bone.

Carl Meadows was a ghost who existed only on paper. Cash McCahill had been missing for nearly a year and was presumed dead by almost everyone. If neither Cash nor Carl survived the procedure, Katzenbach and Katya would tie up a loose end. One more death on their bloody hands would rest as light as a feather on a tombstone and even lighter on their consciences. Assuming they had consciences.

The sooner Cash shed Carl Meadows's skin, the better. Meadows had crossed Stewart Powell, who had plenty of friends in and out of government to do his dirty work. Katzenbach would be the best surgeon to undo what he had done, provided he didn't know that Cash had dimed him out to the IRS.

Cash put fears for himself on the back burner and focused on Tina. As long as Katzenbach remained free to roam the streets of Dallas, and even worse, the halls of the hospital, either he or Gamez should shadow her.

Cash would take the first watch. He sped to Baylor, only to find her private room empty. He asked the receptionist on the floor where the patient in room 403 had gone. "The doctor checked her out two hours ago," she said.

"Dr. Singh?"

"No, the doctor listed on her intake form."

Cash's heart sank. "Katzenbach?"

"That's the one."

***

Cash delivered the news of Tina's disappearance to Gamez. They sat in the kitchen of her apartment, a bottle of Glenlivet and two shot glasses on the table between them. A rising tide of rage swept over Cash.

The detective took the bombshell better than Cash had anticipated. Not well. Just better than expected. Gamez didn't go ballistic and wreck the apartment. Instead, he blew off steam by pacing the room.

Gamez stopped cold. "Are you sure Katzenbach has her?"

"One hundred percent," Cash said. "He signed her out of the hospital."

"How do we get her back?"

"He knows that we know he has her," Cash said.

Gamez pounded the table. "We confront him together."

Cash shook his head. "I go alone. He expects me to come for her. If he smells a cop, Tina will be toast." He kept to himself the fear that she already was. With Gamez wired to explode, a suggestion of Tina's death could set him off.

The detective vetoed plan after plan that left him on the sidelines before finally giving in. He pulled a Glock from his shoulder holster and held it out to Cash. "You'll need this."

"I don't carry."

"Is there something in your past I should know?" the cop asked.

"I had an issue with the law a few years back."

"If it comes down to a choice between a felony for you or a funeral for Tina," Gamez said, "take the felony." Cash accepted the Glock and along with it, the risk of a return trip to Seagoville. Gamez was right, it might take a shootout to save Tina.

"What am I supposed to do while you're riding to the rescue?" Gamez sounded as if he was about to lose his shit.

"Pray," Cash said.

***

It was dark before Katzenbach returned Cash's repeated calls. The doctor delivered a clear message. "Call off the dogs."

"I don't know what you're talking about," Cash said.

"Of course you do." Katzenbach sounded calm and in control. "Your friend from the IRS called to schedule an interview."

The news sucker-punched Cash, leaving him speechless. Shafer had jumped the gun. He summoned the strength to say, "I don't have a friend at the IRS."

"Muzzle Shafer anyway."

Certain that Katzenbach would call him out on a lie, Cash resorted to the truth. "That's not how he operates."

"Funny that you, of all people, would use the word *operates*."

A chill ran through Cash. He recovered quickly. It was more important to get Tina back than to go through with the operation. "Where's Tina?"

"She's safe." The "for now" was silent and implied.

"Let me talk to her."

"At the moment, she's in no condition to speak to anyone."

"Then I need to see her."

"That can be arranged." Katzenbach laid out the conditions for a family reunion. Cash countered with a proposal to meet at a public place. The surgeon's original offer hardened into an ultimatum.

Cash cratered on all conditions.

***

Cash followed the instructions down to the last detail, which included losing the weapon. He arrived alone and unarmed at the underground garage in Katzenbach's office building.

At 9:00 p.m. on a Friday night, the garage was empty except for a silver Mercedes sedan. The Benz flashed its headlights three times, and Cash walked toward the light. Katya unlocked the door, and he slid onto the passenger seat.

Her right hand held a syringe, her left, a swab. "Roll up your sleeve."

Cash balked, fearful that the syringe contained a hot shot that would put him out permanently. "Let's not and just say we did."

"You know the deal," she said. "This is your last chance to see Tina."

He rolled up his sleeve. She swabbed his arm and gave him a full dose of whatever the doctor had ordered. "Now count backwards from ten."

He made it to three before all the lights in the world went out.

CHAPTER FIFTY-NINE

Cash came to on a metal slab, paralyzed and mute. His first thought was that he had reached the last stop before the grave: the morgue. Katya stood to his right, wearing all white like a Nordic angel of death. Katzenbach in scrubs loomed to the left.

Cash floated in purgatory. A tube snaked from his mouth. Unable to turn his head, he had no idea where the tube ended. The beat of a pump reminded him of the breathing machine that had kept his grandmother in a suspended state for weeks, until he had finally given the green light to pull the plug.

Katya and Katzenbach moved outside Cash's narrow range of vision, leaving him to stew in his fears. If he couldn't breathe on his own, he couldn't do shit. He lay on his back, naked as a corpse. He was not bound, but he was rendered motionless by whatever drugs coursed through his system. He could beg for mercy, but only with his eyes.

Heavy footsteps brought the doctor back into Cash's field of sight. "You probably have a thousand questions, starting with where you are."

Good guess, but that wasn't the first thing on Cash's mind. *Where's Tina?*

Katzenbach must have heard the silent question. "I promised you could see Tina, and I'm a man of my word." His voice was cold, clinical. "She's in the next room, on her own gurney. If only you could get up and walk to her...."

Portable lamps clanked on, blinding Cash. Tears filled his eyes. Grief filled his heart.

"Katya gave you a mild muscle relaxant in the car," the doctor said, "a small but sufficient dose to transport you here without too much trouble. For the operation, however, I administered a paralytic."

He adjusted the tube in Cash's mouth and went on. "I can't have you thrashing about or experiencing involuntary muscle movements—not while I'm performing delicate surgery on your face. For the next several hours, the paralytic will shut down your nerves and muscles. That's why you're on intubation."

The surgeon hovered over Cash. "You asked me to reconstruct your face to its former state." His mocking tone made that outcome seem unlikely. "Actually, it was more a façade than a face. A handsome mask hiding an ugly soul."

Talk of a soul sent a shudder through Cash. Or it would have, if he had been able to move a muscle.

"A simple reversal would be one way to go," Katzenbach said, "but it's not our only option. In my experience, all lawyers have turned out to be two-faced, and you've proven no exception. You put the IRS and the DPD on my trail and then lied about it."

Paralysis and the plastic tube prevented Cash from compounding one lie with another. He *had* succeeded in putting the

IRS on Katzenbach's trail but not the DPD. Despite Cash's best efforts, the cops remained focused on Bragg.

The doctor's forefinger traced the contours of Cash's face. First clockwise, then counterclockwise. Cash didn't feel a thing.

"What would you think about actually *having* two faces?" Katzenbach sounded excited by the prospect. "And I mean this quite literally. It would be a huge step forward for the legal profession. Truth in advertising. What clients would see when they look at you with disgust is what they would get."

Cash screamed *NO!* from the bottom of his lungs. The scream died deep in his chest.

The doctor continued to poke and probe Cash's face. "Hearing no objection, I'll assume you're fine with a split personality. I can draw a dividing line from crown to chin and remake half of your face Cash and leave the other half Carl. Your future will be a mashup of your past and present. Not what you were going for, but half a loaf is better than none. Or, in your case, it would be half a lawyer is better than none."

Katzenbach laughed. Cash silently screamed.

"Alternately, I could turn you into a hideous beast, like in the tale *Beauty and the Beast.* What are the odds that any of the belles from your past would give you a second look based solely on who you are inside?"

Cash desperately didn't want to go there.

"Sweet dreams," Katzenbach said before the lights went out again.

***

Pain radiated from Cash's face, providing bittersweet relief from the absence of feeling. The pumping machine and its maddening sound effects were gone. He was breathing on his own, but every breath sparked a wince.

He might have been out for hours or days. He had no way of knowing. Bandages swaddled his face, covering all but his eyes and mouth. With his new identity under wraps, Cash faced an uncertain future. He had a strong sense that Carl Meadows had been erased, or at least partially so. What lay ahead remained a mystery.

The windowless room was empty except for a small table near the bed and two chairs. The walls were bare, period. Katzenbach entered the room, wearing scrubs and whistling a show tune: "I've Grown Accustomed to Your Face." He stopped whistling and said, "Finally woke from your beauty sleep." His words dripped with irony.

The bandages made it hard for Cash to speak. "How long do you plan to keep me prisoner here?" Each word triggered fresh pain.

"You're free to go at any time."

"And Tina? Is she free to leave as well?"

"Oh, Tina is long gone. She and I…we finished our little business transaction. As far as I know, she's back on the job."

Cash didn't believe it, but he didn't disbelieve it either. He struggled to sit up, but the pain and drugs kept him down.

"You should rest in bed another day or so," the doctor said. "The bandages will come off in four to six weeks."

"And what will I find beneath the bandages?" Cash's voice betrayed fear.

Katzenbach turned out the lights and exited the room, leaving Cash in the dark.

CHAPTER SIXTY

THREE DAYS LATER

Cigar smoke fogged Goldy's office, meaning the old man had won the latest round in the cat-and-mouse contest with Eva over his hidden cache of *Cohibas*. He stared at Cash's bandaged face. "Isn't it a little early for Halloween, and who are you supposed to be? The invisible man or the mummy?"

Cash would have laughed or at least smiled but for two reasons. One, it hurt like hell to do either. Two, it wasn't funny.

Eva entered Goldy's office and handed Cash a cup of coffee. "How are you feeling?" she asked.

"Like someone took a pile driver to my face," Cash said.

She sat next to him on the couch. "What meds are you on?"

"Shorter to list what I'm not on."

"You'll be fine," she said.

Cash wished he shared her confidence. There was no telling what Katzenbach had done to his face. At this point, even Carl Meadows was looking good.

"Quit mollycoddling the boy," Goldy said to Eva. "He needs to get back to work. Just when our business started booming, he decided to up and take a vacation."

Vacation? That brought a smile to Cash, much as it pained him.

"First things first," Cash said. "We have to get Bragg out of jail and put Katzenbach in his place."

"Done and almost done," Eva said. "Bragg's out. Except for the body parts, which the real killer planted in Bragg's barn, the cops had nothing to pin him to the killings, and he had solid alibis for most of the murders. The DA dropped the charges yesterday. Now Bragg is threatening to sue the city."

"We nixed representing him in the lawsuit," Goldy said. "Civil cases aren't my cup of tea."

Eva scoffed. "Like you drink tea."

Cash silently seconded the decision to pass on Bragg's bid to bleed the city, though it would likely be lucrative. The plaintiffs' bar was courting the cult leader, and those bloodsuckers had sharp elbows and sharper teeth.

"And Katzenbach?" Cash said. "Has he been charged?"

Goldy and Eva fell silent, as if each was waiting on the other to break the news. Eva took the bullet. "He will be charged."

"With the DCK killings?" Cash said.

She shook her head.

Cash recoiled. "That can't be right. The missing hearts are the key to the murders. Katzenbach had to get rid of the victims' hearts. The side effects of his drug took healthy teens and turned their tickers into time bombs."

"The cops searched his home and office but came up with nothing," Goldy said. "You have a beautiful theory without an ounce of proof."

Cash's temples throbbed. His tone turned strident. "Katzenbach and Katya lured those women to their deaths."

"Good luck proving that." Goldy sounded tired.

"You said Katzenbach would be charged," Cash said to Eva. "If not for the murders, for what?"

"Katzenbach ran drug tests on underage girls without parental consent," Eva said. "That's a crime, and he failed to get rid of all the witnesses. Tina for one. He and Katya also submitted false information to the FDA about their test subjects, lying about their ages, which is another felony."

"Well, at least he's going away for fraud." Cash didn't try to hide his disappointment.

There was a long silence before Eva whispered, "Misprision."

Cash rocketed to his feet. "*What?*"

Goldy gestured for Cash to sit, and he did. "Calm down, son. Katya is copping to fraud and taking the fall for arranging fake documents for the girls and falsifying the FDA paperwork. Katzenbach will plead guilty to the lesser charge of misprision, claiming he discovered Katya's fraud years after the fact and failed to report it."

"That's bullshit!" Cash clenched his fists until the knuckles turned white. "She's covering for him."

"In addition to Katya's testimony," Goldy said, "there were other problems with proving the doctor guilty of fraud." He and Eva exchanged a furtive look. Neither bothered to explain.

"Misprision carries a three-year max, meaning Katzenbach will do a year and some change behind bars, get his license back, and pick up where he left off." When neither Eva nor Goldy pushed back, Cash resumed the rant. "Are you telling me that a year in prison buys Katzenbach a clean slate for eight murders?"

"Not for the murders," Goldy said. "He doesn't get a pass for crimes of violence. That is, if enough evidence ever turns up to charge him."

"What about Tina's kidnapping?" Cash said.

"What kidnapping?" Goldy sounded amused. "She was desperate to leave the hospital, and Katzenbach cleared it for her. Then he offered her a free collagen injection, and she took it."

Cash didn't buy it. He stared at Eva, who looked down at the floor. He turned back to Goldy.

"And me?" Cash's voice rose in volume and pitch. "What Katzenbach did to me doesn't count?"

"What did he do?" Goldy matched Cash's decibel level. "You asked him to operate on your face and signed the consent for him to do so."

"What if he disfigured me?"

Goldy rubbed his chin and said, "Guess we'll have to wait and see."

* * *

An odor of garlic wafted from Gamez's kitchen to the living room, where he, Tina, and Cash sat. Cash would have preferred confronting the two separately but doubted he could pry them apart any time soon.

The couple were on the couch, their legs and arms entwined. "When do you get the bandages removed?" Tina sounded surprisingly upbeat and untroubled.

Cash changed the subject. "Gamez, I heard you bailed from the DCK investigation."

"You heard wrong." Gamez sounded bitter. "After Bragg was cut loose, I got busted down to a dead end beat in south Dallas. What happens to the task force now is out of my hands."

Cash turned to Tina. "What will become of the task force?"

She shrugged. "Don't ask me. I told the chief that if Robbie was off the team, so was I. She called my bluff and sent me to dispatch."

Cash could live with that. Anything that took Tina out of harm's way worked for him.

"In fact," she said, "I'm thinking of leaving the department."

This keeps getting better and better.

"That way I can devote full time to law school. I've got my sights set on landing a job in the DA's office. That's where the decisions really get made."

One step forward, two steps back.

"If you come up with evidence tying Katzenbach to the killings," Gamez said, "you'll have to sell it to a new team of cops."

Who says I take my case to the cops?

"And if you can't find the goods against Katzenbach," Tina said, "then he skates on eight murders, including Brandi's."

"There's more than one way to skin a snake," Cash said, more to himself than to her.

CHAPTER SIXTY-ONE

SIX WEEKS LATER

Cash entered Dr. Sunita Singh's office early for his appointment and sat across the desk from her. If his bandaged face caught her by surprise, she didn't show it. She put down a half-peeled orange. The citrusy smell made his mouth water, but that wasn't the only thing that had his juices flowing. The glass desk offered a clear view of her lean legs.

"To what do I owe the pleasure, Mr. Meadows?" Her tone was playful.

"It's time to remove my bandages, and I want you to do the honors."

She was taken aback. "Shouldn't that be done by the surgeon who operated on you?"

"It was Katzenbach, and he's behind bars."

She groaned. Katzenbach's guilty plea and sentence had been all over the media. The internet buzzed with rumors that he was the DCK killer, but the cops couldn't nail him on that.

In the end, the feds had pulled a Capone and gotten him on the ticky-tacky offense of misprision.

You know that cosmetic surgery isn't my field, right?" she said.

"All I'm asking is for you to unveil the new me." The bandages hid his stab at a smile. "It's as simple as peeling an orange."

She walked to him and leaned against the desk. "What did you have done?"

"It's what I had undone, but that's a long story to share over a bottle of wine and dinner tonight. If I'm back to my old self, we can celebrate. If not, you can comfort me."

"Think positive," she said. "Either way, we'll celebrate."

"Sure. We can always toast you for saving Tina's life."

"That's an overstatement." The doctor's silky voice could calm a tornado. "I ran a few tests, diagnosed her heart condition, and put her on meds. She's not out of the woods, not by a long shot. She may still need surgery down the road."

"Thanks to you, we learned of Tina's bad ticker. Once you had discovered her condition, it was too late for Katzenbach to stage another DCK killing and take her heart. If you had postponed her tests for even a day, she would've been victim number nine. So yes, you saved her life."

Singh blushed, which made her more beautiful. She snipped through the bandages with scissors and slowly unraveled the layers. When the last strand fell away, she stepped back and assessed the surgeon's handiwork.

Cash was afraid to look in the mirror. He scanned her eyes for a reaction but found none, which he took as a good sign. She hadn't gasped or shrunk in horror.

"On a scale of one to ten, what do I rate?" His voice remained steady. "Give it to me straight, Doc."

Her fingers gently explored the contours of his face. She touched a sensitive spot, and he flinched. Their lips were only inches apart, close enough for him to smell coffee on her breath. She stopped probing. "I might swipe right to an offer of dinner tonight. Just dinner. Not a date." She pulled a makeup mirror from her purse and held it up for him to see the final cut.

Cash exhaled with a rush, and his heart raced. It took a while, but his brain caught up with his heart. His breathing slowed.

Now he had a new mystery: Why hadn't Katzenbach fucked him over?

CHAPTER SIXTY-TWO

SIX MONTHS LATER

Every once in a blue moon, the universe gets its shit together. The stars align. A slot machine hits the jackpot. Slow-moving ducks line up in the shooting gallery.

Today, Seagoville served as one-stop shopping for Cash. He had three inmates on his dance card, and all had wound up in his old haunt. The sitting ducks were Solomon Katzenbach, Gerry Freeman, and Big Black.

A dirty doctor, a dirty lawyer, and a down and dirty lifer.

Cash waited in a soundproof room reserved for visiting attorneys, not at all sure Katzenbach would show. To protect attorney-client privilege, a room set aside for legal conferences had to be bug-free. As a precaution, Cash patted down the undersides of the metal table and chairs.

Katzenbach arrived, looking depressingly healthy. He had dropped ten pounds or so, and his tan from yard time accentuated the snowy whiteness of his hair. Losing the beard had shaved a decade from his face.

The enemies sat across the table from each other. Katzenbach broke the steely silence. "If you came to pitch for my business, you're wasting your time. I already have a lawyer. Or did you come to thank me for how well your surgery turned out?"

"I'm not here to do either. I can't represent you because I'll be a witness for the prosecution at your murder trial, whenever that takes place. But I am curious who you hired and what you hired him to do. You signed away your right to appeal in the plea papers."

"Stewart Powell is wiring my pardon and release from prison. It's no stretch for him, now that his daughter will become AG."

Cash seethed. "You have no shot at a pardon." He sounded more confident than he felt. "I don't understand why Powell keeps you on as a client. Sure, it made sense for his firm to have represented you on the patent a decade ago. But shilling for a serial killer? I don't get it. Out of curiosity, how much did you lose when your patent crashed and burned?"

"Who said I lost?" An egomaniac like Katzenbach couldn't keep from bragging, even when the smart play was to clam up. "Worst case, I do a year and some change. If you survived a deuce here, I can do a year standing on my head." He already sounded like a convict.

"A year or so in Club Fed will be a warmup for your life sentence at Huntsville."

"There will never be a murder trial," the defrocked doctor said, "because there's no evidence against me."

"Guess again."

"Take your best shot, counselor. Convince me you've got something besides suspicion and hot air."

Cash balked at the challenge. The goal had been to prod Katzenbach into talking and hope he made an admission or two. Five minutes into the face-off, Cash ditched Plan A in favor of laying out his case. "To begin with, the killer had to be someone the victims trusted enough to meet with alone and at night."

"Or a john," Katzenbach said. "The girls had their regulars. Even Tina. I hear she gives great head, but then, you would already know that."

To keep from strangling the bastard, Cash kept his hands clasped together under the table. "You and Katya lured the women to their deaths. That was the easy part, but creating a fictitious serial killer and framing Bragg puts you in the evil genius hall of fame. The DCK fiction allowed you to hide your goal, which was harvesting the victims' hearts to cover up the damage you did to them years ago."

"I took street trash and turned them into goddesses."

"You made them dead girls walking."

"Katya made a few innocent mistakes in our testing protocol, and we're paying the price for that."

"Not even close to true. You picked trans kids living on the streets as your test subjects, because they were throwaways to you. The girls would sign anything, take anything, and do anything to afford the operations you performed on them. You fucked up their hearts and later killed them to keep from being discovered."

The surgeon scoffed. "The tests took place a decade ago. The killings didn't start until years later. How do you explain that?"

"That stumped me for a while," Cash said. "That is, until I got hold of Rosie Perales's bank records. Remember Rosie? She was your first victim. She figured out what you had done to her and blackmailed you for six months, before you decided it was safer and cheaper to kill her. But you couldn't be sure that Rosie hadn't told the others. Even if she hadn't, it was just a matter of time before they found out. You created the Dice Cold Killer to take care of your current and future problems."

Katzenbach pushed away from the table. "What I hear is a wild-assed theory, without any proof to back it up." He rose. "Come see me when you have evidence. Better yet, don't come back at all. I'll look you up when I'm out, which will be soon."

"The only way you'll leave this place," Cash said, "is in a body bag. You have friends on the outside. I have friends on the inside."

A flicker of fear clouded the doctor's eyes. He started to speak but held his tongue.

Cash got to his feet. "One last question before our final goodbye. Why didn't you disfigure me when you had the chance?"

Katzenbach sighed. "I was sorely tempted, but as a lawyer, you understand the concept of *quid pro quo.* The night I operated on you, Tina really was in the next room, sedated but conscious. She and I made a deal on the spot: your face for my freedom."

"I have my face, but you don't have your freedom."

"Not yet, but thanks to Tina, I soon will. The night of your operation, she and I hammered out her affidavit, in which she swore under oath that she and Brandi went to great lengths to hide their true ages and identities from me and that Katya had handled the paperwork and provided the false documents. That affidavit saved face for you *and* me, and it will be Exhibit A in my pardon application."

The news gut-punched Cash. He didn't respond right away because he couldn't. It was the first he had heard of Tina's affidavit—a boon to Katzenbach that had come at too high a price.

The affidavit cleared up three mysteries. First, it explained why Cash had emerged from the operation looking like Cash. Second, it accounted for Katzenbach's light sentence and galling confidence in a pardon. Sure, Katya had fallen on her sword, but Katzenbach's landing had still been too soft. The misprision charge was a joke.

Finally, he now knew why Tina had seemed chill about how his operation would turn out. She had known all along.

That girl had some explaining to do.

"Tell Powell to stand down on your early release," Cash said. "You'll be carried out of here in no time." At the door, he turned back to Katzenbach and said, "Quite a coincidence that you wound up in the same prison with one of the lawyers who represented you."

"Perhaps a coincidence." The surgeon's smile suggested otherwise. "Perhaps not."

***

"I thought you was dead," Big Black said. Reading glasses lent him a more civilized look. Well, civilized for a brute who had killed men with his bare hands.

"As the saying goes, rumors of my death were greatly exaggerated." Cash gave the prisoner time to catch the drift, if not the source. "Nice specs."

"It's the small print in the books you done brought me over the years," Big Black said. "Got another?"

"You're in luck." Cash placed a hardback on the table.

Big's eyes lit up. "Dickens?"

"No, but it's about people who lived and died in the land of Dickens. Specifically, London." Cash slid the book across the table.

Big picked it up and read the title aloud. "*The Five: The Untold Lives of the Women Killed by Jack the Ripper.*" He looked puzzled.

"Jack the Ripper was a very evil man," Cash said, "and there have been a slew of books about him. He killed at least five innocent women and never got caught and punished for his crimes."

"When?"

"Long ago. In the 1880s. Shortly after Dickens died."

Big Black gripped the book so hard that his knuckles turned white. "The creep never paid for his crimes. That ain't right."

Cash leaned forward and lowered his voice. "Same goes for the person who killed Marty. Like Marty, the women butchered by Jack are still waiting to be avenged." He leaned back. "After you finish reading the book, we'll talk about justice. For Marty and the women."

***

Politics makes strange bedfellows. As does prison.

The fortuity of Gerry Freeman and Solomon Katzenbach sharing a cellblock at Seagoville underscored a mystery that had been gnawing at Cash for months. What was the connection between Powell and Katzenbach?

Sure, it made sense for Powell, Ingram & Gardner to have handled the surgeon's patent and startup. The white-shoe firm had a deep bench of intellectual property and corporate attorneys. In ordinary circumstances, though, the firm wouldn't be caught in the same zip code with a person of interest in a murder investigation, much less one involving serial killings.

"Make it quick." Freeman stood by the door as he spoke. "I'm in the middle of my workout." Prison workouts had produced no noticeable results. The attorney still had the same slight build, pencil neck, spindly arms and legs.

"I dropped by to see if you're having second thoughts about taking the fall for Powell," Cash said.

"Even if I were, and I'm not, what makes you think I would talk to you?"

"Because I've been where you are now, and I listened to Marty Biddle express second thoughts in similar circumstances. Taking one for the team cost him a wife, two kids, and ultimately his life."

Freeman lost the smirk. "Long as I keep quiet, I keep breathing."

Cash smiled. "That's what Marty thought as well. Rhoden too."

Freeman drifted to the table but didn't sit. Beads of sweat dotted his forehead. The wheels were turning inside.

"Jenna Powell can't remain US attorney forever," Cash said, "and her bid to become AG is about to crash and burn. When she's gone, the feds will give you immunity and force you to testify before a grand jury."

"I've got nothing to tell the grand jury."

"Really? Nothing at all? Nothing about how Stewart Powell brought in Rocket Rhoden to represent Marty. Or as the case turned out, to *not* represent the poor sap at all."

The color drained from Freeman's face. He sat but didn't say a word.

Cash slapped the table with both palms and stood. "Good luck convincing your partners, I mean your *former* partners, that you'll commit perjury for them and do another nickel on top of the one you're serving now."

Freeman stared at the table, silent as a corpse.

Cash smelled Freeman's fear. "The question isn't whether you'll talk, but whether you do before Katzenbach does. Also whether you come forward before Powell can silence you permanently." Cash rose and walked to the door.

"The old-timers here say you beat a cartel," Freeman said.

"I outlasted two."

"Even if you had wiped out a hundred cartels," Freeman said, "you still wouldn't be ready for what's about to come down on your head. You have no fucking clue."

"I've got one clue." Cash smiled. "Katzenbach just gave it to me."

CHAPTER SIXTY-THREE

It was dark when Cash left the prison. His Porsche was the last to exit the visitors' lot. With three meetings at Seagoville behind him and three more tomorrow in the free world, Cash should have gone straight home and crashed. But he couldn't rest before confronting Tina.

She balked at meeting him tonight. Cash insisted and convinced her to come alone to the apartment she had all but abandoned. She arrived at 10:33, more than thirty minutes late. He ambushed her in the foyer, and they never moved deeper into the apartment.

Tina had showered and dressed hurriedly, based on the evidence of wet hair and mismatched socks. "This had better be good." She sounded tired and ticked off.

"Whose side are you on?" He almost managed to drain the anger from his voice.

"I don't know what you're talking about," she said, now sounding less tired and more ticked off.

"You gave Katzenbach a get-out-of-jail-free card."

She looked puzzled. "I still don't know what you're talking about."

"Your affidavit," he said. "The one where you minimized his role in the false documents to the FDA and laid it all on Katya. The one that paved the way for his plea to misprision. The surprise he threw in my face today."

"Did Katzenbach tell you *why* I signed the affidavit?" She matched his outrage and raised him a decibel or two.

"He bragged about it." Cash shook his head. "Maybe you're not cut out to be a lawyer, because you made a shitty deal."

"I don't think so." The tremors in her voice carried the threat of tears.

"Whatever he would've done to my face, I could've lived with it."

She laughed. "Vain as you are, if he had carved up your face, you never would've come out of the shadows." Her eyes locked on his. She lowered her voice. "Besides, it wasn't just your face. He had your life in his hands."

"But eight dead women…how can you let him walk away from eight murders?"

"We can still get him for the murders," she said.

"I don't see how. Eight corpses can't testify. Your affidavit burns you as a witness against him. The others he experimented on will be too terrified to take the stand."

"What would you have done if our positions had been reversed?" She choked up but went on in more of a whisper than a voice. "If it had been me strapped to an operating table and paralyzed, how far would you have gone to save me?"

He didn't answer before her first tear fell. It took only one to break him. The rest were overkill. He wrapped his arms around her while she sobbed into his chest.

CHAPTER SIXTY-FOUR

The day after three meetings in the pen, Cash took three meetings outside the box. The first one got off to a rocky start. He tracked down Skyler Patterson at Hanoi Hank's during the lunch break from her trial *du jour*.

He placed a big bowl of even more chili rice on the table and invited himself to join her. "I've been calling you all morning," he said.

"Take the failure to return your calls as my way of saying fuck off."

"And yet here we are," he said. "Fate has thrown us together."

"I wouldn't call it fate. Since I cover the courthouse beat, you know where to find me on my lunch break. Lord how I miss the days you were underground and I could enjoy my meals."

Cash spiked his bowl with shots of tabasco sauce and offered the bottle to her. She passed on the extra indigestion. "Whatever you're selling," she said, "I'm not buying."

"I'm not selling anything. I'm giving you a Pulitzer story that practically writes itself. All you need to do is prepare your acceptance speech."

"The last time you used that line on me, I almost got fired."

"Hear me out."

Her shoulders slumped in surrender. "I will pretend to listen to your new brand of bullshit, if you promise not to bring up either Stewart Powell or Solomon Katzenbach."

"It's not an either-or situation," he said. "This is a tale about Stewart Powell *and* Solomon Katzenbach."

She gave him a pained look. "How do you still have a law license?"

She remained seated, which he took as a green light to go on. "The connection between Powell and Katzenbach is the key to the story."

"Seriously, I have to be back in court in fifteen minutes," she said. "Let me finish my meal in peace."

"Did you know that Powell's firm represented Katzenbach in a patent application?"

She shrugged. "So what? His firm has a whole floor of IP lawyers who specialize in patent work."

"This was a patent for the antidepressant that fucked up Tina's heart. Plus, the hearts of the eight trans women who were killed by Katzenbach."

"Not proven," she said. "Not even charged."

"How about this connection?" His voice turned more strident. "Powell's firm now represents Katzenbach in his bid for a pardon."

Another shrug.

"Since when did Powell's firm do criminal work?" he said.

"In covering the courthouse for eight years, here's what I've learned about your noble profession." Her tone dripped with sarcasm. "If you throw enough money at a lawyer, he'll represent Jack the Ripper."

"Funny you should mention Jack the Ripper."

"Why is that funny?"

"Like Katzenbach, he never got charged for the murders he committed."

She stood and threw her paper napkin on the table. "Well, you did it."

"Hooked you on the story?"

"No, killed my appetite. I'm heading back to court."

He grabbed her arm. "One more thing to consider. Katzenbach invested a ton of time and money in a patent that he later abandoned. He should've been in a world of hurt financially. Instead, he claimed not to have suffered at all. How does that happen?"

That brought Skyler back to the table.

***

Cash accompanied Skyler to the federal courthouse and boarded the elevator with her, bending her ear until she got off on the sixteenth floor. He descended to the seventh floor for meeting number two.

Shafer's office had become more cluttered and cramped. Cardboard boxes had multiplied. Clear floor space had shrunk.

Shafer remained seated behind his desk, neither inviting Cash to sit nor rising to shake hands. The black-and-white picture of the agent's patron saint, Frank J. Wilson, hung on the wall behind him.

"I'm still pissed that you deceived me with a false identity," Shafer said. "What are you here to beg for today?"

"I've come to offer you immortality." Cash pointed to Wilson's head shot. "Future agents will have *your* picture hanging in their offices."

Shafer's deadpan expression ran the gamut of emotions, from A to A: amusement to annoyance. "Does anyone actually buy your blarney?"

"You'd be surprised." Cash invited himself to sit. "I'll get right to the point."

"Please do." Amusement had given way to pure annoyance.

"Something you told me doesn't mesh with a claim made by Solomon Katzenbach."

The agent groaned. "Is that your dirty doctor again?"

"Trust me. He gets dirtier."

"First, I don't trust you. Second, the only person less interested than I in chasing your dirty doc is my supervisor."

"Give me two minutes, and both you and the higher-ups will be chomping at the bit to go after Katzenbach."

Shafer lowered his head, less a nod than a sign of surrender.

"According to you, Katzenbach sank a small fortune into an invention that went bust. That turned out to be true. However, he told me that flushing the patent didn't set him back financially. In fact, it did the opposite. He claims to have had a banner year." Cash paused to let that sink in. "How does that happen?"

Shafer leaned back in his chair and stared at the ceiling. The wheels were turning inside his head. "Let me get this straight. You think Katzenbach killed eight women, but you want to nail him on a tax charge?"

"My hunch is that we're dealing with more than a tax crime," Cash said, "and with bigger targets than Katzenbach."

Chomping at the bit or not, the agent was licking his lips.

***

The third meeting of the day took place on Zoom. Even with the filter on, Regina Delgado looked ragged. Bags under her eyes. Fret lines bracketed her lips.

"I've got a meeting with the AG in ten minutes," she said. "You've got five."

Cash had closed to juries in less time and walked clients from the courthouse. "Give my love and kisses to Karen," he said.

"That's General Belton to you."

"Savor your time in the big office," he said, "because this may be your last visit there."

Her fret lines deepened. "Why? What have you heard?"

"Word on the street is that you're trailing badly in a two-horse race."

"If it's down to two horses, I've still got a shot." She sounded shaky.

"Only if the lead horse stumbles," he said.

"I take it that you have a plan to improve my odds."

"We need to discuss this face-to-face."

There was a pause. "I can fit you in tomorrow morning at ten." Another pause, shorter this time. "Not in my office. There's a coffee shop at DuPont Circle called—"

He cut her off. "I'm calling in a chit you owe a close friend. We do it at my office. See you tomorrow at ten." He hung up before she could counter his counter.

CHAPTER SIXTY-FIVE

The next morning, Cash arrived at the office at 10:15 and found Skyler Patterson, Marty Shafer, and Regina Delgado seated in the waiting room. Skyler looked bored; Shafer, irked; and Regina, pissed. He blew past the trio without a word and entered Goldy's office, uninvited.

Goldy told Cash to close the door, and he did. "Don't know how or why you did it," the old man said, "but you managed to gather in our office, at one time, the last three people on the planet I would ever want to see."

"This is my cast to rehearse a little play I call *Dead Men Talking*.

Goldy shook his head. "Half the time, I don't know what the hell you're going on about. The rest of the time, I don't want to know."

"I've found a way to bring down the house of Powell," Cash said.

"Other than Powell's being a rich asshole who throws his weight around, why do you give a shit?"

"Because he had Marty Biddle killed."

Goldy leaned forward and lowered his voice. "I wouldn't repeat that outside this room—not unless your genius plan involves getting yourself and the firm sued for defamation."

"Follow me, old man. Time to meet our cast."

***

From her collection of college athletic apparel, Skyler had chosen a Sooners sweatshirt today. Cash saw the selection as a nod to Goldy, who had graduated from OU, undergrad and law.

Eva, Tina, Goldy, and Cash fanned around Skyler at the conference room table. The reporter seemed relaxed, even amused. "Hmmm. Outnumbered only four to one. You're going to need reinforcements to take me on."

"This isn't an us-against-you scenario," Cash said. "Believe it or not, we're all on the same side here."

"Not from where I sit." Skyler sounded dubious.

"Did you get any sleep last night?" Cash said.

"Thanks to you, I didn't."

Cash bought that. Skyler's eyes, bloodshot and blinking, told of an all-nighter. "What did you find?" he said.

Skyler pulled a writing pad from her purse and checked her notes. "For starters, Powell's law firm represented Dr. Katzenbach, both in filing the patent application and abandoning it." She flipped to the next page of notes. "It looked like there would be litigation with a competing patent filed by a group in Houston, but Katzenbach waved the white flag."

Goldy harrumphed. "So far, you haven't told us anything we didn't already know."

"Hold your horses, grandpa," Skyler said.

Goldy's face turned red. "Who's she calling grandpa?"

Cash turned to Goldy, "Since my operation, it can only be you. Let her finish."

"Here's something you don't know," the reporter said. "At the same time Powell's firm was representing Katzenbach on the patent, the firm also represented a fledgling hedge fund called Longhorn Investments, formed by Lou Watson."

"Watson and Longhorn are still Powell's clients," Cash said. "In fact, his biggest clients."

"Katzenbach's patent was owned by a public company called Gemini LLC. A private company headquartered in Nevada was the only entity that owned more than ten percent of the Gemini stock."

"So what?" Goldy said.

"Gemini made a public filing with the SEC when it abandoned the patent. Two days before that SEC filing, Longhorn shorted its entire holding of stock in Gemini."

Cash leaned back in the chair. His words were slow to come. "Let me get this straight. Powell's firm represented both Katzenbach's public company and Longhorn, and the latter shorted its Gemini shares two days before the world learned that Katzenbach's patent was worthless." He whistled. "We're looking at insider trading."

"Bingo," Skyler said.

***

In the conference room chair vacated minutes ago by Skyler, Shafer skipped the small talk and went straight to his standard warning. "I cannot and will not disclose to you any confidential tax information. If that's why you asked me here, we can end this meeting now."

"Relax, Shafer," Cash said. "We're in a giving mood this morning. You're about to receive a tip to the biggest tax case of your career."

The tax investigator doubled down on the hard-ass attitude by crossing his arms at his chest. "As long as you understand it's a one-way street, we can proceed."

Cash nodded.

"No strings attached?" Shafer said.

"No strings." Cash let that sink in before continuing. "Something has been keeping me up nights. Katzenbach's invention tanked, but according to your records, he didn't take a hit financially. How was that possible?"

"Maybe he had offsetting gains," Shafer said.

"No maybe about it," Cash said. "Here's the lead for you to run down. A public company called Gemini LLC owned the patent. The company was based in Nevada. Katzenbach was the CEO, and I suspect that a crook named Benny from Vegas was the real owner. Powell's law firm represented both Gemini and a new hedge fund called Longhorn Investments."

"Is there a point to this story?" Shafer sounded less sure of himself. "Powell's firm has cornered the legal market in Texas. It's no surprise that both companies were clients."

"Two days before Gemini filed an 8-K report with the SEC publicly announcing the abandonment of the patent, Longhorn shorted its stock in Gemini and made a killing for its clients."

Shafer's eyes widened. "And you suspect some of that killing went to Katzenbach."

"Not directly," Cash said. "Your job is to see how much of the insider trading money wound its way to the doctor indirectly."

"Didn't you say no strings?" Shafer said.

Cash ignored the question. "And clear your calendar for tomorrow."

* * *

By the time Regina Delgado took the hot seat in the conference room, her temper had ratcheted from a slow burn to volcanic. She and Cash were alone in the room. Her choice, not his.

"I didn't fly all the way from DC on the red eye to sit for an hour in the reception area," she said, "like one of your criminal clients."

"Oh, I wouldn't keep a paying client waiting that long." Cash smiled.

Regina didn't. "I don't like to be kept waiting."

"And yet," Cash said, "you waited." He kept his voice maddeningly calm. "You'll be glad you did."

"My return flight leaves at noon." She checked her watch. "That gives you fifteen minutes before I'm out of here."

"You need to extend your visit by a day."

"Why would I do that?" she said.

"To win the Iron Throne."

Regina leaned forward in the chair. Cash took that to mean he had all the time in the world. He walked to a chalkboard and wrote three names at the top: Solomon Katzenbach, Stewart Powell, and Lou Watson. Under each name, he wrote the name of the corresponding company: Gemini LLC, Powell, Ingram & Gardner, and Longhorn Investments.

He walked her through the cozy relationships among the three men and their companies and highlighted the overt acts of the conspiracy. The filing and abandonment of Katzenbach's patent. The formation of his public company. The suspicious shorting of Gemini stock by Longhorn. The projected windfalls to the co-conspirators.

He stressed Stewart Powell's role in the scheme. He was the thread that tied it all together. After Cash wrapped up, she stared at the chalkboard for minutes before finding her voice. "You'll need an inside witness."

"Maybe two," he said.

"Where are you going to find them?"

"I've already found them," he said, "but hooking them is another story. That's where you come in."

She stiffened in her seat. "Why me?"

He left the chalkboard and took the chair across the table from her. "For obvious reasons, I can't take this to my local US attorney." He paused before delivering the clincher. "Plus, I can't think of anyone more highly motivated than you to make a case against Powell."

She shuddered. "It could backfire on me."

"In which case," he said, "you're no worse off. Powell has lined up every senator for sale to support his daughter for the big job. By my count, that's *every* senator. If Jenna becomes AG, your transfer to the Bismarck office won't be far behind. A South Texas girl like you won't survive a winter in North Dakota. Your only play is to root out the entire Powell clan, starting with the head."

Minutes passed in silence. "I'll need your assistant to book me a room at the Hall Arts Hotel," she said, "and change my return flight to tomorrow night."

Cash smiled. "To be on the safe side, let's book you two nights at the Hall."

CHAPTER SIXTY-SIX

With three roles cast, Cash needed two more players for tomorrow's drama, and he knew where to find them. He spent the afternoon at FCI Seagoville.

Nothing ever changed at the federal pen. Every time he set foot inside, a sense of fatigue drained him. Always the same faces, scenery, sounds, and smells. The sameness of it all sapped the life from inmates and even exes like him.

Warden Stockman hadn't changed either. He still exuded all the warmth of a granite mountain. He didn't so much age as erode, with fissures opening on his pitted face and a thickening neck settling onto broad shoulders.

Like most mountains, the warden had a point of vulnerability, and Cash knew how to exploit it.

"You just can't stay away from this place," Stockman said.

"It's your magnetic personality." Cash managed to keep a straight face. "Plus, I'm here to help you clear an open investigation, along with your conscience."

Stockman scoffed. "What investigation would that be?"

"The murder of Marty Biddle."

The warden winced, a rare show of emotion.

It was time for Cash to exploit the chink in the warden's armor. He laid out the circumstantial evidence linking Stewart Powell, Solomon Katzenbach, and Lou Watson in a conspiracy to short stocks based on an inside tip. As the CFO of Longhorn, Biddle would have participated in the scheme and could have parlayed his knowledge of the crime into an early release.

"To make the charge stick," Cash said, "we need an insider to flip. There are two candidates in your house."

"Who died and put you in charge?" the warden said. "I work for and with the Department of Justice. Last time I checked, DOJ lifted your badge about fifteen years ago and took your law license five years ago."

"I got my law license back."

"But not the badge."

Cash shook his head. "No, not the badge."

"I'll be happy to work with a prosecutor assigned to the investigation," Stockman said.

"We can't go through the local US Attorney's office because of Stewart Powell's involvement in the crime, but I'll do you one better. Tomorrow morning, Deputy AG Regina Delgado will be here to do the honors."

"What am I supposed to do?"

"Follow the script she gives you," Cash said, "and really sell it."

"What will you be doing?"

"Watching the dominoes fall from the comfort of your office."

The warden frowned. "You always were a pushy sonovabitch, but by all means, make yourself at home," he said with a heavy dose of sarcasm.

"One last thing," Cash said. "I'll need to borrow one of your prisoners."

***

Unlike the warden, Big Black had changed. Fresh cuts crisscrossed his face. Scraped knuckles suggested he had landed his share of blows in whatever altercation had sent him to solitary for the weekend.

"You've been fighting again," Cash said.

Big shrugged. "Wannabe in the block had to be put in his place."

Cash didn't have to ask who had won. Big was still standing. The newbie would be licking his wounds in the infirmary.

"Did you bring me a book?" the inmate asked.

Cash placed a paperback on the table: *Hard Candy* by Andrew Vachss. "It's a thriller about the lengths to which a mercenary named Burke goes to punish pervs who prey on the young and weak."

Big thumbed through the pages. "I'll knock this one out tonight. Bring more."

It was a good sign that Big had stopped asking about a release date. It meant the lifer had come to accept the reality of his plight. He would leave BOP's custody in a body bag.

However, if things went well tomorrow, Cash hoped to land Big in a low-security prison in a nicer climate. Perhaps even a camp. Baby steps. Cash kept the plan to himself. No need to raise Big's expectations, only to have them dashed if things went wrong.

"I'll be back tomorrow with another book," Cash said. "Maybe Dickens."

Big eyed him suspiciously. "Two visits in two days. What's up?"

"I have a favor to ask of you."

"Typical fucking lawyer," Big said. "Always a catch."

"This will be a piece of cake for you. The warden will take you to two meetings tomorrow, both here."

"What do I have to do?"

"The menacing look you just gave me," Cash said. "Give it to the prisoners at the meetings."

"I don't have to say nothing?"

Cash smiled. "The look will do."

CHAPTER SIXTY-SEVEN

The next day, Cash gave last minute directions to the players gathered in the warden's office. Five had speaking roles: Regina Delgado, Agent Shafer, Detective Gamez, Tina Campos, and Warden Stockman. Big Black had no lines, but his walk-on would sell the scene or sink it.

Cash had no doubt that five of the six sided with him. Given Stewart Powell's designs on making his daughter the next AG, he stood between Regina and her dream of landing the plum post. Regina would kneecap her mother to score the top job at Justice.

Had Shafer been born a century earlier, he could have been one of Eliot Ness's Untouchables. The tax agent couldn't be bought, not by Stewart Powell or anyone.

Gamez and Tina were still smarting over their dismissals from the DCK task force. Gamez had gone from the fast track to a patrol beat on the graveyard shift. He would crawl over broken glass to get his detective badge back.

In Tina's case, catching the serial killer was to be her swan song on the force. After that, it would be off to law school full-time, with her sights set on the DA's office.

Big Black was invisible to Powell. Poor, black, barely educated, and behind bars for most of his hard-knock life, Big wouldn't be a blip on the rich man's radar.

That left Warden Stockman as the wild card, the only one whose allegiance Cash questioned. On the one hand, if Stockman aspired to climb the ladder at the BOP, kowtowing to Powell could make it happen.

On the other, he shared Cash's obsession with catching Marty Biddle's killer. Stockman saw himself as the Good Shepherd, watching over his flock. He tended white sheep, black sheep, and every hue in between.

In the end, it really didn't matter how Cash came down on the warden. The operation couldn't work without him. Both Katzenbach and Freeman were at Seagoville and under his thumb.

Regardless of how it played out, Cash would see and hear everything from the comfort of Stockman's office. The BOP had installed CCTV in Seagoville, with a direct feed to the warden's computer. The yard, interview rooms, hallways, showers, stalls, and cellblocks were all fair game for surveillance. Cash had the option of viewing one site or up to twelve venues simultaneously.

"It's showtime!" Cash said. "Katzenbach and Freeman need to see each other as they enter their separate interview rooms, but it can't look like we staged it."

Regina laughed. "They won't believe it was an accident that they ran into each other in the hallway."

"Perhaps," Cash said, "but at least we keep them guessing."

"There's no way this will work." Leave it to Shafer to be a buzzkill. "As soon as Freeman and Katzenbach hit the interview rooms, they'll demand to see their lawyers."

"I've thought of that," Cash said. "There are four steps to a successful prisoners' dilemma game. First, the inmates must be dirty, and both of ours are up to their necks in crime. Second, they need to see but not talk to each other on the way to their interviews. Third, our interrogators, preferably a pair of interviewers for each prisoner, should be highly motivated. Again, we have two teams who could make Mother Teresa cop to killing JFK."

"Who's interviewing whom?" Tina said.

"You and Gamez will take Katzenbach," Cash said, "and Regina and Shafer have Freeman."

"And the fourth ingredient?" Tina said.

Cash smiled. "That's the secret sauce that will convince our prisoners to spill their guts, instead of lawyering up."

"But what is it?" Tina said.

"If I told you," Cash said, "it wouldn't be secret." He clapped once. "Is everyone ready to hit their marks?"

No one moved. It looked as if the game might be over before it started. Tina rose, followed by Gamez. Stockman was the last to get to his feet.

"Before you go, let's make this more interesting." Cash handed a slip of paper to each of them. "We'll take bets on who will crack first. K for Katzenbach, F for Freeman. Give your ballot to me on the way out."

"What if neither of them flips?" the warden asked.

"Then we're all fucked," Regina said.

***

Cash tucked the slips of paper in his pocket and sent the players on their way. He settled behind the warden's desk and experimented with the viewing options on the computer. Ultimately, the action would boil down to a split screen between two side-by-side interview rooms.

The guards assigned to escort duty pulled off the *accidental* meeting of Katzenbach and Freeman in the corridor. The prisoners stopped and stared at each other. No words passed between them before they entered the rooms.

So far, all had gone according to plan. Cash split the screen into two halves. The left side featured the Delgado-Shafer duo against Freeman. The right showed Gamez and Tina sitting across the table from Katzenbach.

Cash muted the Katzenbach side and upped the volume on Regina's seduction of Freeman. She introduced herself and said, "I'm here to interview you in connection with an insider trading investigation involving a company called Gemini and your former law firm."

Freeman flinched. Not much but Cash caught it. The inmate recovered quickly and said, "I want to see my lawyer."

Cash silenced the Freeman room and jumped to the other screen. He unmuted the right side in time to catch Katzenbach also demanding to talk to his attorney.

Two minutes into both interviews. Two invocations of the right to counsel. Two rooms silent as tombs. Still according to plan.

On the left side of the screen, Warden Stockman and Big Black entered the room with Freeman. "Pardon the interruption,"

Stockman said, "but I want to introduce Freeman to his new cellmate. Meet Marcus DuPree, better known as Big Black."

Big didn't say a word. He stood and glared at Freeman. This time, Freeman more than flinched. He shuddered.

"Don't apologize," Regina said. "Freeman has asked to see counsel. That ends the interview."

"Good deal," the warden said. "The sooner you wrap up here, the sooner the cellmates can get to know each other."

The warden and Big left one interview room and went to the other. Stockman delivered the same lines to Katzenbach. If anything, Big looked more menacing the second time around.

By the time the warden and Big left the room with Katzenbach, Freeman had already signed two forms: a waiver of counsel and an acknowledgment of his *Miranda* rights. Thirty seconds later, Katzenbach signed identical forms.

Cash pulled the paper slips from his pocket and tallied the returns. Three Ks and three Fs. His ballot tipped the scale to Katzenbach. No reflection on the doctor's mettle. There was simply no way Cash would bet against Tina under any circumstances.

The majority ruled, and Katzenbach delivered the first nail in a coffin large enough for him, Freeman, and several of his partners.

CHAPTER SIXTY-EIGHT

After three hours and thirteen minutes without a break, Tina and Gamez terminated the interview with Katzenbach. There are only so many evasions, rationalizations, half-truths, and downright lies an individual can stomach in one sitting.

On the return from Seagoville to Dallas, Gamez, Tina, and Cash rode in silence to the outskirts of the city. Gamez drove, with Tina riding shotgun. Cash had the backseat to himself.

Cash broke the silence. “I’ll spring for drinks.”

Tina turned to Cash and said, “To celebrate or drown our sorrows?”

“To celebrate,” Cash said. “We have Katzenbach by the short hairs.”

“Not on the serial killings, we don’t.” Tina sounded tired.

“We have him nailed on insider trading,” Cash said, “and that will keep him behind bars for the rest of his life, whether his life expectancy is measured in years, months, days, or hours.”

Tina slid closer to Gamez and rested her head on his shoulder. “Not sure the charge will stick against Powell. You may have scuttled his daughter's shot at AG, but daddy could still walk away."

"We'll see," Cash said, "but don't underestimate the value of taking out Katzenbach and Jenna Powell."

"It's worse than bad if Powell remains free," Tina said. "He's like an elephant. He'll never forget what we did to him, his firm, and his family."

Cash leaned back in the seat and cupped his hands behind his head. "Do you know how you eat an elephant?"

Gamez beat Tina to the punchline. "One bite at a time."

Cash smiled and said, "Savor every sweet bite."

THE END

ACKNOWLEDGMENTS

I was blessed to be born into a family of readers and writers who encouraged a love of literature in their children. Our parents were teachers, and our house was crammed with eclectic books.

I am doubly blessed to find myself in a family of readers and writers. My wife Regina and daughter Jessica, both writers themselves, are infinitely patient, loving, supportive, and fearless.

All gratitude goes to super-agent Jan Miller and her talented team at DuPree Miller & Associates. Jan is more than an agent to our family. She is a longtime friend, confidante, and most importantly, the godmother of our only child.

Thanks also to the great teams at Savio Public and Post Hill Press, who have been there for Cash McCahill and me during the fictional lawyer's journey to date.

I have the great fortune of being a small cog in a group of talented writers who meet weekly to critique each other's works. Our Tuesday night gatherings include Jan Blankenship, Victoria Calder, Will Clarke, Peggy Fleming, Harry Hunsicker,

Fanchon Knott, Brooke Malouf, Julie Mitchell, David Norman, Glenna Whitley, Max Wright, and Kelly Yandell.

In addition to the family and friends listed above, my Austin angel Erin Brown has made invaluable edits to all my Cash books. Likewise, Jayla Howard and Valerie Jackson, two of the bravest women I know, were kind enough to read drafts of this novel and offer helpful advice. In return, Jayla and Valerie have in me an ally for life.

Finally, my trusted assistant Veronica Long has been by my side in and out of the courtroom for twenty-five years. She makes the practice of law fun and could teach Della Street a thing or two.

ABOUT THE AUTHOR

Paul Coggins is a prominent criminal defense attorney in Dallas and the former United States Attorney for the Northern District of Texas. After his BA from Yale, he earned law degrees from Harvard and Oxford, which he attended as a Rhodes Scholar. He has traveled widely and lives in the high-stakes world portrayed in the Cash McCahill novels.

His prior Cash novels were *Sting Like a Butterfly* and *The Eye of the Tigress*. He is working on the fourth installment in the series: *Canary in the Courthouse*.